Acclaim for *Scaling th*

"Every company wants to grow faster, but few have access ιω -
and comprehensive blueprint for achieving scalable, repeatable revenue growth. Tom Mohr's *Scaling the Revenue Engine* provides exactly that - detailed guidance and insights on the key patterns and behaviors that drive revenue growth. From building predictable demand to delighting customers, this book provides everything you need to design, build, and scale your revenue engine."

—**Scott Albro**, CEO, TOPO

"Building a business from zero to IPO is not easy and never follows a prescribed set of steps. Tom's book gives the entrepreneur the tools necessary to build, tune and operate the business's Revenue Engine - the living and breathing machine of all successful businesses. Read his book if you want to ensure your Revenue Engine is operating at peak performance at each phase of your company's journey to an IPO!"

—**Mark Brewer**, CEO, Lightbend

"Tom Mohr's ability to recognize, visualize and communicate the patterns of business makes him an outstanding coach and an insightful writer. *Scaling the Revenue Engine* provides frameworks for understanding (and scaling) businesses of all types."

—**David Kopp**, CEO, Healthline Media

"In Tom Mohr's *Scaling the Revenue Engine*, you'll find practical advice for how to define your ideal customer profile, develop resonant messages and build and execute an accountable, orchestrated, effective engagement plan that yields sound unit economics and accelerating revenues. If you want to scale your revenue engine, I encourage you to read this book."

—**Chris Aker**, Chief Revenue Officer, BirdEye

"Tom Mohr's *Scaling the Revenue Engine* is the 'missing link' business manual. It defines steps based on real-world business experiences and practice, not theory, in scaling and growing a successful business from early stage to sustainable and profitable revenue. A must read for any business leader, whether in a startup or an established company."

—**David Puglia**, Co-founder and CMO, Cuspair

"*Scaling the Revenue Engine* showcases Tom Mohr's unique talent for assembling practical insights and concepts that every CEO can use to grow a business effectively."

—**Tom Grubb**, Chief Strategy Officer, Digital Pi

"At CEO Quest, we help tech company CEOs accelerate company growth— from early stage to $100M in revenue and beyond. Tom Mohr is passionate about company building and works hard every day to equip CEOs with the requisite knowledge and tools to accelerate growth. It's this passion that led him to author *Scaling the Revenue Engine*. You'll find *Scaling the Revenue Engine* to be a practical and powerful guide, whether your company has barely achieved initial product-market fit or is a rising category leader. The book brings together best practices learned through our advisory work at CEO Quest, along with deep research and insights from top business minds. The result is a blueprint CEOs can use to tackle revenue engine challenges and opportunities at every stage in the company building journey."

—**Bill Portelli**, Managing Director, CEO Quest

SCALING THE REVENUE ENGINE

TOM MOHR

 For information, address CEO Quest, 1810 University Way, San Jose, CA 95126, USA. Books may be purchased for educational, business, or sales promotional use. For information, please e-mail Tom Mohr at tmohr@ceoquest.com.

Library of Congress Cataloging-in-Publication Data has been applied for.

ISBN: 978-1-54394-898-1

This book is dedicated to Pageen,
who captivates me daily with her smiling Irish eyes, countless words of wisdom
and routine acts of love. She's the love of my life.

Contents

Preface

In 2007 I co-founded and built a tech company, which became, after a couple of name changes, Digital Air Strike. Over six hard-fought years, we took it from zero to $20M revenue and cash flow positive. It was way harder than anything I'd previously done. It was certainly harder than my previous job as president of Knight Ridder Digital, where we took revenue from $100M to $200M.

My experience taught me great respect for tech startup CEOs. Moreover, it was the impetus to start the company I now run, CEO Quest. At CEO Quest, we deliver tech CEOs the essential component I lacked: a roadmap for scaling. Today I'm privileged to work with a diverse group of CEOs, all outstanding individuals running rapidly scaling companies.

We obsessively seek to help our members make a steady drumbeat of sharper decisions, resulting in company acceleration. I've been able to bring my experiences to bear in a way that helps these great CEOs, which is a privilege. But, the learning path has been a two-way street. In the midst of my advice to them, I constantly find I learn much in return.

My desire to provide CEOs with the very best answers and ideas for company building at every stage of the journey led me to become a keen student of revenue engine best practices. In turn, this galvanized the research for this book, begun over 3 years ago.

1

Revenue Engine Overview

Key Concepts in Chapter 1:

- The revenue engine is the totality of systems and activities that create engagement of prospects and customers
- LTV and CAC comprise the boundary conditions for a successful revenue engine
- The revenue engine is a whole system, comprised of four foundational layers plus the "bow tie" (representing the prospect and customer journey)
- The revenue engine spans the functions of brand marketing, product marketing, growth marketing, sales development, sales and customer success
- Best practice revenue engines tightly orchestrate the right functions at the right stage, considering people, tools, workflow and metrics

This chapter is relevant for the following business models:

- Very Low Customer LTV (<$500)
- Low Customer LTV ($501 - $10,000)
- Mid Customer LTV ($10,001 - $100,000)
- High Customer LTV ($100,001 - $500,000)
- Very High Customer LTV ($500,001+)

Only 0.14 percent of the 60,000 software companies that received funding in the past decade have become unicorns (companies worth $1 billion or more).[1] Thirty percent of these 60,000 lost their entire invested capital, and 70 percent failed to achieve projected ROI (in other words, they had an unsuccessful exit).[2] An article published in the Harvard Business Review noted that 62 out of 100 venture capital (VC) funds the Kauffman Foundation invested in over 20 years failed to beat a small cap public index.[3]

For the founding tech company CEO or senior executive, whose common shares sit under the VC's preferred shares, these statistics are crushing. Over the years, too many founders and senior execs have poured their sweat into companies that yielded little or no equity outcome.

If you are a VC-backed tech company CEO, you are highly motivated to beat the odds.

But how?

Valuation is tied to revenue growth. In most companies, the only path to a financially successful exit for CEOs and their teams is through rapid revenue acceleration. It is on behalf of tech startup CEOs—and to aid in their pursuit of rapid revenue acceleration—that I have written this book.

The prevailing framework for revenue generation treats marketing, sales, customer success, and finance as separate domains with separate accountabilities and arm's length handoffs. Success in this model hinges on hiring experienced domain experts at the top of each function and expecting cross-functional executive cooperation in driving revenue generation activity.

But, after two years of in-depth research into the revenue generation practices of a diverse array of early and mid-stage tech companies, along with a review of the secondary research and the inputs of world-class marketing and sales practitioners, a different framework emerges.

Revenue generation is achieved through coordinated activity across the enterprise. This begins with a clearly defined strategy and results in finely tuned acts of daily customer engagement along the entire prospect and customer journey.

Coordination must occur not just with top executives, but with managers and front line employees too, particularly those at the cross-functional handoff points. The sum of all the strategies, plans, people, tools, workflows, and metrics that create this coordinated revenue generation activity is what I call the "revenue engine."

Best practice revenue engines are built as whole systems, bounded by unit economics, with end-to-end workflows and data flows that support and orchestrate customer engagement. These metrics are tracked at every step and optimized via continuous improvement projects.

The revenue engine's purpose is to maximize repeatable, scalable, ROI-positive revenue and profit growth. You drive ROI by maximizing your customer lifetime value (LTV) and minimizing customer acquisition cost (CAC). You drive growth by optimizing your pursuit of prospects and expansion spending from current customers, working within CAC boundaries.

Before we go further, it's worth examining what we mean by "business model." We tend to think of business models in terms of "media," or "marketplace," or "e-commerce," or "B2C SaaS," or "B2B SaaS (SMB / mid-market / enterprise)." But such descriptions leave opaque the key variable that differentiates them. At least for revenue engine purposes, a clearer way to describe business model is in reference to LTV:

- Very Low Customer LTV (<$500)
- Low Customer LTV ($501—$10,000)
- Mid Customer LTV ($10,001—$100,000)
- High Customer LTV ($100,001—$500,000)
- Very High Customer LTV ($500,001+)

Using this approach, most media, marketplace, e-commerce and B2C SaaS businesses fit into the Very Low Customer LTV business model. Here, the scaling path is via online demand generation (e.g., SEO, SEM, digital marketing, viral social effects). A B2B SaaS company serving SMB customers, on the other hand, would likely fit into the Low Customer LTV business model, and may combine online demand generation with a high-velocity call center for fulfillment.

With the Very Large Customer LTV business model, a complex sales process, high-priced sales executives and multi-dimensional account-based marketing initiatives prevail. As LTV grows, an expanding array of customer acquisition and expansion levers becomes viable.

The point is that revenue engine strategy must start with the math of the business. Customer LTV is the grand arbiter. In order to scale, it is generally recognized that the ratio of LTV / CAC should be 3 or greater, with CAC payback less than 18 months. This boundary condition establishes the revenue generation options available, given your business model:

	Customer Lifetime Value				
	VERY LOW	LOW	MEDIUM	HIGH	VERY HIGH
Typical Customer	Consumer	SMB	Mid-Market	Enterprise	Large Enterprise
Typical Business Model	Online Fulfillment; E-commerce; Marketplaces; Media	SaaS with online fulfillment + inside sales fulfillment	SaaS inside sales + field sales	SaaS field sales + enterprise sales	SaaS enterprise sales
Universe of Prospects	Millions	Hundreds of thousands	Thousands	Hundreds to thousands	Hundreds
Typical Top Funnel	Growth marketing initiatives (SEO / SEM / Affiliate Marketing / Programmatic Display, etc.)	Product marketing and growth marketing initiatives	Brand marketing, product marketing and growth marketing initiatives	Brand marketing, product marketing and growth marketing initiatives	Brand marketing, product marketing and growth marketing initiatives
Time from Lead to Closed Won	Minutes to hours	Days to 2 months	2-4 months	4-12 months	12+ months
Typical Conversion Methods	Fully automated	Partially automated; leads based; inside sales supported by growth marketing and tools for efficiency	Combination of leads based and account based. Standardized workflows for inside and field sales, supported by growth marketing and tools for efficiency	Account based. Nurture campaigns to develop prospects. Multi-level direct selling with field and enterprise sales execs.	Account based. Nurture campaigns to develop prospects. Significant investment in prospect cultivation. Customized account plans. Senior enterprise sales execs.

The path to scaling revenue, then, is to move from highest-ROI customer acquisition tactics, to the next highest-ROI tactics, to the next, always exhausting the potential of each tactic before moving on. You keep adding tactics until the ROI pushes up against the LTV / CAC boundary. As you add these new tactics, you simultaneously work to further optimize the performance of existing ones.

Each component of the revenue engine must deliver peak performance for the other components to function properly. They all work together to efficiently and effectively carry the right buyers and users through the prospect and customer journey, from initial awareness through initial sale, launch, and expansion.

The performance of your revenue engine depends on two factors:

its design and its implementation. What engine have you designed? A Porsche or a Yugo? Even if it's a Porsche—thoughtfully and carefully designed—have you kept it oiled, fit, and trim? Are you using the highest-performing fuel?

The Revenue Engine Framework

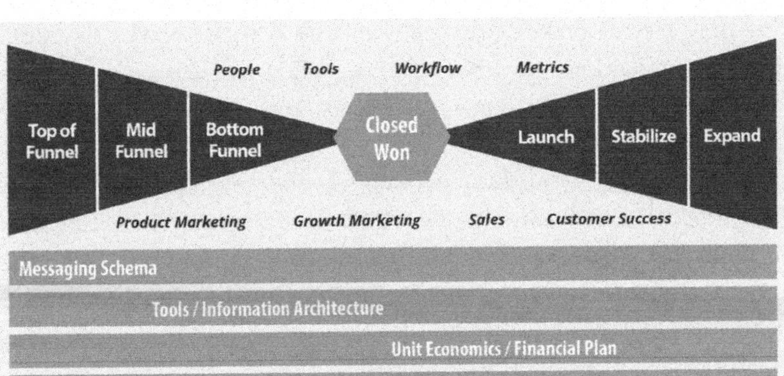

The revenue engine starts with what we call the "Bow Tie"—the top part of the revenue engine framework shown above. The customer engagement journey starts at Top of Funnel, then continues through Mid Funnel, and then to Bottom Funnel, leading to Closed Won— the "knot" on the Bow Tie. Subsequently, the journey continues on to Launch, Stabilize, and Expand.

Sitting beneath the Bow Tie are four foundational layers. The base layer is Mission / Strategy, comprised of:

- Mission, vision, and values
- Customer segmentation
- Value proposition
- Competitive positioning
- Brand identity
- Product
- Pricing and packaging
- Prospect and customer journey

- Channel architecture

Sitting above Mission / Strategy are three more foundational layers: "Unit Economics / Financial Plan," "Tools / Information Architecture," and "Messaging Schema."

These four foundational layers are the building blocks that support all the customer engagement activity that occurs along the Bow Tie. The Bow Tie customer engagement activity is performed by functions (product marketing, growth marketing, sales, and customer success) that coordinate people, tools, workflows, and metrics to accomplish the job.

Regardless of your business model, the revenue engine's core components are consistent. The B2C E-commerce site's customer traverses the Bow Tie in the same sequence as does the B2B SaaS enterprise customer. No matter the business model, the imperative is to design and implement an engine that is fit, trim, constantly measured, and continuously improving.

The Foundational Layers

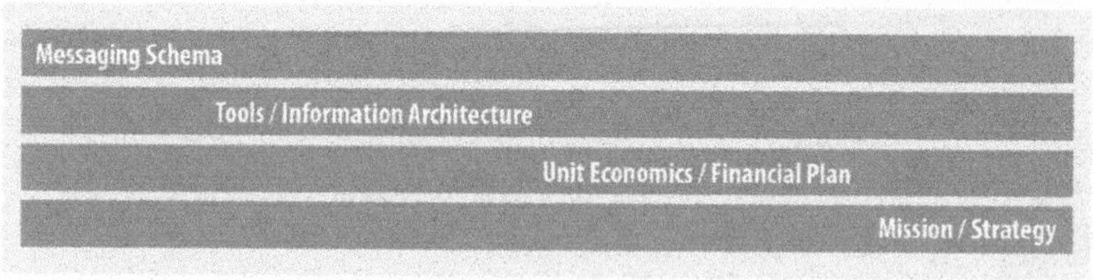

Messaging Schema

Tools / Information Architecture

Unit Economics / Financial Plan

Mission / Strategy

To make your revenue engine perform like a Porsche, you first need to attend to the engine's foundational layers. Let's go through each, working from the bottom up.

Mission / Strategy Layer

Mission, Vision, and Values

These comprise your essential canon, your "north star," which guides purpose, end-in-mind, and norms. Without clarity here, you don't even know if you're cutting a path through the right forest.

Customer Segmentation

Segmentation is vital. It's the starting point for the entire revenue engine. Done well, you will have a tight definition of the specific attributes of your target market and ideal customer profile (ICP).

For each top priority segment, you will know the buyer and user personas, the specific needs and pain points addressed, and the pricing demand curve. These, of course, will evolve over time, so it makes sense for you to regularly reassess your segmentation research.

Value Proposition

Your value proposition defines the core functional value attributes that strongly resonate to your top priority segments, and that you can claim as unique.

Competitive Positioning

Competitive positioning accentuates the value drivers that resonate for your top priority segments. You call out those attributes for which you have a strong competitive advantage. You express these attributes in a way that elevates your brand while boxing in your competitors.

Brand Identity

With clear segmentation, a strong value proposition, and compelling competitive positioning, you are ready to express your brand identity in four dimensions:

- Brand as company
- Brand as product
- Brand as person (the human-like traits of your brand)

- Brand as symbol (logo, other iconography, typography, etc.)

Product

Your product road map is strategy in motion. The mission of product development is to drive revenue growth, so it's important early in development to first understand the "true problem" you must solve. True problems include value problems, velocity problems, retention problems, chasm crossing problems, segment expansion problems, and customer expansion problems.

An outward-in approach works best, leading you to the new features that will successfully address your true problem and meet the needs of your top priority segments.

Pricing and Packaging

Smart pricing is transformational. It starts with understanding the segment-specific pricing demand curve. Key success factors include derisking the entry point (initial pricing), pricing to penetrate, building an expansion of customer spend into the price structure, and capturing cash up front where possible.

Prospect and Customer Journey

It's critical to map the prospect and customer journey. Each step in that journey is a "moment of truth," where the presence and quality of your messaging will influence the decision to proceed. As such, this journey map becomes the foundation for smart step-specific messaging and sales workflows.

Channel Architecture

Channel strategy can transform a business. The first step is to identify all possible paths (partner-based or internal) to the customer. Some common paths include ISV, system integrator, reseller, distributor, comarketer, field sales team, inside sales team, or online channels. Next, you must choose your paths of preference and the specific partners you seek to secure.

After that, you need to engage potential partners effectively, building steadily towards a partnership deal. This requires knowing partner deal best practices and the traps to avoid. Finally, once you have secured the right partnerships and have defined your own direct sales channels, you must manage these pathways to the customer with high fidelity.

Unit Economics / Financial Plan Layer

Unit economics

Unit economics establish the boundaries of your business. To chase revenue without regard to the LTV / CAC viability parameters is both irrational and reckless. On the contrary, you must instrument your business end-to-end so that you have constant visibility into the LTV / CAC impacts of all activities and workflows.

Pricing, variable costs, channel choices, customer acquisition practices, retention and expansion practices, and retention performance all impact unit economics. Metrics dashboards from all workflows should be structured to roll up to summary LTV / CAC calculations.

Financial Plan

Metrics dashboards should start at the lowest level workflows and build up, like a pyramid, to overview metrics for the business. At the top of the pyramid is the financial plan. Here, one should find GAAP financials, headcount schedules, and all key strategic and operational metrics, with trending. All should show both Plan and Actual.

In a perfect world, "actuals" are populated via automatic links to source repositories of data (accounting, contracting, billing, the CRM, and product systems).

Tools / Information Architecture Layer

To optimize revenue engine performance, you have assembled vendor tools. This marketing and sales tools stack must be set up such that data flows seamlessly across the system in support of your end-to-end workflows, always yielding one source of truth. The architecture of your data should:

- Define your customer hierarchy (parent/child/grandchild relationships)
- Define stages of the prospect and customer lifecycle
- Define other key factors (billing arrangements, sales territory rules, etc.)

Messaging Schema Layer

Your messaging schema is your detailed blueprint to guide day-to-day messaging execution at every stage of the prospect and customer journey.

Inside your messaging schema are the statements that achieve:

- Vision lock ("I get what you do and why it's relevant to me")
- Conviction lock ("I'm convinced. Sign me up!")
- Advocacy lock ("I'm a raving fan")

If your business model includes sales development reps, account executives, and customer success managers, then the messaging schema includes six playbooks (otherwise, it just includes the first the first three):

- Brand playbook (the style guide)
- Product marketing playbook (the key focus areas, themes, and positioning objectives; the collateral assets and publishing calendar)
- Growth marketing playbook (the campaign objectives, campaign plan, and testing plan)

- Sales development playbook (personas, programs, use cases and plays)
- Account executives playbook (from "opportunity" to "closed won" plan, pitch deck, plays)
- Customer success playbook (programs and plays).

The Bow Tie

With these foundational layers in place, you can now execute workflows more effectively along the Bow Tie.

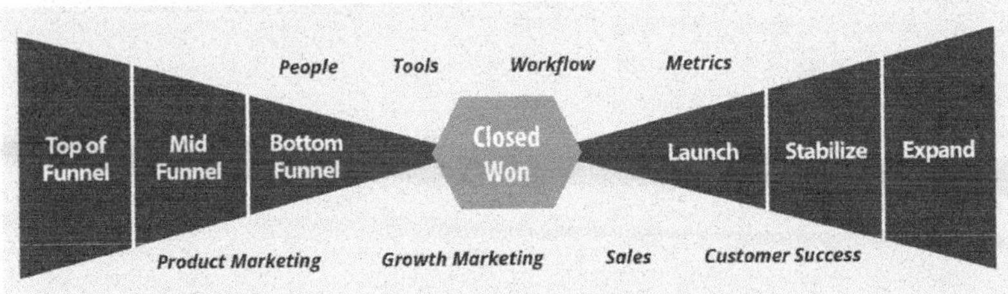

The Bow Tie tracks the prospect and customer journey, which is defined by the prospect's and customer's steps all the way from "disengaged" to "raving fan." Each step is a moment of truth in which you seek maximum positive influence.

The following functional requirements are typical at different stages of the Bow Tie:

	Top of funnel	Mid Funnel	Bottom Funnel	Launch	Stabilize	Expand
Brand Marketing	■					
Product Marketing	■	■		■	■	■
Growth Marketing	■	■		■	■	■
Sales Development		■				
Sales		■	■			■
Customer Success				■	■	■

The Bow Tie is where the "rubber hits the road." As you execute influence at every step along the prospect and customer journey in a highly disciplined way—time after time across all prospects and customers—small, positive increments build up until they accumulate into a mountain of momentum.

Like the design, development, and production of a Porsche engine, it's not easy. It takes a blueprint and lots of hard, iterative work. But it's worth it.

Grab the tools, and get going.

2

Revenue Engine Maturity Model

Key Concepts in Chapter 2:

- To build an optimized revenue engine, have a clear picture of the end in mind
- The earliest stages of company building involve small-scale testing and iteration; you only scale and diversify based on proven results
- Your revenue engine must operate inside a rational LTV / CAC business model
- Your revenue engine maturity levels range from i) Chaotic, ii) Project Centric, iii) Whole System, iv) Quantitative, and v) Continuous Improvement
- An Assessment Tool helps you measure current revenue engine maturity against an end-state standard
- Your maturity assessment yields prioritization of projects, which are best attacked using 60:30:10 approach

This chapter is relevant for the following business models:

- Very Low Customer LTV (<$500)
- Low Customer LTV ($501 - $10,000)
- Mid Customer LTV ($10,001 - $100,000)
- High Customer LTV ($100,001 - $500,000)
- Very High Customer LTV ($500,001+)

Mature or not mature? That is the question.

As a tech company CEO, caught in the throes of crisis du jour, it's often hard to devote any time to a thoughtful, sequential build-out of the revenue engine. You just need more sales now; nothing else matters. But smart tech startup CEOs figure out how to progress steadily through clearly defined stages of maturity while simultaneously delivering the day-to-day unit sales, financial results, and product development outcomes necessary to get funded and to scale.

When you bring your first product to market, you as CEO may well be the totality of your revenue engine. For the Very Low LTV business model, you are the sole conductor of the endless series of A/B tests seeking online traction (what Scott Weiss from Andreessen Horowitz famously called "fruit fly experiments").

If you have a Mid, High, or Very High LTV business model, you're the one reaching out to alpha and beta prospects. You're testing your pitch—validating your product—searching for confirmation that a customer will buy. Even after the first three account executives are hired, you may sell for a while with no marketing department. Then you hire an email marketer, or a growth marketer. Then you hire a sales development rep. Everything is nascent, and in continuous flux.

Early on, smart company building follows a stage-based pattern that multiple experts have sought to define. In his book *Four Steps to the Epiphany*,[1] Steve Blank posited four stages: customer discovery, customer validation, customer creation, and company building. Blank's work focused on the need for a methodical validation of key hypotheses in order to move from stage to stage. Zuora CEO, Tien Tzuo, in a seminal blog post, "Climbing the Mountain,"[2] defined six stages in revenue-based terms: prove the idea = $1M, prove the product = $3M, prove the market = $10M, prove the business model = $30M, prove the vision = $100M, and prove the industry = $300M+. Tzuo called stage-to-stage progressions "switchbacks," each of which demands a big shift in the CEO's leadership approach. Bruce Cleveland and the team at Wildcat Ventures have developed the "Traction Gap Framework,"[3] articulating five early-phase growth stages: Minimum Viable Category (MVC), Initial Product Release (IPR), Minimum Viable Product (MVP), Minimum Viable Repeatability (MVR), and Minimum Viable Traction (MVT). In this framework, the focus is on the requirements necessary to secure the next stage of funding.

Each of these approaches adds nuance to the same fundamental point. In the beginning, company building requires the thoughtful development of core hypotheses, the testing of them via small-scale experiments, and an executional management approach characterized by flexibility and rapid iteration. It is only after the emergence of repeatable success that you begin to scale.

Using Wildcat's Traction Gap Framework then, we can characterize the stages as follows:

MVC

- You have defined your product
- You have defined a massive category
- You have a thesis for how your product serves a persistent need in the category
- You have a thesis for a winning business model and go-to-market path

IPR

- You have beta customers
- You seek customer validation metrics to confirm you have MVP
- The founding team comprises the revenue team
- Proof of MVP creates funding

MVP

- You've built a pared down version of a product that customers will buy
- You have a handful of customers
- Founding team still comprises the revenue team
- Proof of MVR creates more funding

MVR

- You've built a small revenue team (perhaps 2–3 sales reps), have created 1.0 versions of your ideal customer profile, value proposition and sales deck, and have sold to a small but steadily growing list of customers
- You have repeatability, and as you scale you begin to gain increasing traction
- Proof of MVT creates more funding

MVT

- You have begun to implement the people, tools, workflows, and metrics necessary to drive consistent customer and revenue growth
- Customer acquisition is consistent, and retention is solid and improving
- Your unit economics are sound
- You are steadily scaling customers and revenue
- You gain the funding necessary to hit the gas

As you gain traction, the game begins to change. Rapid iteration makes way for an orderly build-out. At each of stage of growth, progress begets funding, and funding begets an expanding team. Your revenue engine builds and diversifies.

For instance, if you are a B2B SaaS business, you add a product marketing function. A growth marketing function. You introduce sales development reps and account execs. The customer success team is created. People, tools, and workflows come together in a grand design. As your revenue engine grows, it becomes more complex and, all too often, unwieldy.

At this point it becomes important to gauge your progress against a standard.

As you leave IPR and MVP and enter into the MVR stage, it's time for your revenue engine architecture to standardize and solidify. Everything becomes more planned out and methodical. From MVR forward, you begin the discipline of regularly assessing the maturity of your revenue engine at the component level. These assessments are critical. They enable you to clarify weak points and prioritize projects.

The Carnegie Mellon University's Capability Maturity Model[4] is a useful framework at this stage. It has five maturity levels:

- **Chaotic:** workflows unpredictable and poorly controlled
- **Project Centric Fixes:** broken workflows fixed one at a time
- **Whole System:** workflows linked end-to-end; design considers dependencies
- **Quantitative:** workflows measured to improve control
- **Continuous improvement:** ongoing, data driven fine-tuning

In Chapter 1— Revenue Engine Overview, we reviewed the four foundational layers and the six Bow Tie components of the revenue engine framework:

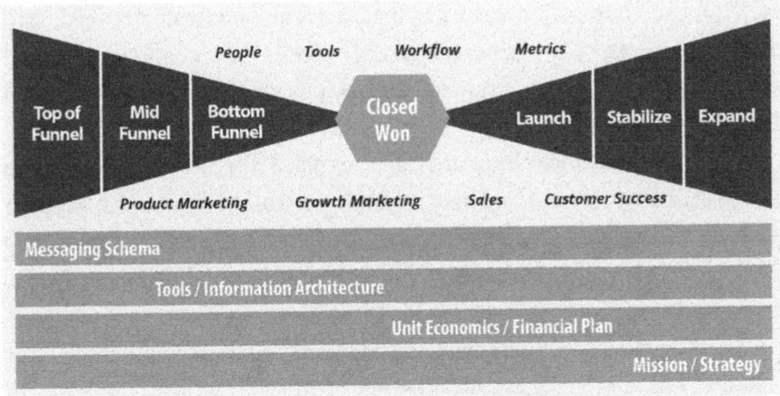

The key is to assess the maturity of each component of the revenue engine, both in the foundational layers and along the Bow Tie, and act on the assessment to continuously improve. For example, a company that has done this well over many years is Eventbrite. It has achieved stage 5 maturity in many of its revenue engine components.

Eventbrite is the leading global ticketing platform and serves customers from SMB to enterprise across major verticals from music events to conferences. Kevin Hartz is co-founder and CEO. Chris Aker, the company's disciplined and hard-charging VP Sales, has worked closely with his Finance and Marketing partners to build a tight prospect and customer engagement workflow.

The foundational layers of Eventbrite's revenue engine are both strategically sound and operationally fit and trim. The company's customer segmentation scheme features four major verticals (music, consumer festivals, endurance events, and conferences), each with sub-verticals. In turn, these sub-verticals are each broken out by SMB, Mid Market, and Enterprise. Across the Bow Tie (the prospect and customer journey), all workflows have been designed for efficiency and to optimize customer engagement. Metrics track each step, and the data is used by teams to continuously improve. Tools further enhance these workflows. Eventbrite's tools stack is tied together by a tight information architecture.

Three sales teams (SMB, Mid Market, and Enterprise) exist for each of the four major verticals (i.e., a total of 12 sales teams), and there are over 50 permutations of pitch decks and integrated marketing campaigns to connect uniquely with the buyer personas in all sub-verticals.

Clear performance standards are in place for every stage of the prospect and customer journey and for all roles. Playbooks support training and enablement of new hires. People are supported to achieve their performance requirements, but everyone is held accountable for meeting them.

Workflows are integrated end-to-end and instrumented for metrics. These metrics are used by teams to continuously improve. In short, Eventbrite's revenue engine is a whole system that is fast approaching stage 5 maturity.

If you are at or beyond the MVR stage, your company's journey towards stage 5 maturity can commence in earnest. It begins with a diagnostic assessment. Take a moment to answer the following questions with a 1–5 rating, with 5 being fully optimized:

Revenue Engine Maturity Assessment

	MATURITY ASSESSMENT				
	1	2	3	4	5
MISSION / STRATEGY					
Mission, Vision and Values: Mission and vision are clearly articulated, and are consistent with your business model and product road map.					
Strategy: Customer LTV and CAC are tracked monthly. LTV is considered the boundary condition for customer acquisition and retention spending (i.e., the LTV / CAC ratio should be >3 and CAC payback should be <18 months).					
Strategy: Given your Customer LTV, you have determined the business model you will live within (lead gen + online fulfillment; lead gen + inside sales; lead gen + inside / outside sales; account based enterprise sales; etc.). Working inside your chosen business model, you are methodically working from the highest-ROI tactics to the next-highest to the next-highest, always seeking to optimize each tranche before moving to the next, always working within the LTV / CAC boundary of >3.					
Segmentation: A segmentation scheme has been built from research into 50+ permutations of product use; for each permutation you have ascertained the value of your product to the buyer given this use, buyer and user personas, degree of product / market fit, sales complexity, total addressable market and competitive intensity. These permutations have been placed into buckets that comprise segments, and from these segments you have chosen your top priority segments.					
Segmentation: From your segmentation research you have gained insights into the roles, activities and pain points of your ideal customer that have informed your product development process. These insights have yielded both enhancements to existing products and new product extensions that have gained significant traction inside your top priority segments. You have an agile product development process that is highly responsive to emerging insights about your target markets.					
Value Proposition: For each top priority segment, you have defined the core functional value proposition that most resonates with its buyers and users, and confirmed efficacy via research.					
Positioning: For each top priority segment, you have created a competitive positioning statement that boxes in your competitors and resonates with the segment's buyers and users, and have confirmed efficacy via research.					
Positioning: You can identify all meaningful competitors. You have created an objective feature by feature analysis to determine your sources of competitive advantage. You have a clear understanding of competitor pricing.					
Brand Identity: You have created your brand identity: brand as product (the unique attributes of each product, and the brand architecture); brand as company (the brand attributes that apply for your company as a whole); brand as person (human-like attributes of your brand); and brand as symbol (iconography, typography, logo, style guide, etc.).					
Product: Your product solves a big pain point, and prospects from top priority segments move briskly from value proposition to purchase. The first mile of the product experience is conducive to rapid adoption. The product boasts high levels of customer retention. You have "crossed the chasm" from early adopters to more mainstream customers. You have developed the features necessary to expand beyond your original top segments to other adjacent segments. You have built expansion capability and new product extensions to increase current customer spend.					
Pricing and Packaging: Your pricing and packaging is based on research into the demand curve of your top priority segments. You have priced to penetrate. You have created introductory pricing that reduces customer risk. Your pricing delivers you competitive advantage. Your pricing scheme builds in expansion capability. You take cash up front.					
Prospect and Customer Journey: You have mapped every step in the prospect and customer journey for your top priority segments. At each step, you have determined the optimal messages the prospects or customers should receive to maximize likelihood they will proceed to the next step.					
Channel Architecture: You have identified every possible pathway to the customer, including direct and channel-based. You have evaluated the economic benefit of channel partnerships. You have identified specific channel partner targets, if any make sense. You have prioritized these targets and have developed an engagement strategy. You have effectively executed your engagement strategy. You have successfully negotiated channel partnerships. You are managing channel partnerships highly effectively, and have all the data necessary to continuously improve customer engagement via these channel partners. You do not have any channel conflict.					

UNIT ECONOMICS / FINANCIAL PLAN	MATURITY ASSESSMENT 1	2	3	4	5
Unit Economics: You have instrumented your end to end workflows to yield metrics. For the operating activities that impact either CAC or LTV, your metrics roll up to an LTV / CAC analysis at the company wide level, but also at the level of channel, program and campaign. These in turn roll into the financial plan. All marketing, sales and customer success activities are captured in these metrics, and you have full visibility from top of funnel, to mid, to bottom, to launch, stabilize and expand.					
Unit Economics: You have a clear understanding of the level of investment that is possible in customer retention / customer success, given your customer LTV. You manage within these constraints.					
Financial Plan: Your financial plan includes full GAAP financials, all company-level operating metrics, sales and marketing productivity metrics and personnel / head count schedules. Everything in the financial plan compares Plan and Actual. Actual data flows into the financial plan automatically. Each month is closed by the 15th day of the subsequent month.					

TOOLS / INFORMATION ARCHITECTURE	MATURITY ASSESSMENT 1	2	3	4	5
Tools: The marketing and sales tools you have acquired have been linked together so that data flows seamlessly. These tools support workflows, simplify work and increase effectiveness. You have no significant gaps in your tools. You are using the best tools available given the requirements you have. Your teams are using the tools properly. The tools are yielding data that populate a unified metrics dashboard of all workflows in the company.					
Information Architecture: Your information architecture has been completely thought through. You have built into all systems a clear definition of the customer hierarchy (i.e. GE vs. the San Francisco Marketing Department of GE), the product hierarchy, the price book, all stages in the customer lifecycle, all supported billing arrangements, etc. There is no re-entry of data required, and there is always just one source of truth with your data.					
Information Architecture: Workflows are stable and metrics-enabled; the handoffs from one workflow to the next are seamless; the people who work within and across these workflows use metrics to continuously improve them.					

MESSAGING SCHEMA	MATURITY ASSESSMENT 1	2	3	4	5
Messaging Schema: Leveraging your segmentation scheme, value proposition, competitive positioning and brand identity, you have developed the following playbooks: Brand Playbook (the style guide); Product Marketing Playbook (the key focus areas, themes, and positioning objectives; the collateral assets and publishing calendar); Growth Marketing Playbook (the campaign objectives, campaign plan and testing plan); Sales Development Playbook (personas, programs, use cases and plays); Account Executives Playbook (Opportunity to Closed Won plan, pitch deck, plays); Customer Success (programs and plays). These playbooks are actively used by your teams for training, and to guide daily work.					

TOP OF FUNNEL	MATURITY ASSESSMENT 1	2	3	4	5
Lead Generation Strategy: You have defined your top of funnel initiatives (brand marketing, product marketing and growth marketing). Depending on your strategy, you have developed orchestrated programs for an online fulfillment model, leads-based marketing, account based marketing or a channel based strategy. Your team is at the right skill level and staffing level, given your requirements. Workflows are being executed efficiently and effectively. You have defined your budget, and are living within it. You are executing programs consistent with your plans. The programs are yielding conversion results which meet your growth objectives consistent with LTV / CAC boundary requirements.					
Conversion Metrics: You have a clear definition of every stage of the prospect and customer journey, from impression to lead to automated qualified lead to marketing qualified lead to opportunity to closed won to customer live and beyond. Every stakeholder in the company agrees on these definitions, and the metrics that track these stages are universally accepted.					
Metrics Driven: You measure every stage of conversion along the prospect and customer funnels, and executives routinely act on this information to develop programs and plans that optimize at every step.					

MID FUNNEL	MATURITY ASSESSMENT 1	2	3	4	5
Mid-Funnel Workflow: If you operate in a leads-based business model, you have clearly defined workflow to qualify and manage a lead. The sales development role is clearly defined, and workflows are optimized between human activity and automated nurture activity. The handoff from SDRs to AEs is executed seamlessly. SDRs and AEs are fully trained. The workflows are fully instrumented with metrics, and the metrics are used to continuously improve.					
Repeatable Performance: If you have sales teams, you have defined clearly the performance expectations of a new SDR and AE. You have defined a remediation plan if early performance falls short. You have clear a performance management and termination path in place. Your sales development and account executive teams are performing at the level necessary to achieve your growth objectives. Your investments in sales development and sales deliver LTV / CAC >3, after accounting for lead acquisition costs.					

BOTTOM FUNNEL	MATURITY ASSESSMENT 1	2	3	4	5
Repeatable Performance: If you have a leads based or account based sales approach, AEs operate within a tightly managed process, moving from Opportunity to Closed Won. You track the conversion rate from Opportunity to Closed Won. This data is used to coach salespeople and continuously improve. This ratio is showing a steadily improving trend. If you operate in a fully automated online fulfillment business model, you have created a highly optimized end to end experience, and you are continuously testing and iterating funnel conversion improvements end to end.					

LAUNCH	MATURITY ASSESSMENT 1	2	3	4	5
Metrics Driven Launch: If a customer launch is required given your product, you have a clearly defined the customer launch process. You have determined the product usage thresholds that determine minimum levels of initial customer adoption of your product. You measure customer performance against these thresholds, and if a customer does not meet the minimum, the launch is not complete and intervention steps are taken. Customers rate the launch process via a Net Promoter Score measure. This NPS score is 50 or greater. The launch team is fully trained.					

STABILIZE	MATURITY ASSESSMENT 1	2	3	4	5
Metrics Driven Stabilization: Post launch, customer data is continuously gathered. The number of actual vs. intended product users, the frequency of use, the depth of feature utilization and customer ROI are all tracked. This data is used to quickly intervene in the event underutilization thresholds are hit, and a remediation plan is initiated. The customer success team is fully trained and optimized. Customer success is high, and logo churn is below 10% a year.					

EXPAND	MATURITY ASSESSMENT 1	2	3	4	5
Repeatable Performance: Expansion of customer spend is fully optimized. Renewals, upsells and cross sells are executed with high fidelity. Customers are experiencing such significant value in the product that they are aggressively buying more, within the constraints of your product offering and business model.					

The answers to these questions should cause you to think deeply about your revenue engine's current state. Do you show mostly 4's and 5's? If so, your revenue engine is well on its way to stage 5 maturity. If not, then perhaps this exercise has helped you define the areas you fall short, and to prioritize where you want to focus next. A helpful next step is to "force rank" your lowest ratings based on the urgency to fix; this will help with project prioritization.

Your maturity assessment and implications can be summarized as follows:

The maturity of your overall revenue engine is a reflection of the maturity of your components. If your foundational layers are not mature, the basic building blocks of your business need work: segmentation scheme, value proposition, positioning, brand identity, product, pricing and packaging, unit economics, messaging schema and so forth. If one or more of the Bow Tie components (Top, Mid, and Bottom Funnel; Launch, Stabilize, and Expand) are less mature, you have bottlenecks to address.

Projects to strengthen foundational layers tend to be harder, bigger and longer; the effects tend to be back-end loaded but very significant. Projects to address bow tie bottlenecks tend to be smaller, more targeted, and faster, with more immediate but more incremental effects.

Moving Up the Maturity Scale

To build your revenue engine into a Porsche takes significant effort. Progress is achieved first by a clear current state assessment, then clarity of vision, then smart prioritization, and finally by hard, detail-oriented project work.

While Bow Tie optimization work is important, great CEOs make a point to carve out management time to chip away at foundational layer projects. Because they're hard, they're easy to de-prioritize, but it's from the foundational layers that the greatest leverage ultimately emerges.

For too many companies, the tyranny of the urgent continuously steals the necessary time and focus away from engine building. These companies often fail to maximize their potential. It takes sustained CEO-level discipline to build, maintain, and continuously optimize a Porsche engine.

Commit!

3

Mission, Vision, and Values

Key Concepts in Chapter 3:

- Mission, vision and values deliver strategic and tactical alignment and a "shared way" of working together
- To create them, a CEO plays multiple roles: Visionary, Politician, Wordsmith, Evangelist and Role Model
- Strong mission, vision and values are force multipliers for growth

This chapter is relevant for the following business models:

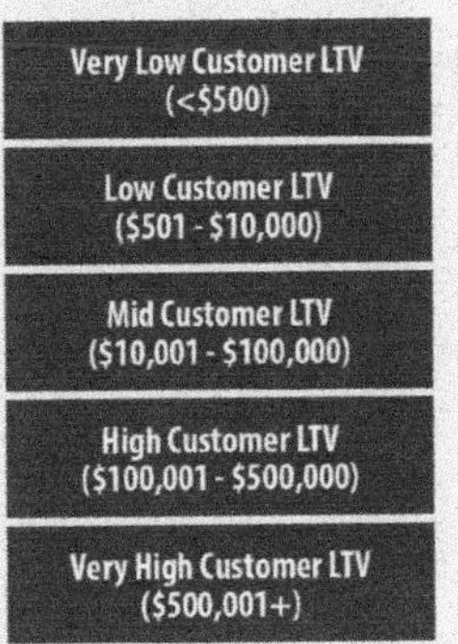

Mission mobilizes. Vision visualizes. Values vitalize.

Mission, vision, and values are the big three. They inform your market focus—the customers you seek, and those you don't. They paint a picture of the world you hope to create. They stipulate the agreed upon norms.

If these bold proclamations are respected, every person in your company will hold every leader in your company accountable. Yes, your top team's actions and decisions must be in full alignment with the proclamations you have made. So too with your brand identity. Mission, vision, and values state who you are and who you aspire to become. For your external facing brand to be an authentic representation of your company, it also must be fully aligned.

A great ***mission*** statement clarifies:

- What you do
- For whom
- Why

A great ***vision*** statement:

- Clarifies what "mission accomplished" looks like: how the world has changed. It defines your future history.

Great ***values*** express the core truth of your aspirational culture. They act as a rallying cry, said with few words, to:

- Clarify
- Direct
- Expect
- Inspire

What's the yield from a focus on mission, vision, and values? Each member of your team possesses a large reservoir of potential. When the mission is clear, you get strategic and tactical alignment. When the vision is clear, you get commitment, perseverance, and even joy in the opportunity to co-create a better future. And when values are clear, you get enthusiastic buy-in to a "shared way" of working together towards common goals. Via this path, passion is unlocked—and with passion, potential. People will stretch further, work harder, give more, and care more. As they experience personal growth, they unleash company growth.

Together, mission, vision, and values comprise your north star. Through the storms of your startup voyage, whenever you lose your way, hold your sextant up to them: the direction forward will become clear again.

Early in my career, I was privileged to witness the power of mission, vision, and values statements to transform a company. It was at the Minneapolis Star Tribune.

The internet had started to explode and multiple threats were on the horizon. I was fortunate to be on the team charged with reinventing the Star Tribune's future. After six months of intensive work, the result was not just a transformational strategy, but a new statement of mission, vision, and values that awakened an incredible period of innovation and growth.

The new mission statement seemed innocent enough: "To enhance the shared life of the community by being the area's leading provider of information and communications that people value." Take note: it did not mention newspapers, or even news. The key phrase was "information and communications."

From this mission spawned an intense period of Web 1.0 innovation. For example, we created an online jobs site based on a resumé database for professionals. This was an early version of the model adopted by Monster and perfected by LinkedIn. We created a real estate website with searchable listings and photos, one of the many early experiments that eventually iterated into the model perfected by Zillow. And startribune.com gained recognition in journalistic circles as a top-tier online news site at the leading edge of innovation.

We didn't understand at the time that online innovation focused on just one market was unsustainable. It took us a few years to work out that the online sites for jobs, cars, real estate and so forth worked best as multi-market platforms. But at the time, that early online innovation elevated our brand and spurred overall growth (the Star Tribune's annual help wanted ad revenues alone hit $90M in the late nineties, and overall revenue grew strongly, approaching $400M).

Similarly, there were new company values: customer focus, employee involvement, continuous improvement, and diversity. These values were taken seriously and spawned a whole new management paradigm at the company: a culture that was innovative, respectful, data driven, and employee involved. We became highly focused on improving customer satisfaction. Sure enough, Gallup researched customer satisfaction before and after these changes, reporting unprecedented improvements.

Mission, vision, and values should be enduring. There are just three times in the scaling of a company where it makes sense to visit or revisit them:

- At company inception
- When you have reached proof of product / market fit—usually around $3M in revenue.
- At a major pivot point—where a change in the core assumptions of your business is required (such as with the Star Tribune)

My focus is on the latter two. In the first, you don't know enough. In the other two, you do. Hard-won experience (such as feedback from your prospects, customers, board, exec team, and employees) yields the data necessary to inform mission, vision, and values.

So how do you do it?

In the drama to create a powerful mission, vision, and set of company values, you as CEO are a five-part actor: visionary, politician, wordsmith, evangelist, and role model. Your goal isn't only to come up with the right words—though that's important. It's also to engage your team so deeply that the words are true, are believed, and come to life—visible both inside and outside of your company.

Visionary

What market do you serve? What problem do you solve now, and how will that change over time? How will your market evolve? How will you drive that evolution?

These questions are informed by:

- A thorough understanding of your market, your customers, and the pain points you seek to address
- Your conviction as to the trends and the disruptions that will mark the evolution of your chosen market
- The role you see your company playing in those trends and disruptions

Politician

In the development of the mission, vision, and values, it's not enough to find the right words. For the words to come to life, you must ignite belief and shared ownership in the hearts of your employees. Here's how:

- Have a retreat with your exec team
- Hold town halls
- Pull together small-group sessions in each functional area of your company
- Walk around and talk with everyone
- Discuss
- Debate

The mission, vision, values creation phase is an excellent opportunity to build belief through active participation. Like a politician, you can test your ideas with employees—discovering what resonates, then iterating and optimizing—until you've landed on words that are true to what you believe, but also incorporate perspectives gleaned from team members at all levels. This bi-directional co-creation simultaneously yields the right words and the team's belief, thus making a powerful impact.

Wordsmith

Words Matter.

- Minimize the number of words per value (1–3)
- Minimize the number of values (3–5)
- Maximize the impact of each

Evangelist

Evangelism starts once the mission, vision, and values are committed to words. The evangelist role is best described by example. Victor Ho is CEO of FiveStars, a company that offers customer loyalty programs for small businesses. Victor and his team have thought deeply about mission, vision, and values, and they work very hard to actuate the words in the daily life of the company.

Fivestars team

FiveStars Mission

"We help businesses and communities thrive by turning every transaction into a relationship."

FiveStars Values

- Shared Humility
- Authentic Relationships

- Warrior Spirit
- Joy Every Day

In developing the list of values that would define the FiveStars culture, the team started from the premise that employees are the most sustainable source of competitive advantage, and the culture you create is your most sustainable product. Victor and his team determined they would build a set of values that were not behavioral, such as "the customer comes first" or "always pursue excellence."

Rather, values would be attitudinal. Victor's team believed that the right behaviors would naturally flow from the right core attitudes.

For instance, the value "Shared Humility" results in the behavior of mutual reliance and a desire to attack problems, not each other. The value "Authentic Relationships" results in direct and honest engagement, being clear about issues while acknowledging each person's struggles and challenges. The value "Joy Every Day" doesn't mean you're always happy—it means that the team exhibits an abiding sense of optimism and stability that helps weather the storms of startup life.

Victor is an evangelist. Here's how:

- Until recently (FiveStars is now over 400 employees), he met directly with every new employee, giving a presentation on the company's mission, vision, and values
- The values are front and center at every town hall meeting
- The values hang on a big banner at corporate headquarters
- Monthly awards are given to employees who uniquely exhibit the values
- Performance reviews now assess an employee's alignment with the company values
- Everyone is expected to be able to quote the mission and values of the company at any time, and they can, and they do

Role Model

As CEO, it's on you to live the words you've created. Your team will learn more from what you do than what you say.

Mission, vision, and values comprise the granite foundation for the castle that is your company. Upon this foundation rests culture, market focus, product vision, brand identity, and more. Designed well, your foundation will soundly bear the load as the castle above it rises and rises relentlessly towards the stars.

Rock on.

4

Customer Segmentation

Key Concepts in Chapter 4:

- Effective customer segmentation is key to your entire revenue engine
- The Use Case Scenario Exercise brings rigor to your customer segmentation research
- Customer segmentation research yields your Ideal Customer Profile (ICP)
- Your ICP gives you the data you need to power effective customer engagement

This chapter is relevant for the following business models:

- Very Low Customer LTV (<$500)
- Low Customer LTV ($501 - $10,000)
- Mid Customer LTV ($10,001 - $100,000)
- High Customer LTV ($100,001 - $500,000)
- Very High Customer LTV ($500,001+)

Smart segmentation sparks scaling.

You have a product. It makes the unworkable workable; the unavoidable and urgent easier. On some dimension of personal or corporate need (status, affiliation, safety, ease of use, cost, speed, etc.), your product connects. Segmentation can only emerge from this: the solid foundation of a compelling product. Without it, you have nothing.

Once you've nailed basic product / market fit, however, proper segmentation is the lift-off point for all future company growth.

Who is your customer? This is the question that customer segmentation answers.

Segmentation is a data-driven filtering exercise. Your segmentation scheme divides the market into buckets, and then clarifies which buckets matter most. Your ideal customer profile (ICP) emerges from your top priority buckets (segments). Here we find the ideal buyers' and users' personas, tasks, expectations and pain points as they pertain to your product.

Let's begin with an example. Zuora is the leading subscription management platform for B2B and B2C companies. It supports recurring revenue billing, multi-channel commerce, global payments, and workflow analytics. The company has raised over $200M in venture funding and is fast growing, with 600 employees serving customers worldwide. Tien Tzuo, founder and CEO, has developed a comprehensive, multi-layer segmentation scheme.

Working bottom-up from a detailed understanding of product use case scenarios, the company has defined three high-level segments: B2B subscription companies, B2C subscription companies, and companies in transformation. The latter segment is populated by companies that are innovating their business models. Each of these three major segments has been further sub-segmented by industry, company size, and geography.

The segmentation scheme is leveraged to clarify brand, tighten messaging, and focus the sales organization. The top-level Zuora brand is distilled into one word: "Freedom." This cascades into three segment-specific brands. For B2B, it's "Freedom to Grow." For B2C, it's "Freedom to Experiment." And for companies in transformation, it's "Freedom to Reinvent."

The sales organization itself is organized into three tiers, based on company size. B2B, B2C, and companies in transformation are all served by the same sales teams within a size-based tier, but messaging is customized to these different audiences, based on their unique buyer and user personas.

Segmentation has also sharpened product road map decision

making. By understanding the unique unmet product needs in each segment, smart decisions have been made to prioritize development.

That's the power of doing it right. Smart customer segmentation:

- Anchors your brand strategy
- Sharpens pricing
- Drives product roadmap prioritization
- Lasers in messaging
- Superpowers lead generation
- Tightens sales workflow

So why do so few tech startup CEOs get it right?

Too often, CEOs either don't segment at all, or they approach the task with a top-down, "gut instinct" approach. Lacking the time or money for extensive research, the next best thing, many CEOs conclude, is essentially an educated guess. But there's a sweet spot that stands between "expensive, time-consuming research projects" and "winging it."

Use Case Scenario Exercise

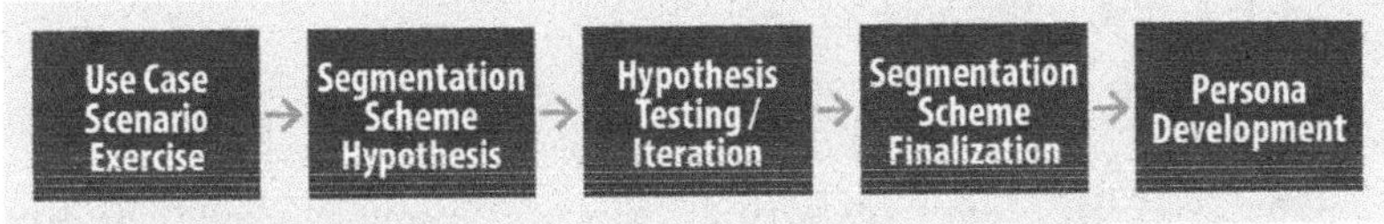

The Use Case Scenario Exercise is the key to finding the sweet spot — the "middle way." It leverages the existing domain knowledge of your team so that you only need to focus on researching the things you don't already know.

To complete the Use Case Scenario exercise, you need to start by coming up with at least 50 different use case scenarios for your product. This ensures you work from the atomic level on up towards a segmentation scheme, versus top down. The 50 use case scenarios are your "raw material" that will eventually yield 1–3 top priority segments. To come up with this number of use case scenarios, or permutations, the first question you will face is, "what segmentation dimensions matter most?" At this stage, you should cast a wide net. You'll narrow later. Here are some dimensions to consider:

B2B:

- Size of company (revenue / employees / market cap / Alexa ranking / etc.)
- Product usage profiles
- Buyer or User profiles
- Product demand indicators
- Technology maturity
- Legacy technology
- Manufacturer / vendor affiliation
- Geography

B2C:

- Gender
- Age
- Income
- Psychographic profiles
- Product usage profiles

Once you have come up with at least 50 permutations, create the following columns in Excel or a Google Sheet:

Column Heading	Column Description
Use Case Scenario	Each entry here is a permutation of the dimensions by which you have chosen to filter
Buyer Persona	A description of the buyer: title or role, key attributes, motivations, psychographic descriptors if relevant
Check Signer	A description of the check signer, if different than buyer: title, key attributes
Influencer(s)	Listing of the influencers: title or role, internal / external; key attributes
User Personas	A description of the users: titles, key attributes, motivations, psychographic descriptors if relevant, types of use
Use(s)	A listing of the type of use by user
Example Co.	If B2B, list 1-3 companies that fit this use case
Time from Opportunity to Close (Months)	How long it takes from the Opportunity stage to Closed Won
Prospect Concentration (H/M/L)	For a given use case, how concentrated are the prospects? Are there 10M prospects? 1M? 100K? 1000? 100? 10?
Sales Complexity (H/M/L)	Given the buyers, influencers and users, and the decision process for a given use case, grade the complexity of the sale
Intensity of Need (H / M / L)	How significant is the pain? How big is the ROI if the pain is solved?
Product Market Fit Rating (%)	Make a judgment as to the percentage that your current product fits this use case: do all the features this use case needs exist yet in your product? 100% = a perfect fit
Estimate of Total Addressable Market	Given this use case, estimate the annual revenue value to you if every person (B2C) or company (B2B) that fits the use case were to buy
Potential Deal Size	What's the annual contract value of a fully optimized customer in this use case?
Competitive Intensity	How many other companies can serve this use case well and at a competitive price?
Positioning Message	Given buyer and user personas and the needs within this use case, what would be a 1-2 sentence positioning statement that would resonate?
Confidence Interval %	How confident are you that all the previous answers are accurate? 100%? 50%?

As you execute this task you'll be forced to think more about your customer and your market. This may cause you to change the dimensions and iterate the exercise a couple of times. That's good! It means you're really thinking it through. It also probably means you're listening closely to your customers and prospects.

Salespeople should be asked to fill out the Use Case Scenario exercise. Top salespeople have good instincts; tap into that.

Once you're done, you might feel that many answers aren't much more than a "gut-level guess." For some questions, such as your estimate of total addressable market, that's OK. If you understand your chosen domain, your guess is probably close enough. For other questions, such as buyer persona, a guess isn't good enough: research will be required.

Once you've completed the use case scenario exercise, check the confidence interval % for each scenario. Any row showing a confidence interval of less than 90% requires further research. Note that you're only conducting research on things you know you don't know. That's much more efficient than the kind of comprehensive research project a bigger company might do. If you're B2B, pick up the phone and call people who fit the use case for which you need more data. Have a good conversation with 20 or more people, so you have enough pattern recognition to gain confidence that you understand the use case. For B2C, you may need to conduct a shopping mall survey or "person on the street" interviews.

Segmentation Scheme Hypothesis

Once you have completed this exercise, identify all the use case scenarios that exhibit:

- A large total addressable market
- High product / market fit
- High intensity of need
- Low to moderate competitive intensity

Depending on your business, you might also place weight on other factors, such as:

- Technology maturity
- Manufacturer / vendor affiliation
- Time from opportunity to closed won
- Potential deal size

Review all the use case scenarios that match your chosen filters. Perhaps you have 15. Is there a way to naturally group them into 3–5 segments? You are looking for common dimensions that create a rational basis for grouping. Within these, is there an obvious prioritization into your 1–3 top priority segments? As mentioned previously, Zuora did just this. The company selected three top priority segments: B2B subscription, B2C subscription, and companies in transformation.

Let's consider the example of an auto industry CRM product. Let's assume this product is targeted to car dealerships with internet incoming lead activity up to 300 leads a month. The following factors are considered primary for the purpose of segment prioritization:

Manufacturer affiliation

- General Motors (GM) affiliated dealers receive an incentive from GM to use a CRM system that is GM certified; this one is certified
- Luxury import dealers have unique needs that are especially well served by this CRM

For those stores that are in dealer groups

- Independent (store level) buying decisions are better than centralized (dealer group level)

Number of internet leads per store

- 100–300 leads is best

Total addressable market

- The larger the better, all else being equal

This leads to a prioritization of two “Top Priority” segments, two “B Priority” segments and two “not now” segments. Box sizes reflect differences in the total addressable market.

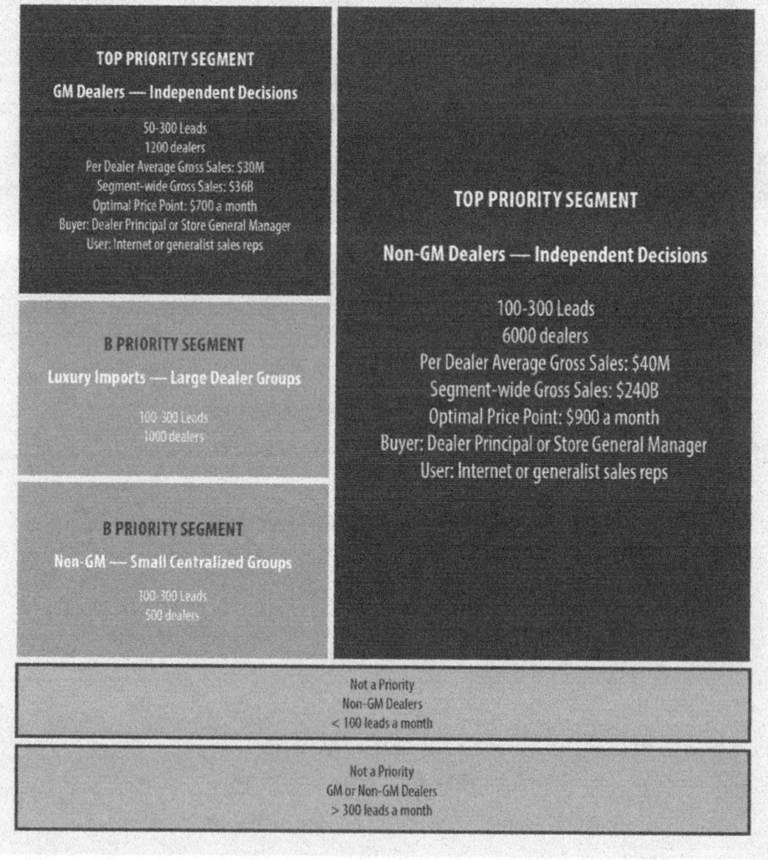

In a strong segmentation scheme, the following information should be known at the segment level:

B2B

- Size of addressable market
- Company profile
- Product usage profiles
- Buyer and user personas
- Pricing demand curve (optimal price point)

B2C

- Size of addressable market
- Buyer and user personas
- Product usage profiles
- Pricing demand curve

Hypothesis Testing / Iteration / Finalization

Since segmentation is central to everything—your product roadmap, pricing, channel choices, sales workflows, messaging—it's important that you test your hypothesis. Go deeper into your top priority segments. Talk to more of the buyers, users and influencers about your product, and their needs. Pitch your product to them, and gauge their reaction on the following dimensions:

- Tasks, expectations and pain points
- Intensity of need / pain
- Degree of interest in your type of pain relief
- Price sensitivity
- Your prospect's perspective on competitive alternatives

Prospect and customer feedback will deepen your understanding, and in all likelihood will cause you to iterate your segmentation scheme a couple of times. But soon you will vector in on a scheme that feels about right. While you will always be open to further iteration and optimization, you are ready to leverage your segment-level knowledge to make decisions.

Persona Development

With your top priority segments now clear, it's time to glean maximum value out of them. This requires building out the buyer and user personas, including:

- Key attributes
- Title / Role
- Tasks
- Expectations
- Pain points
- Value received from your product
- Decision making process / steps
- Motivations
- Risk vs. reward
- Self-interest
- Psychographic patterns
- Buying profile (innovators / early adopters / early majority / late majority / laggards)
- Other generalizable personality tendencies
- Implications for messaging
- Based on key attributes, motivations, and psychographic patterns, what value statements uniquely resonate?
- Implications for prospect and customer journey
- What are the journey steps for your buyers and users, by segment?
- How does persona-specific messaging map to every decision step along the journey?

Ideal Customer Profile

Leveraging your analysis, it's now simple to define your ICP. The ICP will guide your marketing and sales organizations, helping them focus on top prospects and filter out ones that are not on target.

The ICP is a tight description of your top priority segments that can be used by marketing and sales to guide prospect engagement.

B2B

- Company attributes
- Buyer and user persona attributes

B2C

- Buyer persona attributes

If you have a leads-based business model and you have sufficient lead volume, lead scoring tools can help you analytically refine your ICP by determining the correlation between company attributes and purchase behavior.

If you have an account-based business model, the use case scenarios exercise will help you analytically determine your ICP by assessing the sub-segments and specific accounts that exhibit the highest likelihood to buy now, as described in Vinod Khosla's "Rifle Approach."[1]

If you have a B2B or B2C online fulfillment model, you can continuously test assumptions by varying top of funnel targeting and messaging, and testing alternative mid-funnel pathways to the sale.

Summary

A clear segmentation scheme helps you optimize:

Product Road Map

- Focus on development that addresses needs of top priority segments

Pricing

- Optimized for top priority segments, not "stuck in the middle"

Brand strategy

- Value Proposition
- Competitive Positioning
- Brand Identity

Messaging

- What resonates most to the segments that matter most

Lead Generation

- You thoroughly understand the prospect and customer journey
- Campaigns can be designed to match journey steps and optimized messaging

Sales and Customer Success Workflows

- Each step in the prospect and customer journey is a moment of truth
- Segmentation ensures messaging is optimized and helps determine at which steps human intervention makes sense

Channels

- Segment clarity creates channel clarity
- Prioritization of prospects within segments is now possible

This is hard, granular, analytical work. The move from segmentation hypotheses to settled scheme and actionable assumptions is hard-won. But if you put in the effort, the results are inevitable: increased sales acceleration, higher retention and happier customers.

Boom!

5

Value Proposition

Key Concepts in Chapter 5:

- Value proposition is a key stepping-stone in the development of your company's competitive positioning, brand identity, and messaging schema
- Whether your company is B2B, B2C, or B2B2C, your buyer acts on both functional and psychological needs
- The points of value that fulfill these needs, as confirmed by the customer, comprise the starting point for your value proposition
- In your value proposition, you highlight the value points that are of greatest importance to the customer, and that you can defensibly claim

This chapter is relevant for the following business models:

Your venture's value proposition and its valuation are linked.

As a tech company CEO, you understand the power of technology to change the world. Every sector of the global economy is under continuous invention and re-creation; technology's forward march is relentless. In this march, tech companies (led by their CEOs) stride forward in a long, ragged line. Some peter out. Some fall away. Only the best accelerate. For the few who have brought to a big market a uniquely powerful combination of product and message, the investor / team / customer flywheel spins ever faster. As it does, these companies earn the privilege to change the world.

If you're a tech company CEO, perhaps you are one of these. Perhaps your product is so visionary that it has opened a new market. Or so disruptive that it has rebuilt an existing market by delivering a faster, better, cheaper solution to existing needs. Or, maybe your company hasn't yet done this, but possesses the potential to do so.

If your product adds "need it yesterday" value to the market you choose to serve, then your work on "value proposition" will be fruitful. Since your value is real, you will simply need to define the value attributes that best convey that value for the audience you seek to serve. The market into which you bring your product has been defined by your segmentation work (discussed in Chapter 4—Customer Segmentation). With your top priority segments defined, value proposition is the next stepping stone on the path to your brand identity:

- From customer segmentation
- To value proposition
- To competitive positioning
- To brand identity

Since brand identity is the basis for your messaging schema (the top foundational layer in the revenue engine Bow Tie Schema below), it is vital to get it right.

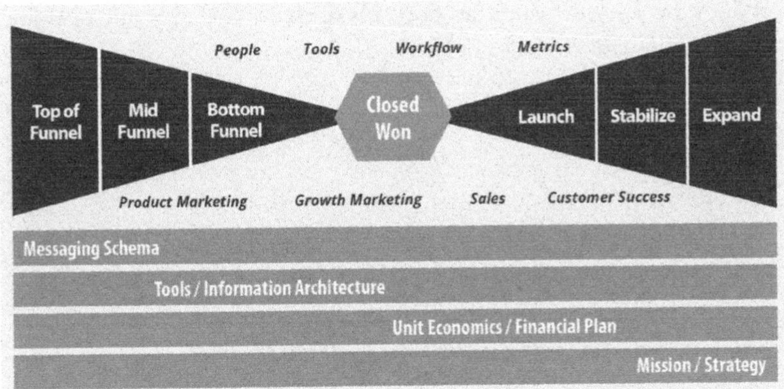

Value proposition and competitive positioning are not the same. Value proposition clarifies the essence of your value to your target customer (internal). Its role is to inform your competitive positioning, which clarifies how you express that value to your target customer (external).

Your segmentation scheme has revealed the key tasks, expectations and pain points of your top priority segments. It has also revealed the personas of your product's buyer and the users. Inside these personas lies the unique psychographic and demographic attributes of the human beings who will make the purchase decision. Whether your business is B2B, B2C, or B2B2C, your prospects have personal needs that must be met, for example:

- To be respected
- To be loved
- To enjoy
- To avoid excessive work
- To be safe (not wrong)
- To be competent
- To be efficient
- To be rewarded

Similarly, for B2B prospects, buyers commingle personal and

company needs and wants as they make decisions. Beyond personal needs, a buyer will consider her company's need to:

- Avoid disruption
- Simplify
- Reduce risk
- Reduce cost
- Increase revenue

So how does one ascertain customer-defined value?

First, consider all needs that your product actually addresses—stated in both functional and psychographic terms. Second, pair each of these needs with the value attribute that fulfills it (i.e., "need for efficiency" is paired with "high-speed"). Third, rank these value attributes based on the importance accorded to each attribute by prospects and customers in your top priority segments.

How will you know you've got it right?

Research. Lots of it. Research takes many forms: surveys, A/B testing, conjoint analysis, customer advisory boards, feedback from customer-facing employees such as salespeople and customer success teams, and regular executive-level engagement with real prospects and customers—often in the customer's own work or living space—are all critical ingredients to create deep customer-centric understanding.

More than anything, it is important to bring the customer's voice into the center of value proposition development. A true understanding of your most important value attributes is hard-won, and never permanently assured. It must be continuously validated. Everything depends on it.

To filter the raw data and gain clarity, it's useful to complete a value attributes chart:

The X axis contains value attributes

The Y axis contains the customer-defined rating (0 to 10)

Place the value attributes on the X axis of a graph from left (most important, according to the target customer) to right (least important)

- Score yourself for each attribute

- Score your competitors

In the example below, if you are green and your competitor is gold, you win on attributes A, B, C, and D (the four most important attributes to your target customer):

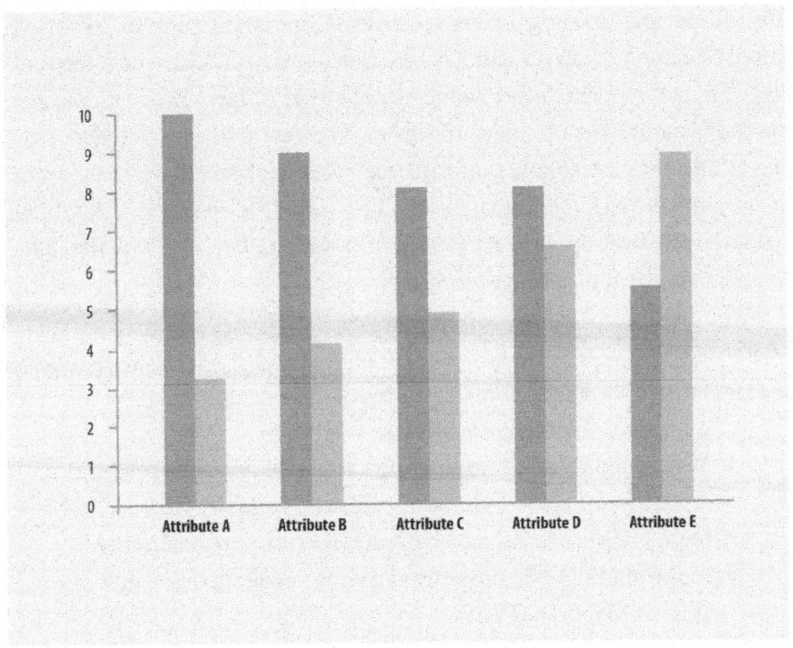

The next step is to use this data to build out a value proposition statement. There are many different variations, but Geoffrey Moore's framework from his book *Crossing the Chasm*[1] gets the job done effectively.

- For (target customers)
- Who are dissatisfied with (the current market alternative)
- Our product is a (description of product category)
- That provides (compelling reason to buy)
- Unlike (the product alternative)

- We deliver (key whole product features for your specific application)

Mark Brewer is CEO of Lightbend, an exciting, fast-growing development platform company. His company provides the leading reactive application development platform for building distributed applications and modernizing aging infrastructures. Companies such as Walmart, Intel, Samsung, Verizon and LinkedIn depend on Lightbend's technology. To get to a stronger value proposition, Mark Brewer commissioned a significant research initiative. The research revealed three key buyer and user personas, tied to three roles: technology leaders, architects, and development managers. Through this research, Lightbend gained deep insights into its position in the market, and how its value is perceived by multiple stakeholders.

The Lightbend value proposition is:

- For technology leaders, architects and development managers at large enterprises
- Who need to modernize aging infrastructure, improve the reliability of their systems, establish new multi-year technical standards, and increase developer productivity
- Lightbend's application development program for the Java Virtual Machine (JVM)
- Leverages microservices and fast data on a message-driven runtime to scale applications effortlessly on multi-core and cloud computing architectures
- Enabling you to modernize at startup speed

Lightbend has gone further. It has leveraged its research to customize the overall value proposition for its three targeted personas. For the technology leader, the emphasis is on modernization and systems reliability. For the architect, the focus is on establishment of multi-year technical standards. And for the development manager, the focus is on developer productivity. These customizations ensure value propositions are developed for each persona that are unique and impactful.

As the Lightbend example underscores, research is the absolute key to a successful value proposition. Research, and when you're done, research again.

Your value proposition is the foundation for competitive positioning. It isn't complicated, but it's important. Get it right, and your competitive positioning statements will be built on solid footing. From competitive positioning comes your brand identity. And from brand identity comes your messaging schema, the blueprint for day-to-day prospect and customer messaging.

With a crisp value proposition in hand, your road trip toward a persona-specific, powerful, and resonant messaging schema accelerates.

Zoom.

6

Competitive Positioning

Key Concepts in Chapter 6:

- Competitive positioning takes stock of your chosen market and your top priority segments, the competitive dynamic, key trends, and your unique value attributes (as highlighted in your value proposition)
- It requires a deep, research-driven understanding of your market, competitors, and the personas in your top priority segments
- A great positioning statement is clear, authentic, and resonant to your targeted personas; it crystallizes your value while boxing in your competitors

This chapter is relevant for the following business models:

- Very Low Customer LTV (<$500)
- Low Customer LTV ($501 - $10,000)
- Mid Customer LTV ($10,001 - $100,000)
- High Customer LTV ($100,001 - $500,000)
- Very High Customer LTV ($500,001+)

Proper positioning packs punch and parts the pack.

Competitive positioning is a bold, defensible claim. You start with the market and top priority segments you serve. You consider the competitive dynamic. You evaluate major trends. You glean your essential value as captured in your Value Proposition (Chapter 5). Using all of these (the market, competitor positions, trends, and your key value attributes), you create a positioning statement that crystallizes your unique differentiated value while boxing in your competitors.

Competitive positioning requires that you:

- Understand your top priority segments and their buyer and user personas
- Define your market and market type
- Research competitors
- Create market maps to position both you and your competitors
- Determine the critical emerging trends in your market
- Create a claim that succinctly conveys competitively advantaged value
- Test, iterate, and optimize

Segments and Personas

In Chapter 4—Customer Segmentation, we reviewed a bottoms-up approach to confirming your top priority segments. Inside these segments are the buyer and user personas that are the target audience for your positioning statement. Their unique psychographic, demographic, and needs-based profiles have already informed your value proposition. Keep those profiles handy.

When you craft your positioning statement, you will find the right tone if you concentrate on "speaking" to your targeted personas.

Market and Market Type

Your top priority segments exist in a market. It might be the multiplayer online gaming market. Or the multi-cloud workload processing market. Or the automotive marketing automation market. Or the health media market. Or the predictive medicine market. Or the logistics market. What's your market? Define it.

Once your market is clearly defined, you can determine its type. As Steve Blank articulated in *Four Steps to the Epiphany,*[1] there are three market type options:

- You compete in an existing market
- You are re-segmenting an existing market (either with a low-priced "good enough" strategy or a niche strategy)
- You are creating a new market

For instance, in 1999 Salesforce entered into an existing market—the CRM market. In 2003, Eloqua created an adjacent but new market—the marketing automation market (now populated by others, such as Marketo and HubSpot). And more recently, in 2012, Insightly re-segmented an existing market (CRM), focusing exclusively on SMB customers.

On the B2C side, Flickr created a new market—the social photo sharing site. Pinterest and Instagram (now the largest social sharing site with over 500 million monthly active users, according to Wikipedia) entered into an existing market, differentiating with new features.

Establishing your market type helps you define the basis for competitive advantage, important in constructing your competitive positioning statement.

Competitors

Research your competitors on the following dimensions:

- Features
- Performance
- Price
- Channel
- Market share
- Brand awareness
- Brand reputation
- Positioning
- For each competitor, review and consider:
- Their website
- Any publicly available research
- Online social reputation

- Substantive online customer reviews about product features/efficacy/ utility
- Conversations with current customers
- Conversations with former customers

How well do competitors address the tasks, expectations, and pain points of the buyers and users in your top priority segments? What positioning can they claim? Where are they vulnerable?

The result of your research will be a grid that looks like this:

	Features	Performance	Price	Channel	Market Share	Brand Awareness	Brand Reputation	Positioning
You								
Competitor A								
Competitor B								
Competitor C								

Market Maps

Using the competitive research data, you can create market maps that sharpen your understanding of your position vs. competitors. For B2B technology companies, it's possible this has been done for you. Gartner's Magic Quadrant[2] measures competitors on completeness of vision (x-axis) vs. ability to execute (y-axis). This map has four quadrants: Niche Players, Challengers, Leaders, and Visionaries.

Here is the Magic Quadrant for the Cloud Infrastructure as a Service market, worldwide:

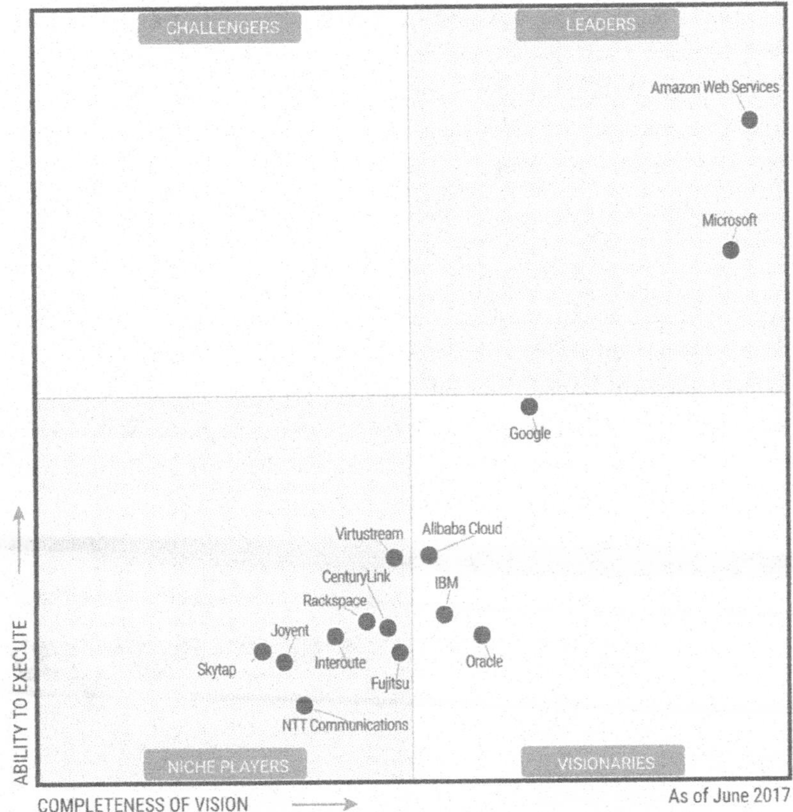

Other market maps that could help you define your unique points of competitive advantage include:

- Price / Performance
- Feature / Technology
- Channel / Margin
- Trend / Competitor

A competitive positioning map may help clarify key dynamics, like the perceptions of prospects and the claims of competitors. With such a map, you can find your own, sufficiently differentiated positioning.

If you are re-segmenting an existing market, your segmentation scheme (often presented as a large square representing the market, divided into boxes representing segments) is a useful contributor to positioning. And if you are creating a new market, it might help to draw a map that puts you at the center and defines the forces creating this new market.

These market maps will help crystalize your points of differentiation and firm up your claims.

Trends

Within your chosen market, it is important to define the critical trends. What emerging problems, opportunities, requirements, and technologies are impacting your top priority segments and reshaping the landscape? What key features are becoming popular? What shifts in market share are occurring as some competitors rise and others fall? Why? Does this dynamic accrue to your benefit or harm?

List the trends. Rank them in priority based on their impact on your growth prospects, and display them:

	Trend #1	Trend #2	Trend #3	Trend #4
You	↑	↑	↑	↓
Competitor A	↔	↓	↑	↓
Competitor B	↓	↔	↓	↑
Competitor C	↓	↓	↔	↔

The answers to trend questions will help you determine whether you are rising on the tide or fighting against the current. If the former, your positioning will more likely be based on a quality advantage. If the latter, price may need to be your advantage.

Create a Claim

You are now ready to craft your bold claim.

This positioning statement must first achieve the "vision lock" threshold: "I get what you do and why it's relevant for me." Then, it must positively differentiate, accentuating your value while boxing in your competitors.

You have already determined whether you're serving an existing market, a re-segmented market or a new market. If entering an existing market, product-centric positioning (feature advantages) makes sense. If re-segmenting an existing market, you're either positioning on price or on niche product advantage. And if entering a new market, you position versus the alternative of doing nothing; positioning is evangelical and descriptive.

The first two market types (an existing market or re-segmented market) enable you to assess your competitive advantage on quality price dimensions.

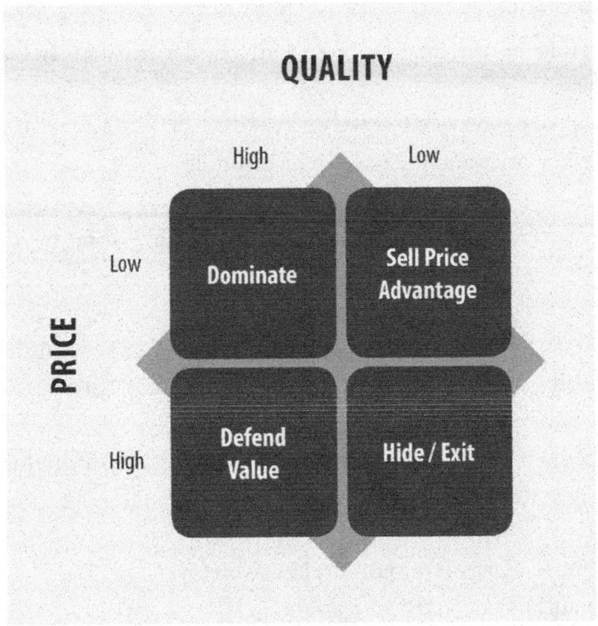

- If you have both a quality and price advantage, you can employ a "dominate" positioning strategy
- If you have a quality disadvantage but offer a lower price, then "sell price advantage"

- If you have a quality advantage but a higher price, then "defend value"
- Of course, if you have inferior quality and a higher price, you must either drop your price significantly or exit

In the writing of positioning statements, Martina Lauchengco, Operating Partner at Costanoa Venture Capital, warns against two pitfalls: the first, the "TMI" (too much information) problem; and the second, the "so simple it's meaningless" problem.

Here's her TMI example:

> "[Data Security Suite], the leading data loss prevention solution, accurately prevents data leakage, secures business processes, and manages compliance and risk by discovering where data is located, monitoring its use, and protecting it, on the network and at the endpoint."

Here's her "meaninglessly simple" example:

> "Better detect and defend your most valuable data by gaining visibility."

The first is mind-numbingly cumbersome. The second doesn't tell you anything. Neither achieves its intended effect: an engaged, interested prospect.

Lauchengco offers three points of advice in the development of a positioning statement:

- Choose clarity over comprehensiveness
- Be authentic vs. authoritarian
- Really know your audience

Here are some positioning statements that achieve these objectives:

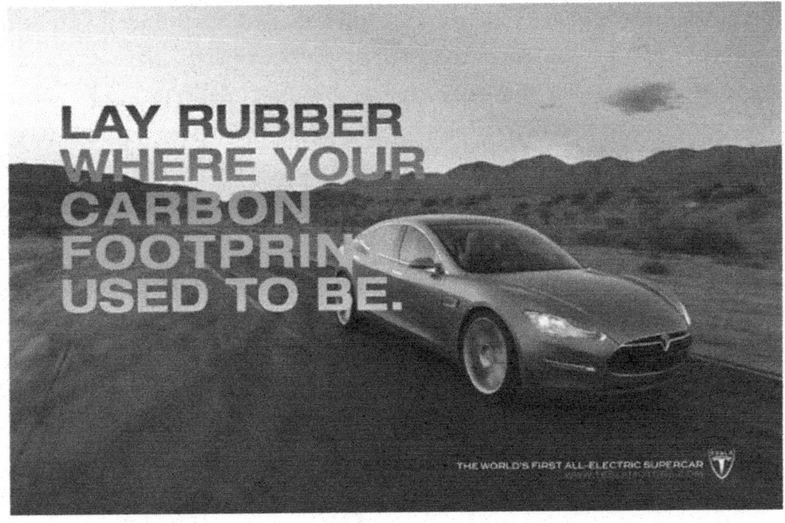

Tesla highlights the advantages most impactful to its socially conscious high-end car buyer. Note that the objective is achieved while simultaneously boxing in competitors. The car market (even electric car market) is an existing market; the positioning statement underscores product advantage clearly, succinctly and powerfully.

Similarly, Salesforce conquers the CRM space with its message, "Salesforce, not software." When first launched, its unique SaaS pricing model combined with cloud-based hosting to provide flexibility, simplicity, and affordability that was not previously available (with legacy CRM systems such as Oracle). While the CRM market existed prior to Salesforce, the predominant model was a software licensing model with on-premise software and ongoing support requirements. Salesforce re-segmented an existing market with a new product delivery model and a new pricing model. The positioning statement emphasizes this product and pricing advantage, and takes advantage of the trend towards SaaS.

Expensify brought simplicity and usability to the expense reporting process, crystallized in its positioning statement, "Expense Reports That Don't Suck." The follow-on phrase, "hassle-free expense reporting built for employees and loved by admins," says it all. For the target buyer and user personas—admins and front-line sales employees—the direct talk works. Unlike other expense report software, which was built with a company-centric mindset, Expensify's positioning statement underscores its employee-first orientation, which differentiates it in this existing market.

In the IT world, containers offer a way to virtualize the operating system. Docker entered this existing market and then grew it dramatically due to its unique product advantages. Docker focuses its positioning on its status as the world's leading open containerization platform for distributed applications. It delivers to developers and sysadmins the development and implementation simplicity they seek. These value attributes are summed up in its positioning statement "Build, Ship, Run" with the follow-on line, "Docker is the world's leading software containerization platform." This, of course, boxes in everyone else.

Lightbend has created a new market. The company's CTO, Jonas Boner, wrote "The Reactive Manifesto,"[3] popularizing the movement from monolith to micro-services based infrastructures. Lightbend provides the leading reactive application development platform for building distributed applications and modernizing aging infrastructures. It uses micro-services and fast data on a message-driven runtime. It enables applications to scale on multi-core and cloud computing architectures seamlessly.

Given this technical description, it would be easy for Lightbend's positioning statement to fall prey to the TMI problem. But it doesn't. "Modernize your enterprise at startup speed" speaks clearly to the technical leaders, architects and development managers at large enterprises who must update their infrastructures to deal with a fast data, distributed world. Positioning to a new market, Lightbend's statement clearly describes the benefit to an audience still coming to grips with the need to change. It also takes advantage of the modernization trend.

Your company's positioning statement will hold center stage in all of your messaging, so it's very important that you put the sweat into creating a good one. Do the research necessary to get it right. Write from the perspective of your target personas. Say something that captures their attention and appreciation.

One positioning statement is sufficient if, on its own, it is adequately salient and resonant for all of your top priority segments and personas. If not, then as with Lightbend, your company-level positioning statement may need to be augmented with positioning statements that are customized at the levels of product, segment, and persona.

Test, Iterate, Optimize

Positioning statements can and should be tested. Get prospect and customer feedback. Talk with salespeople. A/B test via email, paid search campaigns, and website page tests. Iterate. Optimize. Eventually, you'll have a positioning statement you can run with.

Remember, the market will keep shifting on you. Your positioning will need to evolve. Keep your ear to the ground and keep testing.

Position to win.

7

Brand Identity

Key Concepts in Chapter 7:

- Your brand identity builds on the foundation of value proposition and competitive positioning
- Brand identity is comprised of brand as product, brand as company, brand as person, and brand as symbol
- Your Brand Identity Document canonizes your key themes, product descriptions, statements, claims, lists, competitive comparisons, and style details, consistent with your value proposition and competitive positioning
- This Brand Identity Document is the foundation for your messaging schema: the set of playbooks (Brand, Product Marketing, Growth Marketing, Sales Development, Sales, and Customer Success) that provide the fully detailed plans and guidelines for messaging

This chapter is relevant for the following business models:

- Very Low Customer LTV (<$500)
- Low Customer LTV ($501 - $10,000)
- Mid Customer LTV ($10,001 - $100,000)
- High Customer LTV ($100,001 - $500,000)
- Very High Customer LTV ($500,001+)

You are whom you can credibly claim to be.

Brand identity is the comprehensive expression of your aspirational self-image. Built upon the foundations of smart segmentation, distinctive value proposition, and clear competitive positioning, it is the final step in brand development.

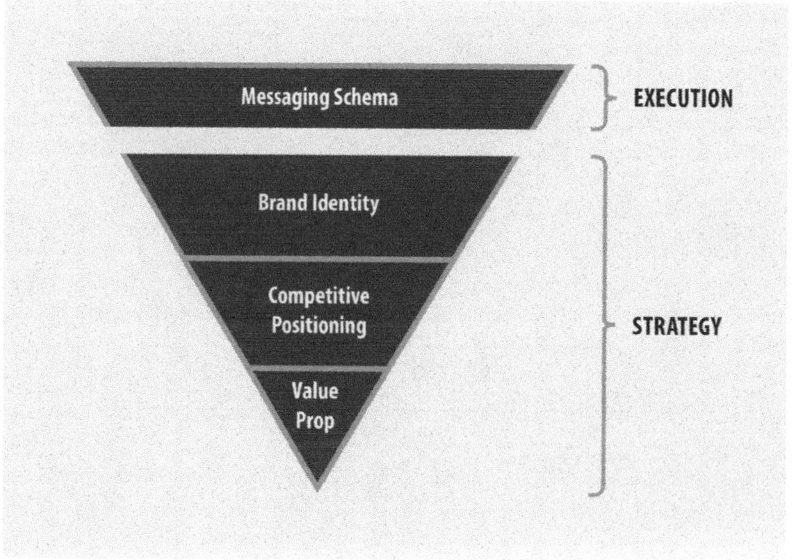

It's important to remember that your brand's value ultimately depends on just one thing: the meaning attached to it by the buyers and users in your target market. For these people, this meaning emerges from a slow, steady accumulation of many impressions. These impressions come from your own messaging, the statements of your current and past customers, and the claims made by your competitors (and their current and past customers).

Your messaging is the primary lever you have to positively shape brand meaning.

The work you do to think through and build out your brand identity should yield messaging so artfully developed and executed it controls the narrative.

UC Berkeley marketing professor, David Aaker,[1] asserts that a company's brand identity is made up of four brand dimensions:

- Brand as company
- Brand as product
- Brand as person
- Brand as symbol

For instance, Apple has a developed a "brand as company" that celebrates creativity, independence, and empowerment, anchored by the positioning, "Think Different." Its "brand as product" is also distinctive: MacBook, iTunes, iPad and iPhone all feature strong product brands in full alignment with the overall Apple brand. Apple has evoked "brand as person" in multiple campaigns over the years—from the Viking woman taking on Big Blue in the 1984 Macintosh commercial, to the "Mac guy vs. PC guy" advertising, to iPod's dancing silhouettes campaign. And of course, Apple's library of pitch-perfect logos, icons, color schemes, and typography comprise the company's "brand as symbol."

Your brand identity must be built to ensure these four brand manifestations are successfully cultivated in the minds of your target audience. At each stage of the prospect and customer journey, your messaging job changes: from creating awareness, to building understanding, to establishing relevance, to capturing interest, to building confirmation. Then, after the sale, you must build purchase affirmation and create a confident, happy customer who wants to recommend your brand to others.

Andrea Tucker, CEO of Strategy Applied, summarizes these messaging jobs into three major stages of commitment:

- Vision Lock ("I get what you do and why it's relevant to me.")
- Conviction Lock ("I'm convinced. Sign me up!")
- Advocacy Lock ("I'm a raving fan!")

Achieving these stages is not simple. Every word and image must be task-focused, brand-true, stage-relevant, and segment-specific. It doesn't just happen. To get there, it's helpful to build out a brand identity document.

The brand identity document, discussed in detail below, is the foundation of your messaging schema. The messaging schema is the library of playbooks that take messaging to the level of detail necessary to guide daily work. The messaging schema includes between three and six playbooks. For all companies, there are playbooks for brand, product marketing and growth marketing. For those companies that have sales teams, there are three additional playbooks (sales development, account executives, and customer success).

The brand identity document includes your value proposition and competitive positioning statements. It articulates the major supporting themes and product-level statements, data, lists, comparisons, and use cases. It also defines the brand's visual expression.

The brand identity document has the following structure:

Brand Identity Document Structure

I. Value proposition

II. Competitive positioning statement

III. Supporting themes

A. Theme 1 (statement that conveys theme and passes "vision lock" test)
   1. Variation 1 by segment and/or persona
   2. Variation 2 by segment and/or persona, etc.

B. Theme 2

C. Theme 3, etc.

IV. Products

A. Product 1
   1. Product benefit statement that passes "vision lock" test
      a. Variation 1 by segment/persona
      b. Variation 2 by segment/persona, etc.
   2. Supporting statements, data, lists, competitive comparisons, and use cases that substantiate claims and pass "conviction lock" test
      a. Variation 1 by segment/persona
      b. Variation 2 by segment/persona, etc.
   3. Best practices, case studies, Q&A, and "how to" assets that validate purchase and pass "advocacy lock" test
      a. Variation 1 by segment/persona
      b. Variation 2 segment/persona, etc.

B. Product 2

C. Product 3, etc.

V. Brand visual expression

A. Architecture
   1. Relationship of master brand to sub-brands
   2. Naming conventions
   3. Hierarchy

B. Symbols
   1. Icons (logos, etc.)
   2. Typography
   3. Color scheme

C. Personality
   1. Human-like traits
   2. Avatars / mascots

The process to create your brand identity document includes the following steps:

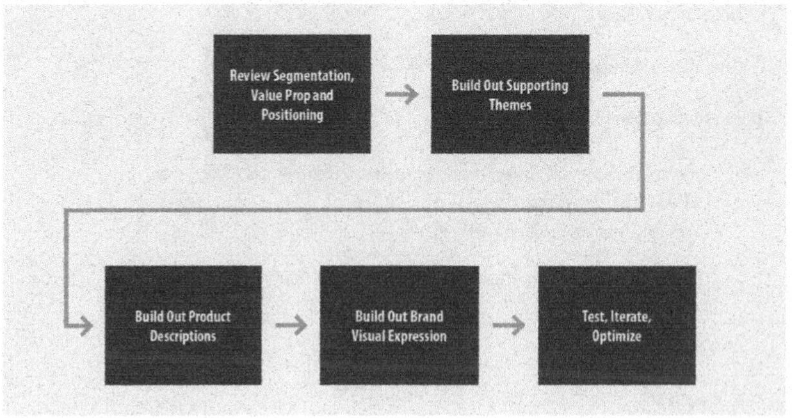

Review Segmentation Data, Value Proposition, and Competitive Positioning

Your value proposition and competitive positioning statement have already been written. So the next step is to develop a short list of supporting themes—the themes that will bolster your competitive positioning statement. Start by pulling together a list of all conceivable themes that could be contenders for the top two to four supporting themes.

This starts by looking over your segmentation data. Within your top priority segments (see Chapter 4—Customer Segmentation), users and buyers have tasks, expectations and pain points. Which ones matter most? Add the most important of these to the themes list.

Next, consider your brand awareness and reputation. With the buyers and users in your top priority segments, how do you fare in terms of aided and unaided brand recall? If you aren't known at all, you have a big communication challenge but at least you are working with a clean slate. If you are known, what's your reputation? What attributes do buyers and users associate with your brand? The most frequently recurring positive attributes should be added to the themes list.

Now turn to your value proposition (see Chapter 5, Value Proposition). It is made up of six components:

- For (target customers)
- Who are dissatisfied with (the current market alternative)
- Our product is a (description of product category)
- That provides (compelling reason to buy)
- Unlike (the product alternative)
- We deliver (key whole product features for your specific application)

These components can be converted into themes, such as:

- "We serve SMB businesses."
- "Current expense reporting systems are overbuilt and cumbersome."
- "We're in the expense reporting market."
- "Our product is simple and user-friendly for small businesses."
- "We're simpler and cheaper than competitive alternatives."
- "Our scan and display features make expense report submission a breeze."

Use this exercise to tease out additional potential themes and add them to the list.

Now consider your competitive positioning statement (see Chapter 6, Competitive Positioning). Does any other important theme come to mind? Add it to the list as well.

Build Out Supporting Themes

You should now have a fairly comprehensive list of potential themes. Do they naturally group together? Do some themes emerge that most powerfully support and expand upon your competitive positioning statement? Rank them in order of importance. Only the top two to four will make the cut, so choose carefully.

For each chosen theme, turn it into a clear statement that achieves vision lock. Test your choice of themes and theme statements with customers and prospects. Iterate and optimize.

Build out Product Descriptions

Consider each product's unique value, consistent with the overall company value proposition. Determine the product benefit statement that achieves vision lock.

Sitting underneath the vision lock statement for each product is supporting information. This includes supporting statements, data, lists, competitive comparisons, integration requirements, stories, use cases, price information, the attributes of your team and the level of support you deliver, and so forth. The purpose of this support is to achieve conviction lock.

Finally, these product descriptions will include the content that helps you achieve advocacy lock: documentation of best practices, case studies, Q&A, "How To," and so forth.

Different segments and personas may require product benefit statement variations. If so, vary accordingly. With prospects and customers, test, iterate, and optimize to confirm clarity and resonance.

Brand Visual Expression

Brand Architecture

Smart brand architecture simplifies and clarifies.

For some companies, brand architecture is irrelevant. The product and company are synonymous. Healthline.com is the health website (the product), and Healthline is the company. But for many tech companies, product features proliferate or new products are added. When this occurs, a well conceived brand architecture becomes important.

Let's start with a simple example—the naming hierarchy for a company with a single dominant product that has various configurations or product bolt-ons. You might, for instance, have a Silver, Platinum or Gold offering. Or you might have an updated version of a product—the Pro 2.0 or 3.0, etc.

ClearCare, a platform for home care agencies, matches this description. The company organizes its brand hierarchy starting with ClearCare, the product platform. The platform is presented showing four categories of use: "Grow your Agency," "Manage Caregivers," "Deliver Care," and "Optimize Operations." Under each category, product features are shown, following a simple descriptive naming convention. In turn, these flow into pricing, as follows:

One Platform

So You Can Get Back To Care

GROW YOUR AGENCY	MANAGE CAREGIVERS	DELIVER CARE	OPTIMIZE OPERATIONS
CRM	Caregiver Marketplace	[illegible] Scheduling	Billing & Payroll
Referral Source Tracking	Applicant Tracking	Smart Telephony	Overtime/ACA Tools
Marketing Tools	Caregiver Portal	Family Room	Reporting & Analytics
Readmission Tracking	Employment Screening	Worksafe Central	Payment Processing
Preferred Partners	Work Comp Insurance	Tele-Health	Tax Credits

Startup	Base	Platform	Franchise
Get started quickly and see immediate results	Differentiate your agency with 25+ tools to help you grow	Integrated features for maximum client growth and time savings	Tools specific to large, franchise and multi-unit brands
See All Features	See All Features	See All Features	See All Features
Scheduling	**Everything in Startup, plus:**	**Everything in Base, plus:**	**Everything in Platform, plus:**
Billing & Payroll	Family Room	Background Checks	HQ Portal
Sales CRM	Caregiver Portals	E-payment	Multi-Unit Territories
Telephony	Readmission Tracking	Earn Tax Credit	Specialized On-boarding
On-Boarding	Marketing Tools	Save on Worker's Comp	Bulk Workflows

As you scale, your product line will expand. You may build separate business units. You may acquire companies that bring along brand equity you want to keep. Inevitably, if you are successful, brand architecture will become more complicated. To solve for these growing complexities, you will need to choose a brand architecture that falls into one of four alternative approaches:

1. Strong Master Brand / Strong Sub-brand

- Sub-brands are strong, but they also have a strong link to the master
- Example: Microsoft

The advantage of this approach is that it ensures the sub-brands are independent, while still leveraging a strong master brand. The risk of this approach is that if the master brand weakens, the sub-brands can suffer. Also, to become strong, each sub-brand requires significant marketing spend.

2. Branded House

- Strong master brand with distinctive but subordinate sub-brands
- Example: Virgin

The branded house architecture carries the benefit of marketing efficiency. Marketing spend is focused on building the master brand. Sub-brands are supported, but are closely linked to the master brand. Challenges include situations in which the sub-brand can't break out from under its master, or in a competitive space, the sub-brand might find the master brand more of an anchor than a lever in creating positive differentiation.

3. Endorsed Brands

- Brands stand alone, but are endorsed by a master brand
- Example: Google

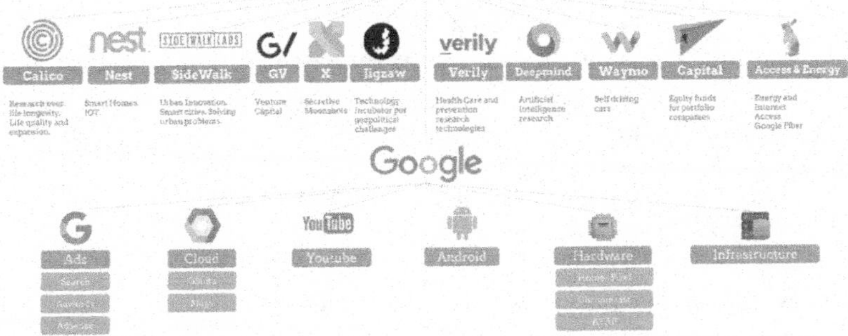

This type of brand architecture delivers the benefit of strong independent brands, while still affording affiliation leverage with a strong master brand. The downside is that each independent brand requires significant independent investment. Also, if the master brand is damaged, there could be negative affiliation risk.

4. House of Brands

- Brands stand completely alone; master brand is not visible
- Example: IAC Media

The advantage of this approach is that every brand is completely independent. Each brand can serve disparate markets and segments uniquely with no negative affiliation impacts. On the other hand, the "house of brands" approach requires the highest level of marketing investment. And of course, there's no leverage from a strong master brand.

The secrets to smart brand architecture are clarity, consistency, and simplicity. Figure out your audience and your purpose, and build a framework that achieves it.

Personality

Leveraging the buyer and user personas you discovered in your customer segmentation work and a deep understanding of the problems you solve, you can express your brand with human-like traits. This is powerful. It makes your brand more accessible and adds emotional and self-expressive benefits to the core functional benefits you deliver.

Brand as person is closely linked to your internal culture and values. Whom you profess to be, expressed in human-like traits, must be aligned with whom you are, as seen by your customers in their interactions with you.

List the human-like traits of your brand. Perhaps it's "cool person" (e.g., Mac) vs. "nerd" (e.g., PC). Or "warm and welcoming." Or "smart." Or "creative."

For an example of a company that does this well, consider Mancrates.com. This e-commerce site for men's gifts is quintessentially and irreverently "male." Guys are pictured with heavy machinery and heavy tools and there's a tongue-in-cheek "manliness" about the entire site. The company creates a fun, accessible, "manly" ambiance for customers that separates it from the pack.

Symbols

Your naming, logo, typography, color scheme, branded images, icons, mascots, and other visual assets comprise your "Brand as

Symbol." These are designed to accentuate the core themes of your brand. What metaphors do you want to invoke? What affiliations? How do they advance your positioning and connect to your top segments and their buyers and users? Choose wisely. Then test, iterate and optimize.

Bringing it All Together

Consider Healthline, one of the most highly visited consumer health websites in the world and the fastest growing in the top four. Its CEO, David Kopp, and his team updated the Healthline brand in 2016.

The team started with a restatement of vision: "A stronger, healthier world," and mission: "To be your most trusted ally in your pursuit of health and well-being." Their value proposition reads as follows:

> "For health seekers who want to be well-informed and self-empowered, Healthline is their most valued and trusted resource. Unlike other consumer health information publishers, we provide experiences that pair authoritative, approachable, actionable content with compassion and a commitment to a healthier world."

As part of their work, the team defined the brand's key themes. These themes inform all content:

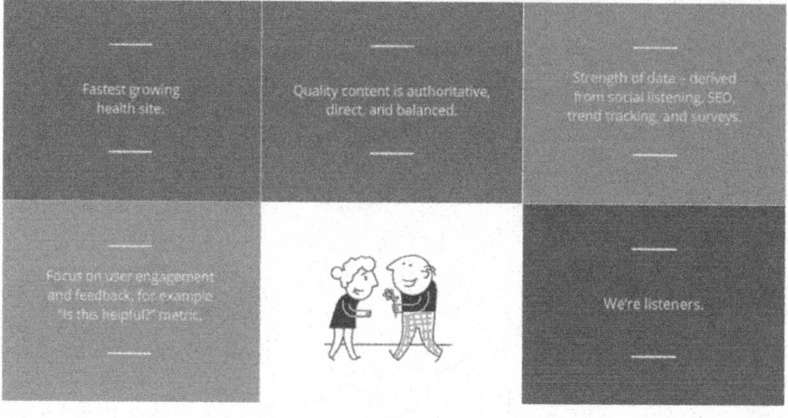

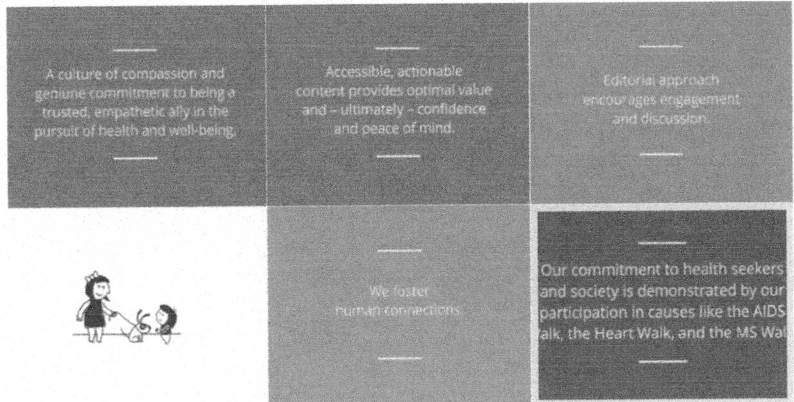

The Healthline personality is described as follows:

our brand personality

healthline is **trustworthy.**
we are **smart**, **passionate,** and **progressive.**
we're **open**, **caring,** and, above all, **we're human!**
we demonstrate **genuine empathy** in all our interactions.

Here's the logo:

There is a defined color palette (no, it's not variations of grey):

Illustrations are part of the brand look and feel:

Carry grocery bags with your forearms instead of your hands

The future is now. No. Not later, now. Right now!

From "29 Things Only A Person With ADHD Would Know"

...you sweat a lot. For no reason other than you're breathing.

From "Don't Sweat It..."

Healthline typography guidelines are below:

Our brand font is Open Sans. With upright, open forms and a neutral, yet friendly appearance, it helps make our content more approachable.

‹

ingenuity

we are smart, innovative, and inspiring changemakers.

[empathy

we feel with our users and are committed to being their true ally in their lifelong pursuit of health and well-being.

›

The Process

The work to build out your brand identity is often undertaken with the help of a strong brand consultant or agency. Customer and prospect testing and iteration are important to get it right.

Work on brand identity is work on the essence of your being as a company. For that reason, it is very important that the entire executive team critically review and provide feedback on the brand identity document. Once defined and finalized, your brand identity is a canon that must be protected and scrupulously followed. Your top team will be the most critical protectors and evangelists. Buy-in is key.

The foundational work you do on brand identity will be expressed in your messaging schema playbooks and ultimately in thousands of messages and millions of impressions sent to your prospects and customers. Each impression will add slightly to the meaning of your brand in the minds of the people you care about most. This is the work that ensures each message resonates like a tuning fork.

Perfect pitch.

8

Product

Key Concepts in Chapter 8:

- Your product roadmap is strategy in motion: it governs the prioritization of development projects and must yield long-term revenue and profit maximization
- Product development velocity governs output: it's achieved via right skills and staff levels, agile development methodology, clear prioritization, and leader team alignment
- To prioritize, ascertain your "true problem": value, velocity, retention, chasm crossing, segmentation, or customer expansion
- At every stage of development, test and iterate with prospects and customers to confirm assumptions

This chapter is relevant for the following business models:

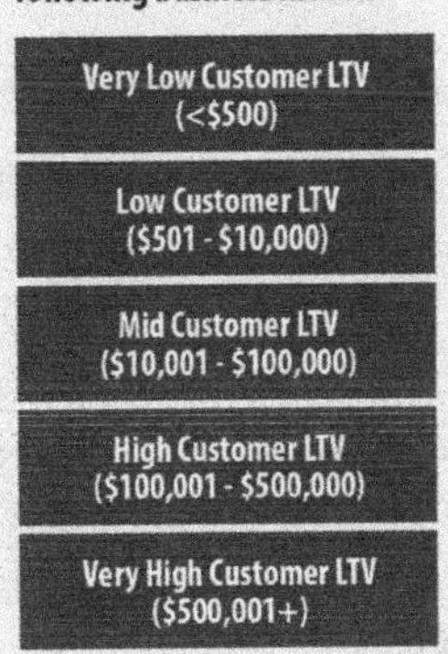

Your product exists to meet a true market need, and by doing so, to drive revenue. As such, it is a key component in the revenue engine—one of the main building blocks of the Mission / Strategy foundation layer.

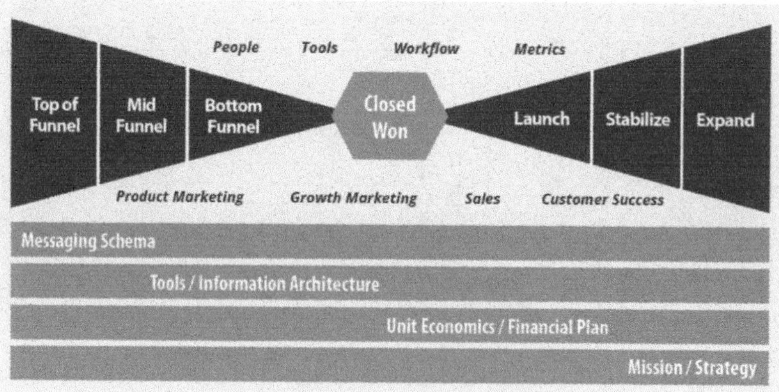

Since your product is the central source of customer value, your product roadmap is an essential tool in optimizing revenue growth. Your roadmap prioritizes the projects you believe are the most critical to drive increases in value. It's strategy in motion.

Product development is both resource-intensive and time-consuming. So it is important that you have a well thought through plan for how to expend your resources and time. The choices you make—of what to do now, what to do next, what to do much later, and what not to do at all—are pivotal.

It starts with your team. Do you have top talent in product and engineering? Your product development capacity will be gated by the competency of your team, especially your top execs. Make sure you have placed the very best into these positions.

It's now widely understood that the agile development process is the optimal way to build software. You probably employ this approach. With it, requirements and solutions evolve through collaboration. Small cross-functional teams meet daily to review work. Development is modular, not monolithic. Early delivery is encouraged, with a continuous improvement mindset. Work is organized around monthly design sprints, and 1–4 week production sprints. By this method, you iteratively develop and rapidly release small increments of software at a time.

Decisions on infrastructure and architecture also impact development velocity. Until you prove product/market fit, it makes sense to build with quick hacks and minimum time to a viable product. That's because if your product is off, you have not over-invested. But, as the product proves itself and begins to scale, you should refactor into a microservices architecture. A microservices-based systems architecture is more responsive, resilient, and capable of leveraging the cloud.

Agile development methods and microservices-based systems architecture are just enablers of great products. It all comes down to the product itself, and a great product must win in the marketplace.

As CEO, when it comes to product development, you must maintain a delicate balance between discipline and flexibility. On the one hand, the market keeps changing, so emerging insights will impact development priorities. On the other hand, the product development machine works best when it works methodically. Jerking priorities around creates massive inefficiency and endangers quality. Striking that balance is an act of leadership judgment.

As CEO, do you frequently bring the latest product idea right to a software developer who can "just make it happen?" Does your VP Engineering regularly declare, "Only I know what the client needs?" Does your Sales VP push for the rapid completion of some shiny new feature "to make sure we hit the quarter?" These are signs of a poorly designed product development system. Poor design creates problems and drains valuable resources. For example, business and engineering teams become misaligned. Product quality suffers. Production slows. Responsiveness to the market declines.

Here is a quick quiz:

- Given your requirements, do your product and engineering teams lack the skills necessary to execute your product plan with very high fidelity at every level of the stack?
- Are your teams too small given the development load?
- Do your product and engineering teams exhibit inefficiency in development?
- Do you fall short of the requirements for a true agile development process?
- Do you have a "shiny object" problem, whereby priorities are excessively re-juggled?

- Are your sales, marketing, product, and engineering teams misaligned on product vision and priorities?

If the answer to any of these question is yes, you have basic problems that must be addressed before you can address product roadmap optimization. Start by putting in place the right people, the right infrastructure and architecture, the right sized teams, a rationalized development process, and a disciplined priority-setting approach.

Start small and scale carefully. It is better to execute well on a few critical priorities, than to execute poorly on everything.

Once you are sure your basic product development system is sound, you are ready to turn to the question of prioritization.

The first prioritization decision is to weight infrastructure work versus product work. As CEO, it's important to support your VP of engineering in the allocation of resources to infrastructure projects. They are vital. They will yield scalability, reliability, and development velocity down the road, even though they will slow market-facing product development in the short term. Fight the instinct to starve these projects in favor of market-facing product work. That's almost never a good decision.

With infrastructure projects built into the product roadmap, the remaining resources can be dedicated to market-facing product projects. Which ones do you work on first? Too often, these priorities are comprised of your case list submitted by current customers. The loudest complaints yield the highest prioritization.

This is a certifiably bad approach. The cases that fly in from highly engaged customers are necessary—but insufficient—contributors to prioritization decisions. As CEO, you should be at least equally concerned about the voiceless: the customers who exhibit little or no usage of your product, the prospects who considered but never bought, the prospects who like your features but value safety (i.e., are waiting on security features, enterprise reporting features, etc.), and the prospects and segments that "should see value" but won't buy.

The smart process for product roadmap decision-making looks something like this:

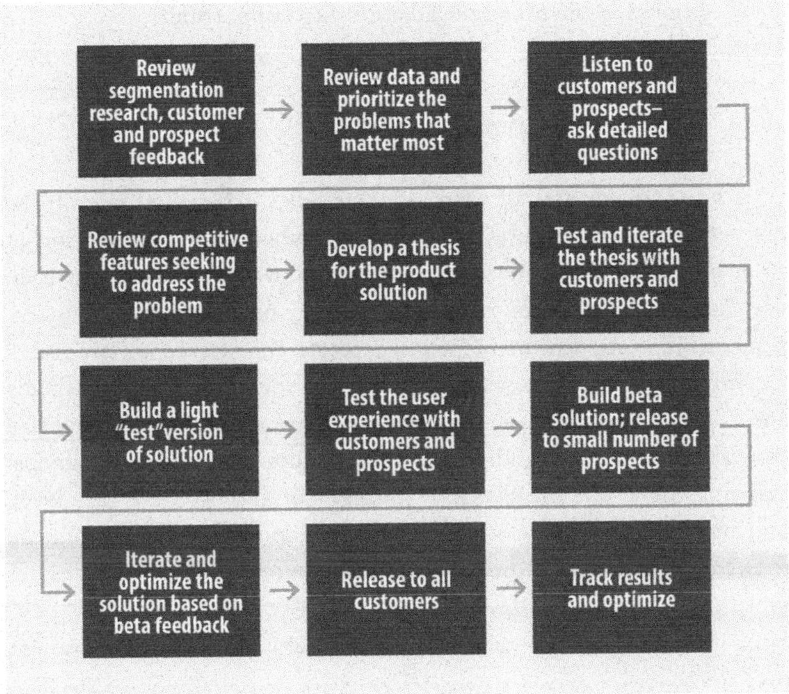

Selecting the Problems to Tackle

The first step in making smart product roadmap decisions is to figure out your "true problems." You might have a:

- Value problem—can't efficiently acquire customers
- Velocity problem—customers like the product once they've bought and become familiar with it, but the conversion fall off (from initial interest to engagement to trial to purchase to familiarity and high satisfaction) is excessively steep
- Retention problem—can sell the product, but product limitations yield excessive churn
- Chasm crossing problem—can't move beyond the innovators and early adopters within your top priority segments
- Segment expansion problem—can't move from initial top

priority segments to the adjacent high-opportunity segments
- Customer expansion problem—can't get existing customers to increase purchases or expand use

True problems are not found in your office. They are found in the marketplace. In Chapter 4—Customer Segmentation, completion of an atomic-level "use case scenario exercise" was advocated. For each use case, you were asked to answer a series of questions. One question was to estimate in percentage terms the degree of product / market fit. Through research such as this, you clarify how prospects and customers within specific use case scenarios currently perceive your product's value, and where the product falls short. By understanding these true problems at the segment and even use case level, and by ranking your segments by their importance to your future growth, you can determine what development initiatives matter most.

A "true problems" analysis might yield product development projects that:

- Alter or even pivot the product to address a value problem within existing top priority customer segments, so that initial sales increase
- Improve the onramp to your product to increase new customer adoption velocity for customers within existing top priority customer segments
- Improve retention by making changes to the product that address the reasons for churn
- Fortify the product to address the safety / dependability / reporting needs of early and late majority customers within existing top priority segments
- Build out the product to address the needs of new customer segments you seek to enter
- Build premium product extensions that allow you to offer premium packages for existing and new customers / segments

- Build new products to serve adjacent needs which you can sell to existing and new customers / segments

Let's consider each type of "true problem."

The Value Problem

If the true problem is value (i.e., you can't efficiently acquire customers because they don't see the value), you have your work cut out for you. You must first validate whether it's a messaging problem. If you have confirmed messaging is not the issue—in other words, prospects understand what you offer but they don't want it—then you must conclude that your entire product thesis was wrong.

If you're in this situation, you have no choice. You must go back to basics and validate:

- Within the customer segments you seek to serve, what exact problem are you trying to solve, down to the use case level?
- For each use case, do both buyer and user experience enough pain from the problem that they will pay you to solve it?
- What exact requirements must the solution address?
- What list of specific features is required to deliver on these requirements?
- Can you build it?
- How long will it take you to build it?
- How many resources will be required to build it?
- If you build it, are there enough ready-to-buy prospects to justify your investment and build a big business?
- Given what you've already built, is there an alternative problem you can solve that is faster to build, less resource intensive and / or opens you to a larger growth opportunity?

Since you did not adequately validate your assumptions the first time around, it's important to do so now. You will face pressure (possibly even from your investors) to move quickly, but truth is much more important than speed. The marketplace, your prospects, and the competitors are all in motion. Finding the true, enduring pain that only you can solve takes work. Where do these needs and emerging trends within top priority segments intersect with your capabilities? This is the essence of product strategy. Talk to more prospects, not less. Make home or office visits; don't just call. To the best of your ability, step into the lives of your prospects and customers and figure out exactly how this next iteration of your product will make their lives better.

The Velocity Problem

If this is your problem, the customers who have purchased your product and have begun to use it properly are happy. The problem is that not enough have overcome the hurdles to become a paying customer. Either the product wasn't designed to engage the prospect at Top or Mid Funnel stage in the first place, or when prospects do initiate engagement, the initial experience falls short and they fall away. For either reason, prospects don't convert at a high enough rate to become buyers and engaged users.

Here, the issue lies in the "first mile" of the customer experience.

The first mile is the initial-use product utility that provides a glimpse into the full product experience, the welcome and introduction tour, the on-boarding experience, explanatory copy, and the empty states and default settings that greet the customer—i.e., the customer's initial product experience.

If this is your challenge, Scott Belsky's post, "Crafting the First Mile of Product"[1] is spot on. Belsky encourages you to assume that all prospects are lazy, vain, and selfish. They need to understand, within 15 seconds, "why am I here," "what can I accomplish," and "what do I do next." They want to receive a benefit for their time very quickly. If the first mile experience can be designed in a way that allows the prospect to "do" something that delivers immediate utility and is ego-gratifying, that's best. As Belsky puts it, "Do is better than Show is better than Explain."

The initial user experience must be simple. The empty states, such as dashboards that do not yet show data, should be designed to deliver some value. The default settings, such as tabs, pre-populated fields, and templates should contribute to a seamless, confidence-building experience.

Belsky argues that the first mile experience should consume at least 30% of total development time in the development of your product. Critically, it should be built early in the development cycle, not at the very end.

The Retention Problem

When you can sell to the customer but you can't retain her, there is one piece of good news. At least you know that the value you claim to deliver resonates. In solving a retention problem, you must first figure out whether churn occurs due to your failure to deliver on the value you have claimed, whether the wrong customers are buying in the first place, or whether there is another supporting requirement that falls short.

For instance, you might claim a business benefit from your technology that the customer simply doesn't experience. That could either be because your product is incapable of delivering the benefit, or because the customer didn't use the product properly.

Alternatively, the product might deliver the promised benefit, but its purchase might come with an unanticipated collateral cost. Problems integrating a new product into legacy technology are often the culprit. More often than not, such problems result in organ rejection. Another source of churn can result from the effect of your product on customer employees. For instance, if your product displaces labor, the impacted employees could be instigators of churn by sabotaging successful implementation.

There are many possible reasons for churn. It's on you and your team to figure out those reasons and to address them. You may even need to consider whether your choice of top priority segments must be revisited. Leverage data to see churn patterns. Talk to and visit enough customers to have high confidence you understand what creates churn.

Only then will you be ready to develop new product solutions to attack the problems.

The Chasm Crossing Problem

As Geoffrey Moore noted in his classic book, *Crossing the Chasm,*[2] innovators and early adopters are different from early and late majority customers. The latter value safety over innovation. Not only do they require validation that your product has become the emerging standard, but they seek specific product features that reduce risk. For instance, mainstream B2B customers will require high levels of security and identity protection. They may require robust enterprise reporting features and may need the product to offer proof that it's delivering its intended ROI.

The feature requirements of early and late majority customers can be gleaned by attempting to sell what you already offer. Interested mainstream customers will balk when they learn you don't have this or that. It's then incumbent upon you to develop a way to rigorously capture the "this" and the "that." As you assemble the list of required features, you can further test your emerging chasm crossing thesis with more mainstream prospects until you have high confidence you understand what's needed. At that point, you're ready to build.

The Segment Expansion Problem

Perhaps you have built a product that has been widely adopted by your top priority segment. Your success has been exciting but you can see on the horizon that your first segment will soon cap out. To continue your rocket ship growth rate, you must conquer new, adjacent segments.

When this is the true problem, it's common for CEOs to make a key mistake. They overestimate the similarity of the existing segment to the next segment, opting to forego thorough analysis of the new segment's unique use case scenarios and needs. The result is too often a "lipstick" makeover that does not fit the new segment's true needs nor solve its true pain points.

Once again, the solution is clear but hard: deeply engage the buyers and users at the use case level. Gain a thorough understanding of the pain that must be solved and the requirements that must be met. Then involve prospective customers in your development process so that by the time you're done you have built a product you know your next segment will buy.

The Customer Expansion Problem

If your product enables customers to increase the quantity purchased, but your customers are not buying increased quantities at the rate you had expected, you have a customer expansion problem.

Start by figuring out the nature of the bottleneck. Alternatives include:

- Not satisfied with the quantity already purchased (churn risk)
- Have bought enough already; don't need more
- Don't know how to buy more
- Haven't been encouraged / reminded to buy more
- Want to buy more, but facing some impediment (within or outside the product)

Since these are existing customers, the task to thoroughly understand the bottleneck should be relatively easy: just reach out to enough of them to gain pattern recognition and confirm your assumptions. Once you understand the bottleneck, you can design the product features that will overcome it.

Solving the Problems: Product Design

Once you have definitively prioritized the problems you will tackle, the real work begins. This work will consume product manager and engineering time, so it needs to get onto the product roadmap. Changing a product roadmap is like turning an ocean liner. It's reasonable to expect that any shifts in priority will need to be made gradually so as not to disrupt existing projects midstream (unless, of course, it is determined that existing projects are off strategy).

True problems in hand, you are ready to design a product concept that will attack and solve them. Since development is costly, it's key to validate your product concept with low-cost methods first.

The sequence of work should look something like this:

- Review competitor solutions; determine existing best practices (to achieve feature parity) and feature gaps
- Develop a solution thesis, with storyboards
- Test the thesis / storyboards with prospects and customers; iterate
- Build a light version of the product; test and iterate
- Build a beta version of the product; expand to a meaningful number of customers; test and iterate
- Full release

Final thoughts

As CEO, your decisions in the product arena will profoundly impact your company's viability and ultimate valuation. So it's best not to screw it up. Start by making absolutely sure you have the right team in place. Build a modular systems architecture. Create a disciplined, agile development process. Think outside-in. Work hard to ascertain your true problem. Ensure top team alignment. Design and test every proposed solution, recognizing that the objective is to increase long-term customer value as measured by revenue and profit growth. Great products prove their worth via unit economics: high LTV and efficient CAC. Your product roadmap decisions are some of the most important decisions you'll make. Do your homework, and choose well.

Epiphanies are hard won.

9

Pricing & Packaging

Key Concepts in Chapter 9:

- Price to maximize the area under your demand curves
- Price to penetrate: customer acquisition is oxygen
- Price to expand: expansion is the cheapest way to grow
- Mitigate introductory-phase risk for your customer
- If possible, get cash up front to massively reduce the cash needed to scale
- Keep it simple: confusion is death

This chapter is relevant for the following business models:

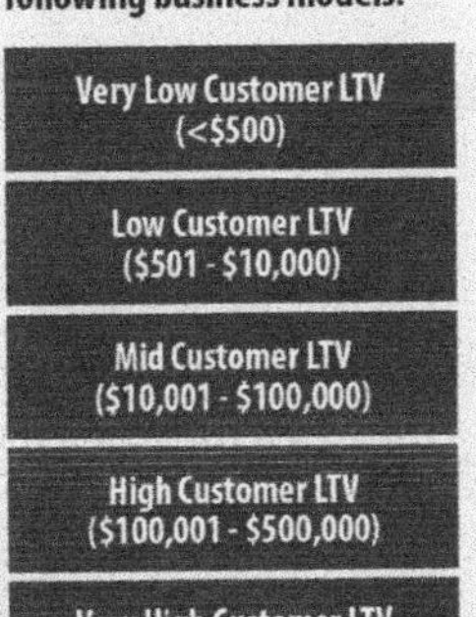

Precise pricing powers profit.

In Microeconomics 101, you learn that companies should price to maximize the area under the demand curve:

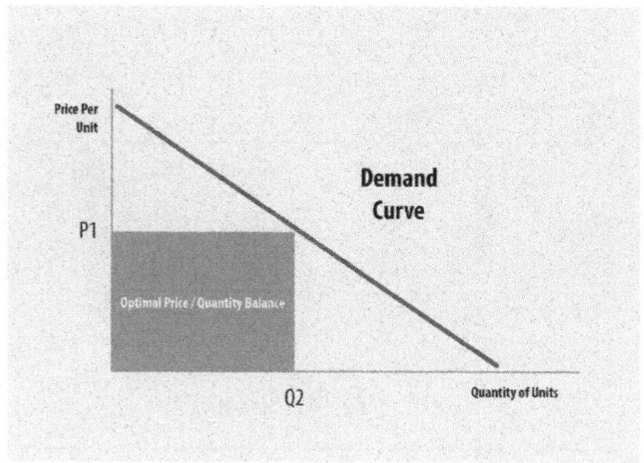

Demand curves should be estimated by segment. For a SaaS product, the x-axis ("Price per Unit") becomes "Price per Package," with Package indicating the average package for the segment (made up of a defined quantity tier). The y-axis ("Number of Units") becomes "Number of Customers," like this:

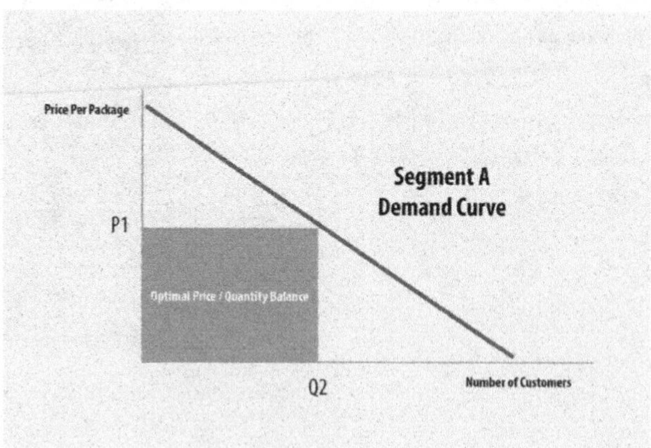

Estimating the demand curve is about estimating price sensitivity. In the case of an annual subscription for a consumer product, demand at $49 a year might be 40% greater than demand at $59 a year. Whereas with a large enterprise sale, the difference in demand between a $5M a year price and a $6M a year price might be modest.

Since you want to capture maximum value, understanding the relationship between price and demand is critical.

Segment-specific market dynamics will cause demand curves to vary. Sometimes they are very flat—where a slight change in price significantly affects the quantity. Flat demand curves are more likely at lower price points, or where competition is high and competitive pricing is visible. Commodities, airline tickets, and many online consumer and SMB subscription products all show flat demand curves. Sometimes they are steep—where demand is relatively insensitive to price. This is more likely to occur at higher price points, particularly when competitive alternatives are not obvious. Mission critical enterprise systems often fit this description.

What drives the slope of the demand curve? Here are the factors:

- The degree of pain experienced
- The economic value of relieving that pain
- The competitive alternatives, and price visibility of alternatives
- Ability to pay
- The personas of the buyer, influencers, and users

A dynamic that is often seen in enterprise SaaS products is demand curve inversion. Buyers may exhibit declining demand above a certain price point, but also below a certain price point. This makes sense: a buyer may perceive that if the price is too low, the vendor will not be able to provide adequate levels of customer support nor guarantee key service level agreements (SLAs).

Such a curve looks like this:

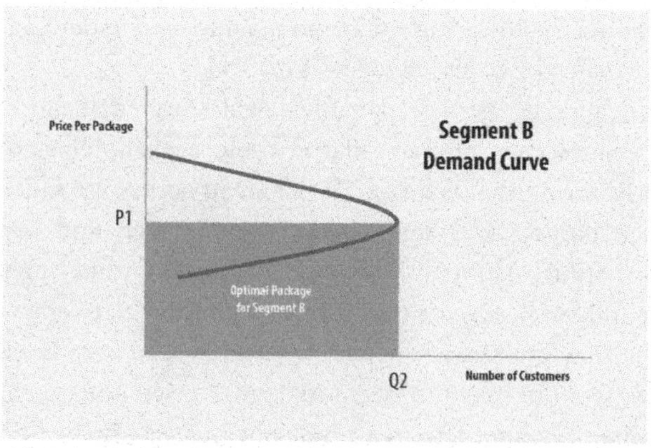

Since demand curves may vary by segment, it is sometimes possible to differentiate pricing by segment to take advantage. But this only works when sufficient segment separation exists (e.g., national boundaries—higher price in Canada than the US). The buyer in a high price segment won't take kindly to seeing similar customers in an adjacent segment receiving a lower price, so be careful.

Airlines have figured out how to get away with significant segment-based price variation for the same product. The weekday warrior business traveler segment pays top dollar. The consumer traveler pays a lot less, if and only if they include a Saturday in the trip (the normal family vacation / weekend getaway use case). Airlines have succeeded in capturing additional volume at a lower price without driving down the high paying customer segment's price. If you choose to vary price by vertical or use case segment, find some credible basis of price differentiation, as the airlines have done.

Another example of segment-based price variation is in B2B software. Some software companies price on-premise software implementations differently than hosted implementations, even though the product architecture is the same.

Your determination of the demand curve will be an educated guess. But there are practical steps you can take to ensure more "educated" and less "guess." For each of your top priority segments:

- Calculate the financial ROI of your product at different price points
- Plot competitor pricing on a graph
- Assess your degree of feature advantage vs. competitors
- Consider the references your customer will use to price compare—i.e. "my ERP costs this much per month, therefore this CRM should cost less"
- Assess ability to pay—are there natural price ceilings?
- Determine whether there are persona-based factors that might impact your assessment of the demand curve: for instance, are your buyers innovators, early adopters, early majority buyers, late majority buyers or laggards?

To get further clarity on price sensitivity in your top priority segments, ask your prospects reference questions:

- "Would you expect our product to cost more or less per seat than Salesforce.com? How much more / less in percentage terms?"
- "Here is our product. Here is adjacent category Product B. Which would you expect costs more? "
- "If you had to choose our product with 'abc' features for $1000 a month, Competitor B with 'bcd' features for $1500 a month, Competitor C with 'def' features for $500 a month, or Competitor D with 'ghi' features at $2000 a month, which would you choose?" (Conjoint Analysis)

Steve Blank, in *The Four Steps to the Epiphany,*[1] suggested the following two questions:

- If I gave you this product for free, would you take it?
- If I charged you $1 million a year for the product, would you buy it?

Blank asserts that answers to these two questions (such as, "What are you, crazy? I'd never pay more than $400,000 per year.") will provide insight into the customer's price sensitivity.

Ask enough of these questions to enough customers, and patterns will emerge. Once you have plotted the curve, you can quickly determine the price / quantity / commitment package that seems optimal for the segment. Before full rollout of any pricing scheme, your "educated guess" must be tested with a sample, iterated, and optimized.

Price to Penetrate

If you are an early-stage startup, customer acquisition is vital. You can't allow the price to be the barrier to adoption. So all things being equal, lower is better. Of course, the degree of pain, the level of competition and competitor price points, the degree of market momentum and excitement about your company and its technology could lend you more upside. But step cautiously.

The more you are disrupting an existing market (replacing existing competitors) v. creating a new market (green field), the more you'll need to undercut the competition to win big.

Even if you're creating a new market, a premium pricing strategy increases incentives for competitors to enter.

In the marketplace space, (Airbnb, Expedia, eBay, etc.) a common pricing scheme is called "the rake." The marketplace platform company charges a percent of the gross value of the transaction that was executed on the platform—that's called the rake.

Bookings.com is Europe's version of Expedia.com. It's a big part of parent company Priceline. At the time Bookings.com entered the market, the prevailing "rake" was 30%. Bookings.com priced their rake at 10%. This was a bold strategic move, and it proved decisive. Merchants flooded to Bookings.com, creating a more compelling consumer experience, which in turn created a happier merchant, in a virtuous upward cycle. It was only many years later, with the marketplace fully established, that Bookings.com introduced a prioritization scheme where merchants could bid up the rake in return for more preferential visibility. The result is that Bookings.com's rake is now estimated to be above 30%.

Bill Gurley, in a blog post titled "A Rake Too Far: Optimal Platform Pricing Strategy,"[2] applauded the strategy:

> "You start with a low rake to get broad-based supplier adoption, and you add in a market-driven pricing dynamic that allows those suppliers who want more volume or exposure to pay more on an opt-in basis... This also allows you to extract more dollars from those suppliers who desire to spend more to promote themselves (without raising the tax on those that don't)."

In the same post, Bill notes the estimated rakes for various marketplaces:

Company	Rake	Notes
Open Table	1.9%	Reservation fee / average meal per person
Homeaway	2.5%	Estimated (low due to use of listing model instead of transaction)
Comparison Shopping	6.0%	Estimated
ebay	9.9%	This is partially listing fees, partially marketing fees, and part PayPal.
oDesk	10.0%	10% on top of all work billed
AirBNB	11.0%	3% + 6-12% depending on size of transaction
Expedia	11.9%	Per 2012 10-K
Amazon Marketplace	12.0%	Guess based on rate table
Fandango	12.5%	Fee charged to user / ticket price
PriceLine	18.5%	Per 2012 10-K
TicketMaster	26.0%	Estimate for tickets sold by TM (non box office) - very har to discern
Steam	30.0%	Rate Card
iTunes	30.0%	Rate Card
Facebook Credits	30.0%	Rate Card
Groupon	38.2%	Calculated from 2012 10-K. Does not include direct goods.
Shutterstock	70.0%	From S-1

Despite Bill Gurley's rave reviews, it would be wise to proceed with caution here. With rakes so high, are Bookings.com, Groupon, Shutterstock, and perhaps even Facebook and iTunes opening the door to competitors by creating a big incentive for customers to seek alternatives?

Price to Expand (Upsells / Cross-Sells)

David Skok, in his blog post "2016 Pacific Crest's SaaS Survey,"[3] shows the difference between the customer acquisition cost (CAC) per dollar of annual contract value (ACV) for a new customer, an upsell, and expansion sale or a renewal:

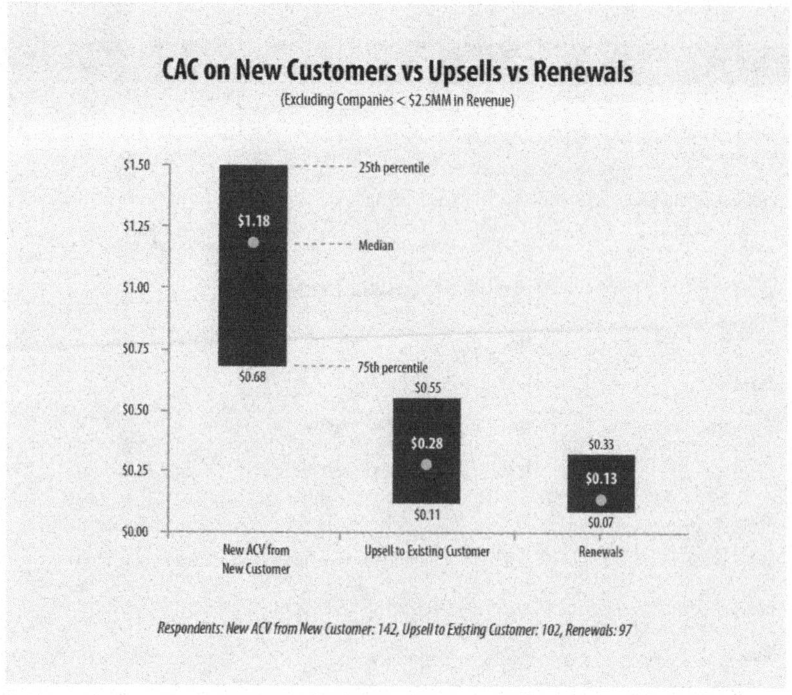

Given its cost efficiency, a pricing and packaging scheme that is optimized for expansion is powerful. There are multiple methods available to accomplish this:

Usage-based pricing, with tiers

- # of units multiplied by the price within a range of use; the price point goes down as you move upward through the tiers
- A risk of this approach is that there's as much flexibility to reduce as to expand usage

Annual commitment to a capped quantity tier, with overage charges

- Has the benefit of capturing the price for 100% utilization regardless of actual usage
- As usage rises above the cap, there's an automatic overage charge for the above-cap quantity (does not require that you upsell the customer)

Cross-sell products

- A la carte product offerings create expansion potential

In my work with tech startups, I have observed that in many SaaS companies, 50%—70% of revenue growth comes from expansion revenue. So, design your pricing and upsell strategies to take advantage of this critical leverage point.

Mitigate Introductory-Phase Risk

Demand is impacted by the customer's perceived risk. Customer risk is higher at the beginning of the product purchase cycle. For this reason, it is not uncommon to see risk-mitigation introductory pricing. Freemium, free trial, pay per use and proof of concept pricing are methods to encourage initial trial.

The 2013 version of the Pacific Crest Survey[4] (focused exclusively on SaaS companies) notes that about 25% of companies surveyed made use of freemium with modest revenue results; try before you buy (free trial) was used by 2/3 of all companies and drove significant revenue impact:

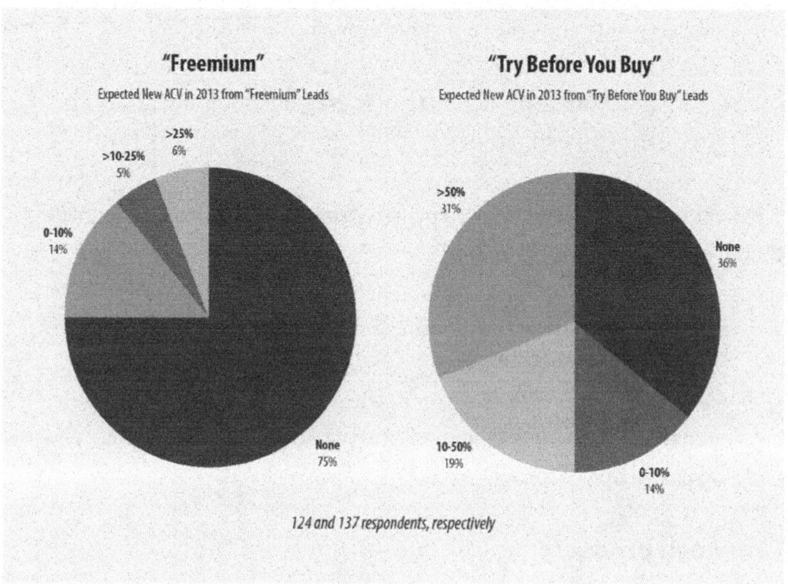

The "try before you buy" approach makes sense because:

- It attracts high-quality prospects who expect to "pay-up" if interested
- Given a high conversion rate, companies can invest in customer success
- The cost to the company is contained since non-paying prospects are timed out—typically after 30–45 days.

Get Annual Cash Up Front

Annual contracts are better than month-to-month contracts. Cash up front is better than month-to-month billing.

It's hard to overstate the significance of cash up front to your company's future success. Without cash upfront, there is an enormous funding requirement. This is at best dilutive, and under more precarious performance scenarios could be deadly. Nino Marakovic, from Sapphire Ventures, in a TechCrunch article titled "Getting More Cash out of SaaS: Timing is Everything,"[5] created the scenario of two identical SaaS companies whose only variation was annual cash up front vs. paid monthly. Both companies shared the exact same GAAP bookings, revenue, and operating income:

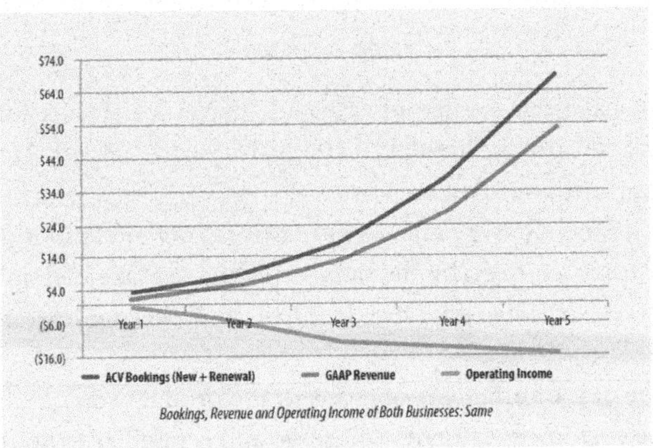

Bookings, Revenue and Operating Income of Both Businesses: Same

But Company A required annual cash up front. Company M billed monthly. Here's the cash effect:

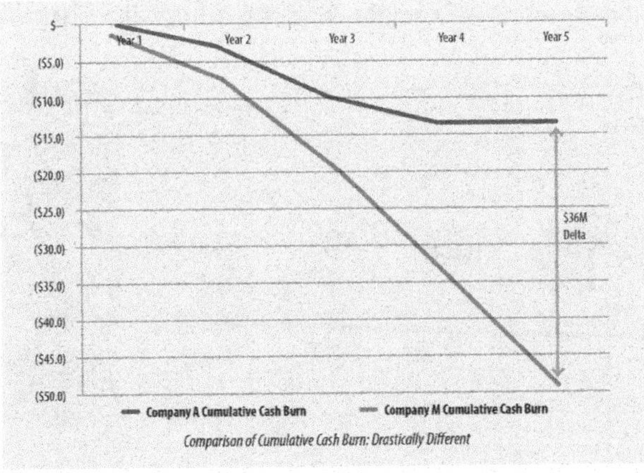

Comparison of Cumulative Cash Burn: Drastically Different

In the example, the increase in cash required to support the monthly pay model—i.e. funding—was $39M.

If possible, require annual commitments, and get cash up front. But be prudent. If cash up front creates too high a hurdle given the competitive environment and intensity of demand, your best choice may be a month-to-month payment schedule.

Keep it Simple

You might have the most sophisticated "maximize the area under the demand curve" pricing model in the history of mankind. However, if it's not simple it's dead on arrival.

For instance, Oracle databases are priced by the number of processors. Salesforce is priced by the number of seats. Make it simple.

Essentially, pricing simplicity features the following:

- The unit of pricing is relevant to the product you offer and the customer segments you serve and is familiar to your prospects
- Alternative packages are clearly and rationally differentiated
- There aren't too many alternatives: three to five is a good range

For a B2B SaaS company, it might look something like this:

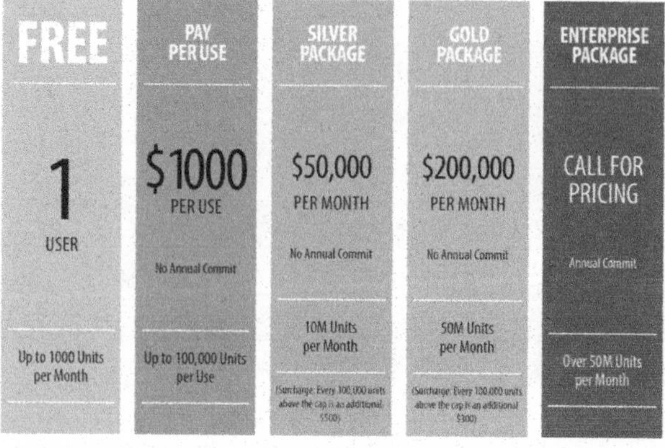

Summary

These pricing considerations all come together in the design of your pricing scheme. Throughout this review of pricing and packaging, we have excluded from pricing design the gross margin of your product. While it is true that high software margins must prevail for a startup (the Pacific Crest study showed the median margins at 76%), smart pricing decisions are always "outside in." Make your pricing segment-centric; let gross margin be an outcome, not a decision driver.

There you have it. If you can price to maximize the area under your demand curve, price to penetrate, price to expand, mitigate introductory-phase risk, get your annual cash up front, and keep it simple, you will have built a market winning pricing scheme.

Price to perfection; the results will be priceless.

10

Prospect & Customer Journey

Key Concepts in Chapter 10:

- Each step in the prospect and customer journey is a moment of truth with your company's future at stake
- As you map each step, your efforts inform sales workflow, marketing campaign structure, and message design
- With the steps clear, you can determine how to maximize impact at each step
- By doing so, your odds of moving the prospect along from step to step will grow, creating revenue momentum

This chapter is relevant for the following business models:

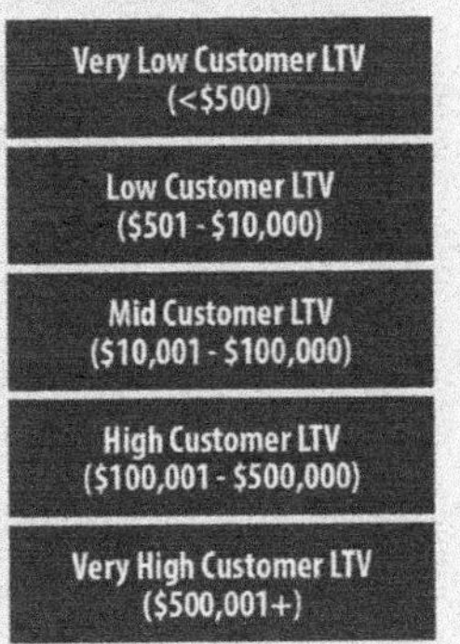

You win the jackpot when the buyer journey becomes a jet stream.

You've defined your priority customer segments. Your team is clear on your target users, the value your product provides, and its competitive advantages. You are consistent with your brand, and you are priced and packaged to disrupt and win. The next step in the execution of your mission and strategy is to define a crystal clear prospect and customer journey.

It's all one journey—comprised of both prospect and customer steps—from awareness, to consideration, to purchase, to implementation, to expansion. You seek to maximize reach and conversion. At Top of Funnel, the goal is to cast a wide net, at least within your high priority segments. From then on, the goal is to continue to deepen the prospect or customer's commitment, so they proceed on the journey towards purchase or expansion.

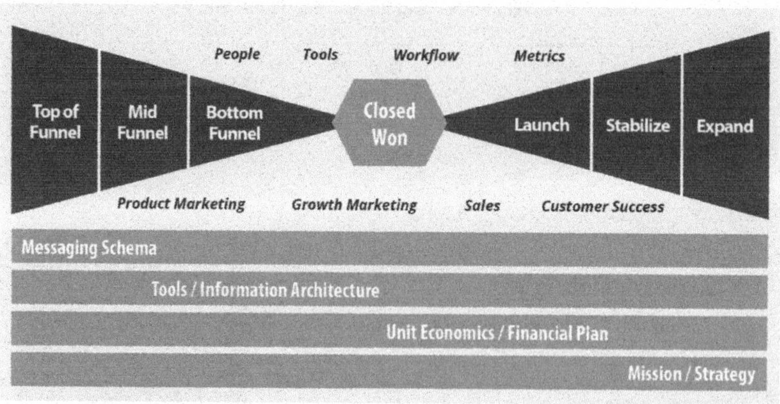

The degree of customization and the amount of human intervention needed along the journey vary based on business model. Both of these factors increase as customer LTV rises. For example, if your product is a media website, a B2C marketplace, or a freemium SaaS product with a very low LTV (under $500), the journey will be the same for all prospects and customers. It will most likely exist entirely in the digital domain. However, if your product has very high LTV (greater than $500,000), the journey will be multifaceted and account specific—including online content, emails, calls, trade shows, lunch and learns, in-person meetings, and so forth.

Don Loonam and his team bring together people, process, and technology with exacting rigor to yield maximum reach and conversion.

The secret to the company's success is the diligence with which

Don and his team mapped every possible pathway of a prospective student from initial interest in a degree program to final enrollment.

His pathway map spreads like a complex root system. The team considered each step with precision, optimizing message content and delivery. Measures are in place for each step. Importantly, the team continuously reviews each step to identify the potential for further optimization. Whatever can be automated is automated, and any steps requiring human intervention have tight scripts and clear performance metrics. Don and his team bring together people, processes, and technology with exacting rigor to yield maximum reach and conversion.

Regardless of your business model, the stages of the journey are consistent, at least at a high level:

- Prospect need / interest / problems / pain is experienced
- Prospect prioritizes the need, interest, problem, or pain for fulfillment or resolution
- Prospect researches alternatives and seeks input of influencers
- Prospect discovers our product
- Prospect seeks to try / test / demo our product
- Prospect (buyer) talks to influencers / seeks references for our product
- Prospect (buyer) involves other users in review of our product
- Prospect (buyer) assesses ROI / financial rationale for our product
- Prospect(buyer) compares to alternatives
- Prospect (buyer) purchases our product
- Customer (buyer / user) experiences launch of our product
- Customer (buyer / user) begins to implement our product
- Customer (buyer / user) experiences our support in the use of our product
- Customer (buyer / user) assesses our product
- Customer (buyer) decides whether to optimize, expand, wind down or cancel our product

It's helpful to capture these steps in a flow chart so you can visualize the prospect's and customer's product consideration points.

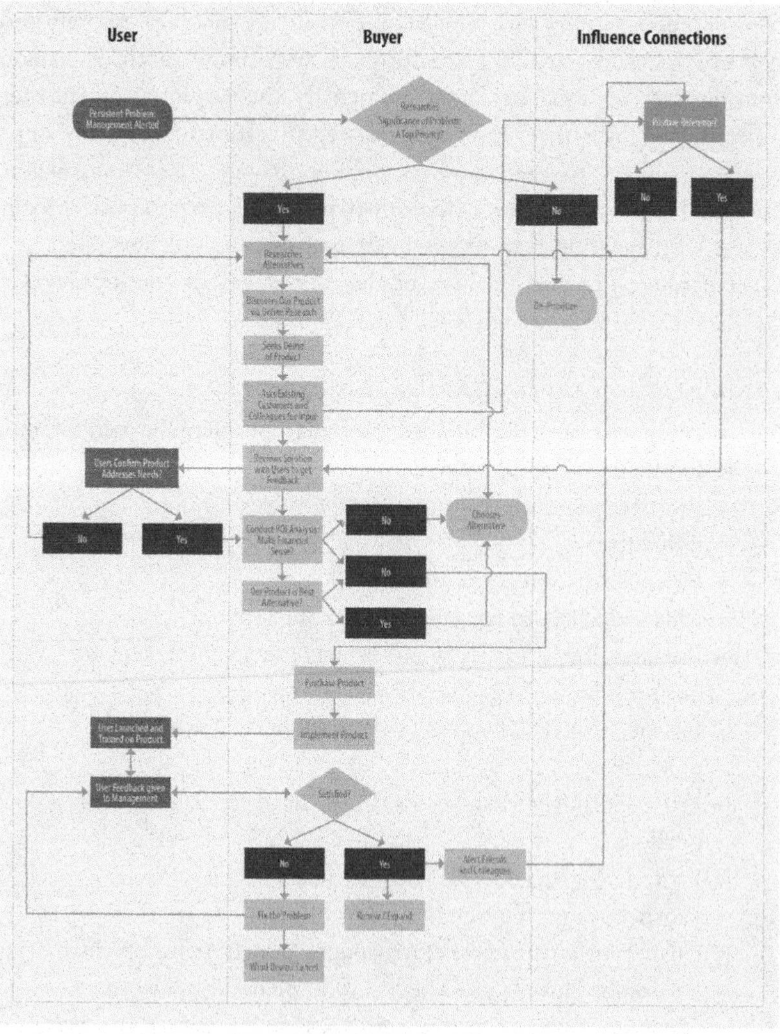

By breaking out these steps, you can identify actions and metrics to measure and positively influence the outcome of each step. This work is developed more completely in your Messaging Schema, but at a high level it looks something like this:

Step	Action	Function	Metrics
Prospect need / interest / problems / pain experienced	Viral social sharing. Thought leadership content that exposes the pain and its consequences.	Product marketing. Growth marketing.	Impressions. Visits. Click thru rate. Inquiries.
Prospect prioritizes the problem for resolution	Thought leadership. Freemium model.	Product. Product marketing. Growth marketing. Sales Development Reps (SDRs).	Impressions. Visits. Click thru rate. Inquiries. Downloads. Automated Qualified Leads (AQLs). Connects to decision makers.
Prospect researches alternatives	The first-mile product experience for freemium. Customer references on website. Features list on website. SEO and SEM initiatives to associate our site with competitive keywords. Trade show presence.	Product. Product marketing. Growth marketing. SDRs.	Impressions. Visits. Click thru rate. Inquiries. AQLs. Booth visits.
Prospect discovers our product	SEO. SEM. Digital advertising. Email marketing. Webinars. Events. Telemarketing.	Product. Product marketing. Growth marketing. SDRs. Business Development Reps (BDRs). Account Execs (AEs).	AQLs. Marketing Qualified Leads (MQLs). Sales Qualified Leads (SQLs). Sales Accepted Leads (SALs).
Prospect seeks demo of our product	Qualification: Budget / Need / Authority / Timing. Pitch deck. Demo protocols — product download, SaaS trial, direct sales demo.	Product. SDRs.	SQLs. SALs. Opportunities.
Prospect talks to influencers / seeks references for our product	Thought leadership. Customer Success programs. Salesperson references. Sales follow-up.	Product marketing. Growth marketing. Customer success. Account execs.	# / % Opportunities.
Prospect buyer involves users in review of our product	Social ratings. Sales introductions. User-focused content on website, such as Q&A for users. "User Guide" pitch deck.	Product marketing. Growth marketing. Account execs.	# / % Opportunities.
Prospect buyer assesses ROI / financial rationale for our product	Salesperson collaborates with prospect on ROI analysis. ROI Calculator on website.	Product. Product marketing. Account execs.	# / % Opportunities.
Buyer compares to alternatives	Salesperson competitive review. Feature by feature competitive comparison grid.	Product marketing. Account execs.	# / % Opportunities.
Buyer purchases our product	Pricing review. Technical diligence. Legal diligence. Contract completion.	Product. Finance. Legal. Account execs.	# / % Closed Won.
Product is launched	Onboarding steps.	Account execs. Customer Success.	Days to Live. % of Users Trained.
Buyer and Users implement product	"First mile" product experience. Best practice webinars. Self-training features.	Product. Product marketing. Customer Success.	% of Users Active. % of Features used.
Buyer and Users assess the product	Success Programs and Success Plays implemented. CSM response to health indicators. Optimization steps.	Product. Product Marketing. Customer Success.	User activity. Usage intensity. Feature utilization. NPS Score. Cases.
Buyer and Users either optimize / expand or wind down / cancel	Success Programs and Success Plays implemented. CSM response to health indicators. Optimization steps. Expansion sales actions. Renewal actions. Churn recovery actions.	Product. Product marketing. Customer Success.	User activity. Usage intensity. Feature utilization. NPS Score. Cases. Upsell revenue. Downsell revenue. Churn rate.

Depending on your product and target customer, it may make sense to create segment-specific or persona-specific variations of the prospect and customer journey. This exercise might deepen visibility into variations in decision-making factors and decision process steps for prospects and customers in different top priority segments.

Clarifying the prospect and customer journey steps is foundational. It allows you to isolate the actions, functions, and results metrics related to each.

You can then track performance at each step which will inform everything, including product design, messaging, online demand generation activity, thought leadership, sales actions, and customer success support.

As noted in Chapter 7—Brand Identity, there are three stage-based objectives in messaging. The first is vision lock, "I get what you do and why it's relevant to me." The second is conviction lock, "I'm convinced. Sign me up." The third is advocacy lock, "I'm a raging fan." When you join the messages that achieve each of these "locks" with the appropriate steps in the prospect and customer journey, you optimize the potential for your prospect or customer to move steadily from step to step.

This foundational work also supports channel strategy. With a clear understanding of the prospect and customer journey, you can more easily identify the partnerships that increase prospect access or improve conversion. For instance, back in the early 2000's, CareerBuilder determined that a substantial number of job seekers were going to MSN Jobs and AOL Jobs to find job postings. So the company worked hard to beat out Monster for the channel partner rights to populate the job postings in those two locations. By winning those two partnerships, CareerBuilder surpassed Monster in traffic volume, and ultimately beat them in revenue.

All steps in the journey are moments of truth. At each step, you must take the actions necessary to win or keep your customer. If you act well, you gain competitive advantage.

You win inch by inch, step by step.

11

Channel Architecture

Key Concepts in Chapter 11:

- Channel architecture, which defines your customer pathways, can be a force multiplier for revenue and market share growth
- Channel alternatives include a variety of partner-driven and internal customer pathways
- Partnerships are long-term commitments: take the time to get them right
- Executing channel strategy takes time and requires clear accountability with measurable milestones and consistent communication between all stakeholders

This chapter is relevant for the following business models:

- **Very Low Customer LTV (<$500)**
- **Low Customer LTV ($501 - $10,000)**
- **Mid Customer LTV ($10,001 - $100,000)**
- **High Customer LTV ($100,001 - $500,000)**
- **Very High Customer LTV ($500,001+)**

Channel is critical: choose carefully.

Channel strategy is a key component of your revenue engine, the final building block in the Mission / Strategy foundation layer.

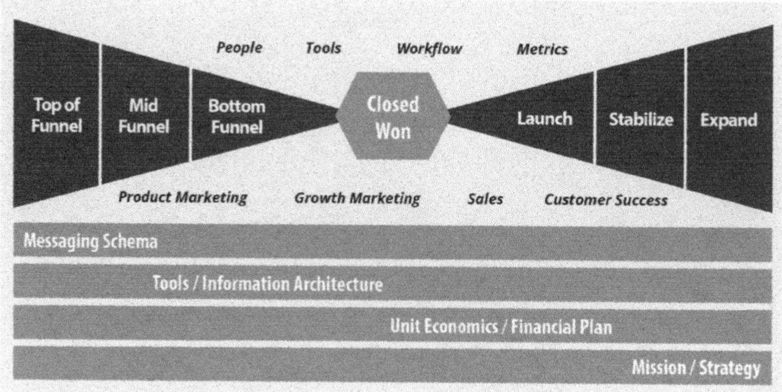

The full set of building blocks in the Mission / Strategy foundation layer are:

- Mission, vision, and values
- Customer segmentation
- Value proposition
- Competitive positioning
- Brand identity
- Product
- Pricing and packaging
- Prospect and customer journey

Channel architecture

Channels are your pathways to the customer. The channels you choose, and the weightings you give them, will significantly impact the breadth of your reach and the quality of your prospect access.

If done well, channel strategy is a force multiplier that will drive significant revenue acceleration and market share growth.

However, it's critical to choose your channels carefully and then execute each with high fidelity. While many aspects of revenue engine strategy are like software (easy to iterate and optimize), channel is more like hardware (hard to modify once built).

Given the fact that channels are time-consuming and hard to build and often difficult to unwind, it's especially important to think through major questions up front:

- Given the size of the potential outcome at scale, projected time to profitability, risk profile, and degree of implementation difficulty, what channels make the most sense to prioritize?
- If your channel choices imply finding partners, who has more leverage—you or your partner?
- What is the best approach to pursue the chosen channels including, where relevant, partner selection and deal negotiations / close?
- What investment weight should you allocate to each channel?
- How will you optimize ongoing channel execution?
- What level of involvement do you want your company to have with the end client during and after the sale of your product?

Channel choices run along a spectrum that includes both external (partner-driven) and internal (directly-controlled) channels. Each requires analysis including a careful risk / reward analysis to prioritize your channel selections.

The maintenance, support, and ongoing optimization of any channel are major commitments of focus, time, and resources.

Excessively limit your channel choices, and you limit your upside. If you open up too many channels without sufficient infrastructure, support, and funding, you may court disaster.

Depending on your business model, you can choose among nine channel alternatives (blue is your channel partner; green is you):

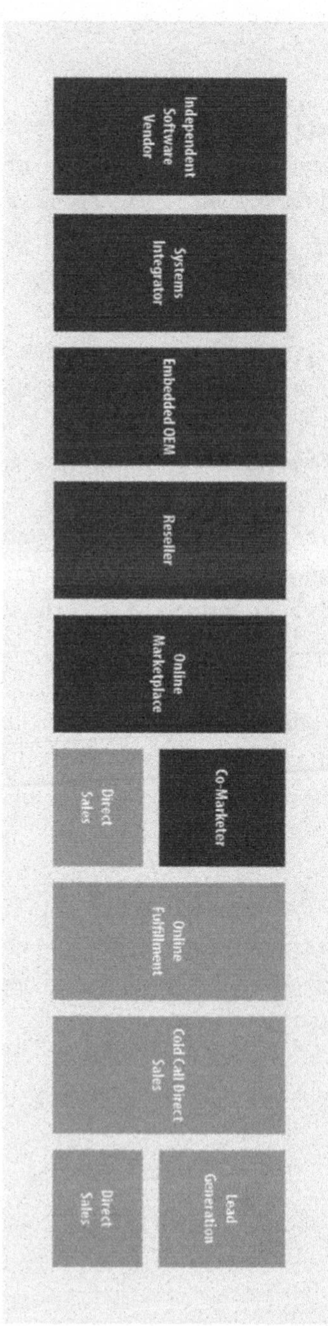
Channel Alternatives
Independent Software Vendor
Systems Integrator
Embedded OEM
Reseller
Online Marketplace
Co-Marketer
Direct Sales
Online Fulfillment
Cold Call Direct Sales
Lead Generation
Direct Sales

1. Independent software vendor (ISV)

    - **Examples:** often vertical-specific
    - Sell / distribute software for specific markets
    - ISV may choose your software to distribute

2. Systems integrator

    - **Examples:** large (Accenture) to small mom and pop shops
    - Help companies rebuild and optimize workflows
    - May choose your software as part of their toolkit and bring it into their customer's company
    - Systems integrator usually remains involved post-sale to launch, stabilize and optimize with your company's support

3. Embedded OEM

    - **Examples:** IBM; Toyota
    - Your product is white labeled and integrated into their products, which is sold by them
    - OEM owns direct post-sale support with its customer but may turn to your company for indirect support

4. Reseller

    - **Examples**: can run the gamut from a large company with a multi-location sales force to small, even one-person independent contractors
    - You are primarily responsible for marketing
    - Reseller sells
    - Reseller prices your product and pays you a wholesale price
    - You usually own post-sale support

5. Online marketplace

- **Examples**: Salesforce App Exchange, Amazon Business, eBay, iTunes
- Your product features in the marketplace
- Marketplace extracts a "rake" from you for each transaction (2%—35% of transaction value)
- You own post-sale support

6. Co-marketer / direct sales

- **Examples**: Microsoft, IBM
- Your product and co- marketer's product work well together
- You commit to promoting each other's products and to selling collaboratively
- Each company finalizes the sale of its owned product separately
- You own post-sale support

7. Online fulfillment

- Your website enables the customer to buy online via an automated workflow
- You own post-sale support

8. Cold call direct sales

- No significant marketing effort
- You sell, you support

9. Lead gen / direct sales

- Marketing generates leads and turns them into MQLs
- Sales sells
- You support

Choosing Channel Strategy

So how do you make the decision as to which channels to pursue, in what order, with what level of investment? Here are the consideration factors:

- Company Stage
- Top Priority Segments
- Buyer Journey Attributes
- Product Characteristics
- Traffic Based / Lead Based / Account Based Marketing
- Channel Capacity
- Unit Economics
- Deal Structure
- Brand
- Ecosystem / Partner Dynamics
- Pricing and Packaging Strategy

Company Stage

Consider a B2B SaaS business. In the beginning, angel funding gives you barely enough fuel to develop your minimum viable product. The CEO and co-founders execute the first few sales. You gain enough traction to raise a seed round and create a small sales team. There's no marketing budget; it's all about cold calling. Then, with further traction proof, you raise more funding. You now begin to make investments in marketing—in online demand generation, thought leadership, trade show booths, and so forth.

At every step, you made educated guesses as to your top priority segments, the buyer and user personas tied to each segment, the value proposition, competitive positioning, brand identity, pricing, and packaging. All of these are hypotheses, and they must be fully validated by your team before considering channel partnerships.

After you see a steady pattern of profitable, repeatable sales, retention, and expansion, you can put channel partnerships on the table.

A rational channel staging might look like this:

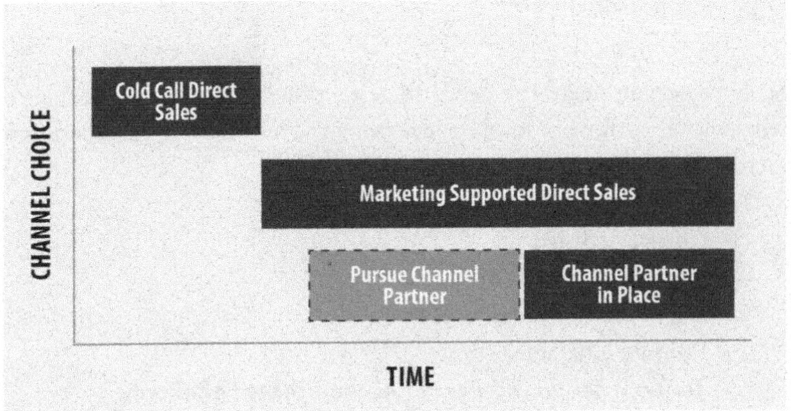

Top Priority Segments

A channel partnership is potentially a powerful way to enter a new segment or accelerate growth in an existing one. But such partnerships must be executed with care. An ill-considered segment-based channel strategy runs the risk of two types of friction:

- Channel conflict
- Price variation

The first is channel conflict. Channel conflict occurs when two sales teams are chasing the same customer—a typical result when no clear rules exist to define each sales team's selling domain. How do you create clear rules? They may be geographic, vertical, size-based or any other binary criterion. The rule could even be "jump ball": the first partner to bring in the deal wins. In healthy segment-based channel partnerships, the rules are crystal clear. Avoid fuzzy rules. They result in channel conflict.

The second friction problem is price variation. Price variation between channels can inflict great harm. If customers get the identical product at a lower price via one channel versus another without sufficient rationale for the difference, then you invite upon yourself strong customer dissatisfaction and brand harm. Assume perfect market knowledge and make sure any channel-based price variation is completely defensible.

Buyer Journey Attributes

At every step of the buyer journey (Top, Mid and Bottom funnel), channel considerations are paramount. At Top of Funnel, for instance, the challenge is to create awareness. One way to achieve this is via your direct channels (cold call, lead generation-to-sales, etc.). But ISVs, systems integrators, resellers, online marketplaces, and co-marketers can increase reach significantly.

On the journey from initial awareness to sale, a partnership with a trusted brand can transfer validation. For instance, when Siebel was an early stage startup, it executed a systems integrator partnership with Andersen Consulting (now Accenture) that put the company on the map and sparked rapid scaling. Later, its co-marketing partnership with IBM further accelerated growth. Ads in the Wall Street Journal promoted "IBM and Siebel," creating a perception that Siebel was bigger than it was at the time. The rest was history.

Such brand affiliations reassure the buyer and reduce perceived risk. This increased buyer trust yields confidence and conviction. For you, it yields a shorter sales cycle and increased conversion rate.

Product Characteristics

Can you sell your product completely independently or does it depend on another product? Most software solutions, both B2B and B2C, must interface with the customer's legacy software environment. Multiple integrations into diverse legacy solutions might need to be mastered by your company. But sometimes one (e.g., Salesforce) or only a couple (e.g., iOS / Android) of products are dependencies. Or, a key integration with a major player might open up a significant new market segment for you. Where any of these scenarios are true, a co-marketing partnership or embedded OEM deal with the company that owns the legacy technology might make sense.

Traffic Based / Lead Based / Account-Based Marketing

If you are a media or a marketplace company, you depend on traffic. In the early 2000's, CareerBuilder negotiated two separate deals, one with AOL and the other with MSN, to switch both partnerships from Monster to CareerBuilder—and announced the agreements to the press on the very same day. A fire hose of job seeker traffic instantly shifted from Monster to CareerBuilder, quickly propelling CareerBuilder to the top of the job board space.

A wide array of online marketplaces exists for B2B companies. For several tech companies, Amazon and eBay are powerful channels. Many others take advantage of vertical-specific marketplaces such as GetApp. When combined with a company's direct online demand generation activity, these marketplaces can be potent lead and sales accelerators.

Perhaps you run a B2B company with High or Very High LTV. In this case, you have the capacity to execute an account-based marketing (ABM) approach: you can mobilize a sustained, multi-dimensional engagement strategy for each prospect. A large channel partner such as IBM or Microsoft might give you access to a subset of customers that would otherwise be hard for you to reach. As long as you clarify assignment rules by geography, vertical, use case, size, or "jump ball" to avoid channel conflicts, such partnerships can be powerful. If done right, they allow you to divide and conquer, capturing more ground faster.

Channel Capacity

Whether you choose a direct- or a partnership-based channel or both, building channels out takes a lot of work. So it's important to determine the total addressable market by channel. Each has access to some subset of your top priority segments. For each channel, if you assume that every potential buyer buys, what is that maximum sales capacity?

This number is obviously an important factor in your channel decisions. Of course, it's not the only consideration. You must also factor in the degree of likelihood you can execute a partnership, negotiation time, speed to scale, and unit economics. But it all starts with the simple question: "If we perform very well within this channel, does it amount to much?"

Unit Economics

Every channel alternative comes with its unique unit economics. It's important to confirm that the economics make sense before you invest much time developing a channel.

In calculating unit economics for each channel alternative, it's not enough to know the revenue split. Unit economics are a function of LTV (driven by the revenue split and the length of the average customer) and CAC (the cost of customer acquisition). So closely consider the cost side. Ask yourself this critical question: "Who is responsible for what?"

- Marketing
- Customer acquisition
- Customer support
- Customer success
- Expansion sales

An understanding of your unit economics by channel will help you clarify which channels are viable. A unit economic analysis is also a significant input as you consider how to weight investments in each of your channels.

Deal Structure

In channel partnerships, there are many moving parts. The following deal terms are critical:

- Term, renewal, and termination rules
- Who owns what (especially with regards to data)
- Minimum partner performance rules
- Product SLAs
- Hosting SLAs

- Support SLAs
- Authorized segments definition
- Channel conflict resolution rules
- Selling rules
- Sales training
- Pipeline data visibility rules
- Post-sale customer support / expansion rules
- Pricing/ deal economics

Let's focus on these three:

- Who owns what
- Minimum partner performance
- Pipeline data visibility rules

First, all things being equal, it's best for you to retain responsibility for messaging and post-sale customer interactions. Your partner will be a communicator of your brand messaging, but you should retain control over that messaging. Similarly, it's best if you can retain ownership of customer support and customer success unless you can be confident that your partner will execute these functions at the same level of quality as you. A choice to hand these functions over to a channel partner should not be made lightly.

Second, be sure to establish clear financial performance requirements for your partner. Failure to achieve minimum performance levels after a sufficient cure period should free you to terminate the entire agreement. It makes no sense to have a partnership in place that doesn't perform to minimum standards.

Third, work hard to negotiate access to your partner's prospect pipeline data. With access to this data, you will understand the funnel conversion dynamics of all your channels. This information will give you the metrics necessary to coach your partner and will help you further optimize your direct marketing and sales performance. Getting the data flows right is a critical channel partner success factor.

Brand

In an embedded OEM deal, you're making a choice to bury your brand so be sure it's worth it. Ask yourself these questions: Is the deal so substantial it transforms your company? Does it open the door to other significant deals (e.g., does one sizable auto manufacturer OEM deal give you the inside track to three more)? Can you compartmentalize the deal to one segment, while you pursue a branded strategy with other segments?

In all other types of channel partnerships, your partner has at least some influence on your brand reputation. You must ensure that your brand is represented to prospects and customers properly. Affiliation with your brand may be a driving factor in a partner's interest in you. Or it may be the other way around. Or both.

Regardless, the marketing, messaging, sales training, and sales performance management actions of your channel partner not only impact the partner's success but they also directly impact the perception of your brand in the marketplace.

So be sure you have the deal structure in place that ensures you can demand excellence in execution and brand fidelity.

Ecosystem and Partner Dynamics

Since channel partnerships tend to be rigid, long-term deals with onerous termination protocols under a non-performance scenario, it's important that the motivation to perform is very high on both sides. This motivation is affected by the dynamics in the market.

If new technology is disrupting a dominant legacy company and you are a player in this new technology, there is the potential for a solid partnership. The more mission critical the partnership is to your partner's success, the more the CEO and top team will be hard at work to drive towards success.

On the other hand, if the relationship is tactical (i.e., one of many sales partnerships) where success or failure is of no significant consequence to the partner, then the likelihood of partnership success is much lower.

Pricing and Packaging Strategy

As previously noted, pricing practices are often a source of channel conflict. It's never a good thing for one customer to be able to price shop from channel to channel. Take, for instance, systems integrator and reseller partnerships.

It's critical that you either negotiate price parity with your direct channels or have bright segment boundaries with clear and defensible price variation rationales.

One essential challenge to master is how to manage pricing as your product evolves. As you add product features, you may choose to introduce new packages at new price points. These will require negotiation with your partners. Make sure your partnership deal terms include a transparent mechanism through which to introduce changes in pricing and packaging.

Channel Partner Pursuit

After defining the channel partners you seek to work with, the next step is to execute an efficient and effective plan of pursuit, a function of the business development role. For channel partnerships, it can be a long odyssey. It's not uncommon for major partnerships to be 2–3 years in the making.

How do you track progress? As CEO, you must measure your VP Business Development's progress by the achievement of milestones along the journey. The sequence of steps looks something like this:

- Choose top priority channels
- Within these channels, define all potential partners
- Rank potential partners based on impact capacity, degree of shared motivation, deal likelihood, projected deal terms, and compatibility
- Map the partner engagement and partnership negotiation process
- Measure progress along each step of the journey

As CEO, you should meet weekly with your head of business development. Expect steady movement from stage to stage towards a deal.

Channel Execution

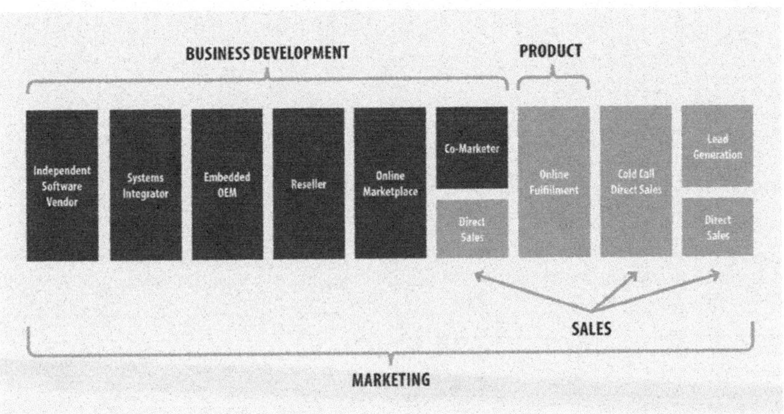

Eventually, you will have a completely implemented channel strategy with productive partnerships in place. Marketplaces will feature your products. But they won't simply morph into an explosion of leads and sales on their own.

Just like your direct channels, partner relationships require precise management. Implement quotas and track weekly pipelines across all partner channels.

If you have a traffic or leads-based partnership, you'll conduct ongoing A/B testing to optimize keywords, product descriptions, and pricing. If you sell via an ABM sales approach through a major reseller, you might embed a senior sales executive in the partner's office. The quarterly planning, monthly review, and weekly accountability disciplines you execute with your channel partners will be instrumental to your success.

In sum, your chosen channels are where the rubber hits the road.

Drive intelligently.

12

Unit Economics

Key Concepts in Chapter 12:

- Unit economics drive data-driven decision-making
- Two unit economics measures reveal a company's financial health and viability: the ratio of LTV to CAC, and the payback period on CAC
- Multiple factors impact both LTV and CAC, depending on business model
- Everything in your company-wide metrics dashboard is anchored by unit economics, and performance should be judged accordingly

This chapter is relevant for the following business models:

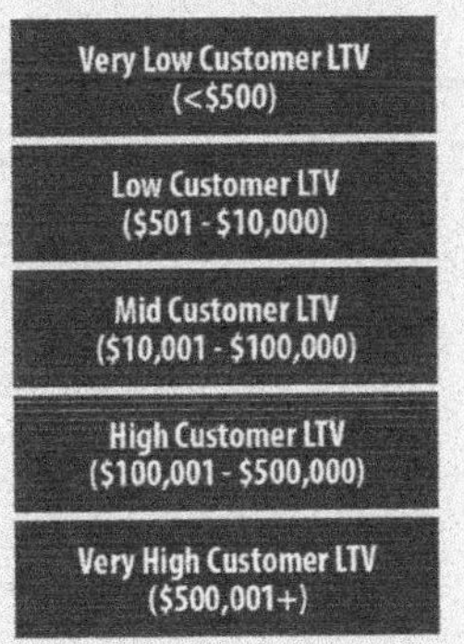

Unicorns became unicorns via unit economics.

Data-driven decision-making is key to a fit and trim revenue engine. Your metrics dashboard is your window into engine performance, giving you the necessary visibility and intelligence to see problems and fix them. So it's important to design your metrics infrastructure so that your unit economics are clear. Unit economics pair with the financial plan to comprise the second foundational layer of the revenue engine.

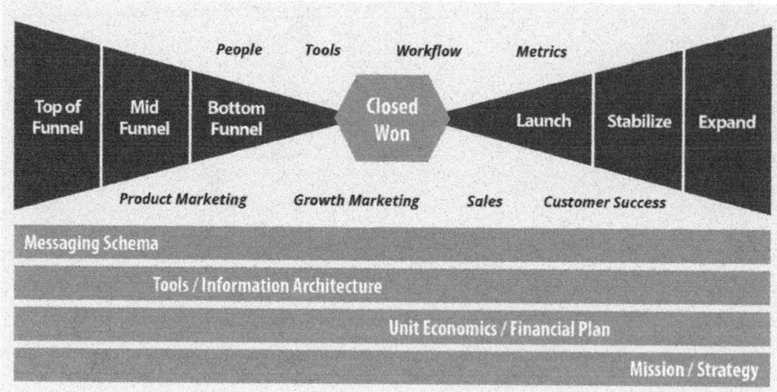

Metrics exist to point you towards maximum profitability and growth. Depending on the business model and other factors, your metrics may assess profitability and growth by:

- Segment
- Product
- Channel
- Marketing program / campaign
- Sales region
- Salesperson

Of course, if you have a Very Low LTV (<$500) business model, metrics exclusively measure digital engagement, lead or traffic acquisition, conversion, and retention along the prospect and customer journey. No human interaction occurs. If, on the other hand, your business model falls into the Low, Medium, High, or Very High LTV buckets, you will likely measure sales teams and their engagement steps as well as automated top of funnel steps.

Metrics are derived from data sensors instrumented into workflows. They either indicate healthy engine performance or alert you to overheating. Effective instrumentation is hard, detail-oriented work (which is why most startups don't execute it well), but it's important.

Build your metrics dashboard and financial plan based on unit economics. If you don't, you'll be driving blind and risking engine failure.

Other than fixed cost analyses, all metrics ultimately flow into unit economics. Two unit economics measures reveal a company's financial health and viability:

- The ratio of an incremental unit's lifetime gross profit (LTV) to its selling cost (CAC)
- The payback period on CAC

Payback is often expressed via the "magic number" calculation, which takes the growth in gross profit in the current quarter versus the previous quarter multiplied by 4, then divides that number by the marketing, sales and retention costs (CAC) of the prior period. If that calculation > 1, you have a payback period of under a year.

Investors generally seek LTV / CAC > 3, and a magic number > .75 or so. If a company outperforms, it should hit the gas. If (after the initial ramp-up and testing phase) it persistently underperforms, a company should hit the brakes, test, and iterate with small teams and small budgets until performance rises above these thresholds.

The calculations of LTV and CAC differ by business model:

SaaS:

- LTV: gross profit per customer over the course of the average lifetime in a given cohort
- CAC: All marketing and sales costs divided by number of customers for that same cohort

Ecommerce:

- LTV: Gross profit per customer over the course of the average lifetime in a given cohort

- CAC: All marketing, traffic acquisition, and conversion optimization costs divided by number of customers for that same cohort

Peer to Peer Marketplace:

- LTV: Gross profit over the course of the lifetime per seller in a given cohort
- CAC: All marketing, traffic acquisition, and conversion optimization costs divided by number of newly acquired sellers for that same cohort

B2B2C Marketplace:

- LTV: Gross profit per business customer over the course of the average lifetime in a given cohort
- CAC: Marketing and sales costs to acquire the business customer plus marketing costs to acquire the consumer divided by the number of newly acquired business customers for that same cohort

Media:

- LTV: Gross profit per thousand impressions for a given cohort—i.e. monthly revenue minus any variable support costs (storage, etc.), divided by gross monthly impressions in thousands
- CAC: Marketing and sales costs to generate revenue plus traffic acquisition costs divided by gross impressions in thousands

Multiple factors drive LTV. Using historical data, you can calculate the LTV for the average customer, as follows:

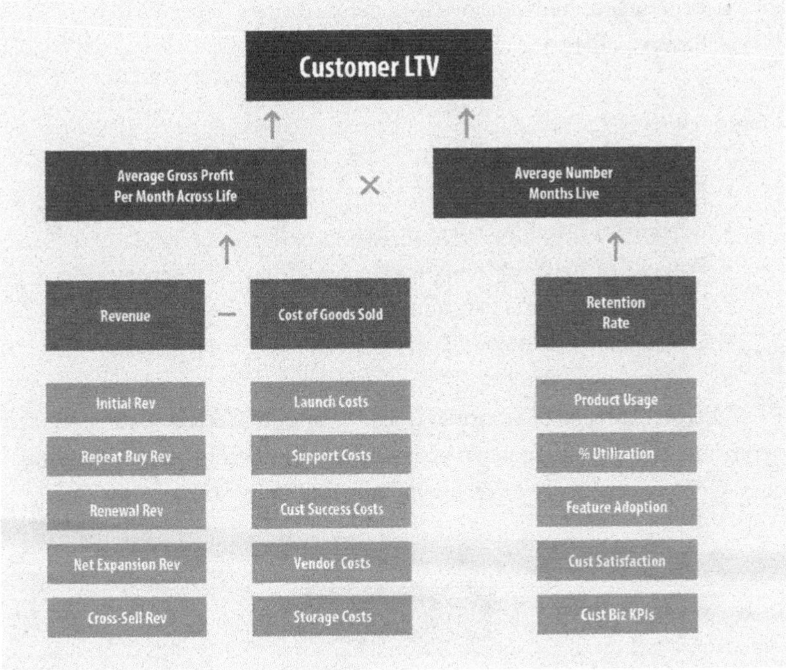

Depending on your business model, your metrics dashboard will track trends for:

Revenue:

- Average initial deal size
- Repeat purchases
- Upsells (expansion) in dollars
- Downsells (contraction) in dollars
- Cross-sells in dollars

Cost of Goods Sold:

- Launch cost per customer
- Support cost per customer
- Customer success cost per customer

- Product-related vendor costs per customer
- Storage costs per customer

Retention Rate:

- Product usage
- Percent of intended users utilizing
- Percent of features being used
- Level of reported customer satisfaction
- Customer's business outcomes from using the product

Multiple factors also drive CAC. Using historical data you can determine the average cost to acquire a customer. For a B2B SaaS business, CAC is a measure of reach and conversion efficiency:

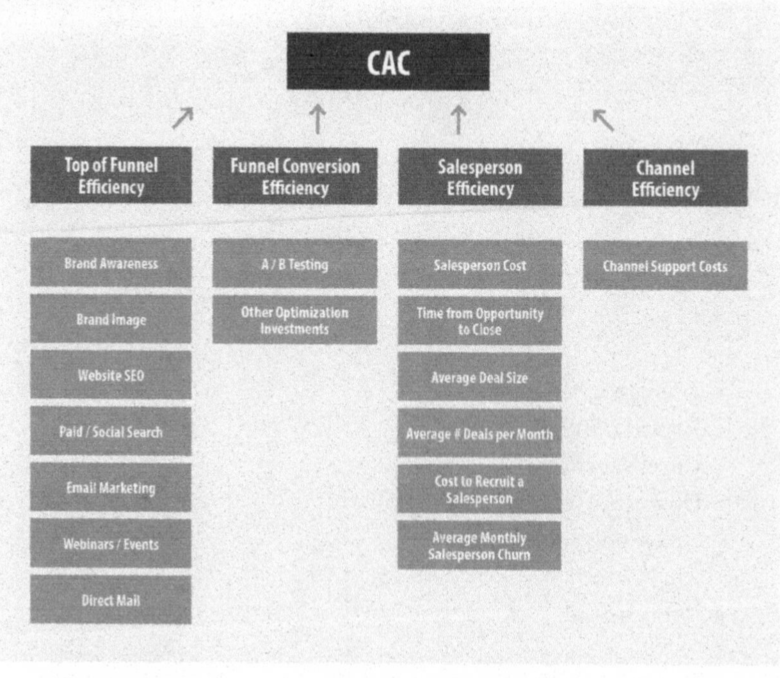

As with LTV, there are multiple contributors to CAC. At a high level, these are:

- Top of Funnel costs
- Mid and Bottom Funnel costs
- Channel costs

Your metrics dashboard tracks these CAC drivers so that you can continuously increase the efficiency of each dollar spent.

In pursuit of your growth goals, you may add:

- New segments
- New products
- New channels
- New marketing programs / campaigns
- New sales regions
- New salespeople

As you do so, tracking on all these dimensions is vital. Create a dashboard for each. Your metrics dashboard must tell you whether each new initiative has met the LTV / CAC and "magic number" hurdles. If a new initiative falls short, then test, iterate and optimize. Don't give up too quickly—you may be just a couple of tweaks away from success. But neither should you hit the gas, at least until your optimization efforts yield the required performance outcomes. Once they do, of course, it's pedal to the metal time.

Prospect Journey Metrics

Your metrics dashboard tracks performance along the prospect journey, from top of funnel, to mid, to bottom. It's best to track by channel. If you have a Low to Mid LTV business model, your metrics dashboard might look as follows:

Prospect Journey					
Email Marketing	Digital Advertising	Search Advertising	Social Advertising	Landing Page Propagation	Events
Cost of campaigns	Cost of campaigns	Cost of campaigns	Cost of campaigns	Cost of campaigns	Cost of events
# Emails sent					# names captured
# / % Emails bounced					# / % qualified names
# / % Emails opened					
# / % Click	# / % Click	# / % Click	# / % Click	# / % Click	
# / % Lead data entry initiated	# / % Lead data entry initiated	# / % Lead data entry initiated	# / % Lead data entry initiated	# / % Lead data entry initiated	
# / % Lead data complete	# / % Lead data complete	# / % Lead data complete	# / % Lead data complete	# / % Lead data complete	
# / % AQL	# / % AQL	# / % AQL	# / % AQL	# / % AQL	# / % AQL
Attribution Rule Applied					
# / % MQL	# / % MQL	# / % MQL	# / % MQL	# / % MQL	# / % MQL
# / % SALs	# / % SALs	# / % SALs	# / % SALs	# / % SALs	# / % SALs
# / % Opportunity	# / % Opportunity	# / % Opportunity	# / % Opportunity	# / % Opportunity	# / % Opportunity
# / % Closed Won	# / % Closed Won	# / % Closed Won	# / % Closed Won	# / % Closed Won	# / % Closed Won
Average $ LTV per customer					
LTV / CAC	LTV / CAC	LTV / CAC	LTV / CAC	LTV / CAC	LTV / CAC

Be cautious with your attribution rules. Attribution of marketing touch points to a closed won deal runs the risk of false precision. If too much time has passed between the marketing touch point and the sale, the influence of the touch point is most likely low. This is especially problematic with High and Very High LTV business models, with their typically long sales cycles. Remember that the purpose of attribution is to establish correlation. You want to determine that a given marketing input yields a predictable sales outcome. If there's an easier path to correlation, take it. It may be best to just A/B test or time series test the yield from one step to the next—i.e. from an inquiry to a lead or a lead to an SAL—than to focus excessively on attribution of closed won deals.

Customer Program Metrics

Net new expansion revenues and LTV can be tracked based on various programs:

Webinars: Product Updates	Events	Customer Success / Sales: Renewal 2 months out	Customer Success / Sales: Expansion Opportunity
# Registrants	# Registered Current Customers to Booth	# customers have renewal in 2 months	# customers ready prospects for expansion conversation
# / % Registrants with full lead form data	# / % sent follow-up email	# / % calls made	# / % calls made
# / % Attendees	# / % emails bounced	# / % connects	# / % connects
# / % sent follow-up email	# / % emails opened	# / % full conversation / discovery assessment held	# / % full conversation / qualifying assessment held
# / % emails bounced	# / % Follow-up action taken	# / % require 30 day Success Plan	# / % full conversation / discovery assessment held
# / % emails opened	# / % qualified expansion prospects	# / % Sales call held	# / % qualified expansion prospects
# / % Follow-up action taken	# / % Sales call held	# / % Renew	# / % Sales call held
# / % qualified expansion prospects	# / % Expansion sale successful		# / % Expansion sale successful
# / % Sales call held			
# / % Expansion sale successful			
LTV / CAC	LTV / CAC	LTV / CAC	LTV / CAC
Magic Number	Magic Number	Magic Number	Magic Number

Channel Metrics

The effectiveness of channel partnerships can also be measured through the lens of unit economics:

Revenue share partnerships:

- If your partner books gross revenue and you receive net revenue, your LTV will be lower than direct selling, but your CAC will be small—possibly zero: usually a net positive, all else being equal

Traffic or lead acquisition partnerships:

- If the incremental traffic or lead volume is predictable and the value of traffic in LTV yield is clear, then the investment in the acquisition can be measured in LTV / CAC and Magic Number terms and judged accordingly
- If the investment is fixed and traffic or lead volume potential is less predictable, there is increased risk that the investment will fall short of the LTV / CAC or Magic Number threshold

And of course, once a channel partnership is in place, a metrics dashboard to track partnership performance should be implemented and regularly reviewed with your partner.

Company-wide Unit Metrics Dashboard

The result of building unit economics into everything is a metrics dashboard hierarchy that looks something like this:

Metrics Dashboard Hierarchy

I. Company Overview dashboard

- A. **Revenue pipeline metrics**
  1. Reach
  2. Conversion
  3. Number of sales
- B. **Overall LTV**
  1. Average price / deal size
  2. Retention rate
  3. Cost of goods sold per sale
- C. **Overall CAC**
  1. Top of funnel cost per sale
  2. Mid and bottom funnel cost per sale
  3. Channel cost per sale

II. Segment-based dashboard

- A. **By Product**
- B. **By Channel**
- C. **By Program**
- D. **By Sales Region**

III. Product-based dashboard

- A. **By Segment**
- B. **By Channel**
- C. **By Program**
- D. **By Sales Region**

IV. Channel-based Dashboard

- A. **By Segment**
- B. **By Product**
- C. **By Program**
- D. **By Sales Region**

V. Program-based Dashboard

- A. **By Segment**
- B. **By Product**
- C. **By Channel**
- D. **By Sales Region**

VI. Sales Region-based Dashboard

- A. **By Segment**
- B. **By Product**
- C. **By Channel**
- D. **By Program**
- E. **By Salesperson**

Looking at the same data from multiple angles heightens clarity. Marketing, sales, customer success, the product team, and the exec team can use these dashboards to continuously optimize profitability and growth.

Metrics dashboard design is important. If you're a SaaS business serious about creating a metrics-driven company, David Skok's SaaS Metrics 2.0[1] is a must read.

It's the most comprehensive, well-researched blog out there on unit economics and metrics infrastructure for a SaaS based company. In fact, it's so good it's worth reading no matter what your business model is.

Check out this company overview dashboard from Skok's blog. It highlights key drivers of unit economics for a SaaS business:

SaaS Metrics 2.0 Scroll right to see the dashboard --->

For companies that book annual contracts

Bookings	Jan	Feb	Mar	Apr	May	Jun
Bookings $,000's (new custs)	$ 264	$ 276	$ 294	$ 312	$ 324	$ 348
Average ACV (new contracts)	$ 6,600	$ 6,571	$ 6,837	$ 6,783	$ 6,750	$ 6,692
Average Contract Term	1.3	1.4	1.4	1.5	1.4	1.6
Average Months Paid Upfront	5.5	7.0	5.0	6.5	5.8	6.2
ARPA - Avg MRR (for new Custs)	$ 550	$ 548	$ 570	$ 565	$ 563	$ 558
ARPA - across installed base	$ 514	$ 521	$ 530	$ 538	$ 552	$ 562
ARR	**Jan**	**Feb**	**Mar**	**Apr**	**May**	**Jun**
New ARR	$ 264.0	$ 276.0	$ 294.0	$ 312.0	$ 324.0	$ 348.0
Churned ARR	$ (100.8)	$ (134.7)	$ (108.3)	$ (107.4)	$ (106.2)	$ (106.1)
Expansion ARR	$ 24.0	$ 29.9	$ 25.8	$ 16.1	$ 83.9	$ 41.2
Net New ARR	**$ 187.2**	**$ 171.3**	**$ 211.5**	**$ 220.7**	**$ 301.6**	**$ 283.2**
Starting ARR	$ 4,800	$ 4,987	$ 5,158	$ 5,370	$ 5,591	$ 5,892
Ending ARR	$ 4,987	$ 5,158	$ 5,370	$ 5,591	$ 5,892	$ 6,175
Churn Metrics	**Jan**	**Feb**	**Mar**	**Apr**	**May**	**Jun**
Total # of Customers	808	825	845	866	890	916
# of new Customers	40	42	43	46	48	52
# of churned Customers	(24)	(25)	(23)	(25)	(24)	(26)
Net New Customers	16	17	20	21	24	26
% Customer Churn	3.0%	3.1%	2.8%	3.0%	2.8%	2.9%
% ARR Churn	2.1%	2.7%	2.1%	2.0%	1.9%	1.8%
% ARR Expansion	0.5%	0.6%	0.5%	0.3%	1.5%	0.7%
% Net ARR Churn	1.6%	2.1%	1.6%	1.7%	0.4%	1.1%
Renewal rate (# of Custs)						
Renewal rate (ARR $'s)						
Customer Engagement Score	121	120	125	126	130	135
Net Promoter Score	28	27	29	32	33	35
Unit Economics (new customers)	**Jan**	**Feb**	**Mar**	**Apr**	**May**	**Jun**
LTV	$ 21,738	$ 16,834	$ 22,519	$ 23,457	$ 24,572	$ 25,716
CAC	$ 8,750	$ 8,571	$ 8,605	$ 8,261	$ 8,125	$ 7,692
LTV to CAC Ratio	2.5	2.0	2.6	2.8	3.0	3.3
Months to Recover CAC	19	19	18	18	17	17

Brandon Christie, currently head of product monetization at

Captora and formerly an analyst at the VC firm NEA, is an expert at trend visualization. Here's a cohort analysis he created:[2]

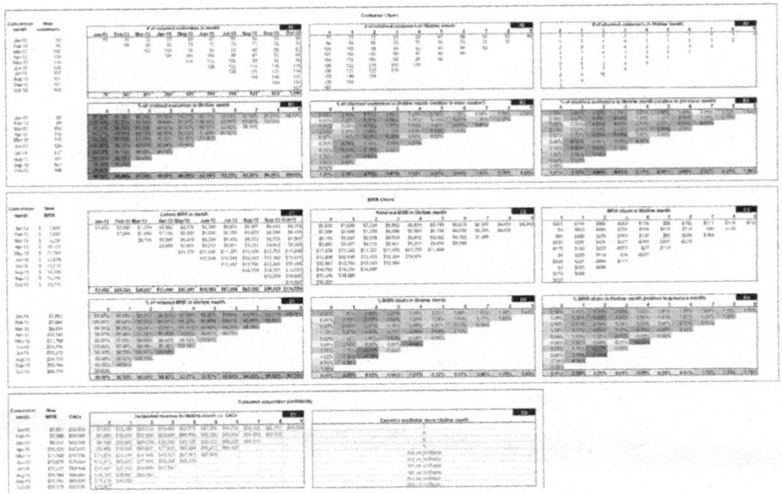

It gives you a sense for the metrics infrastructure you must build to run a fit and trim revenue engine.

Measure on.

13

Financial Plan

Key Concepts in Chapter 13:

- Your financial plan is at the summit of your company's metrics hierarchy, a powerful tool for planning
- Your financial plan supports data-driven decision-making when it captures all inputs that drive your business model, and shows both the state of your business today and a financial road map for the future as its outputs
- To ensure high data fidelity, financial plan inputs should be automated wherever possible via interfaces with core business systems
- Forecasts are best derived via both top-down and bottom-up analyses--presenting a plan for revenue growth that is reasonable and rational from month to month given the cost inputs and historical data

This chapter is relevant for the following business models:

- **Very Low Customer LTV (<$500)**
- **Low Customer LTV ($501 - $10,000)**
- **Mid Customer LTV ($10,001 - $100,000)**
- **High Customer LTV ($100,001 - $500,000)**
- **Very High Customer LTV ($500,001+)**

Financial plans face facts and forecast accordingly.

The financial plan is part of the Unit Economics / Financial Plan foundational layer in the Bow Tie schema.

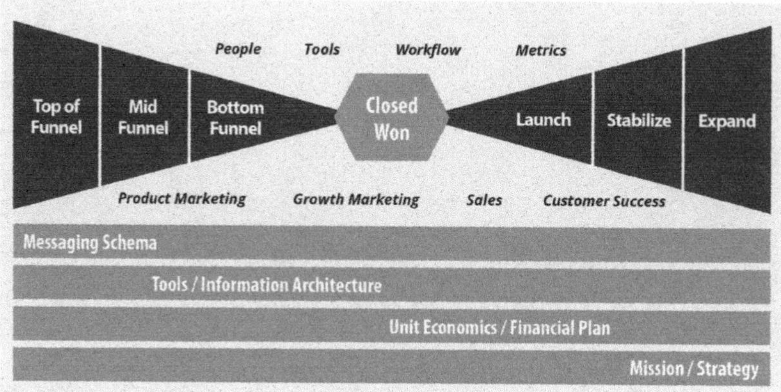

It exists for several significant purposes:

- To deliver GAAP financials to investors for auditing
- To provide investors sound and supported growth and profitability projections
- To plan sources and uses of cash to assure company viability
- To compare projections to actuals
- To present monthly company overview metrics
- To constitute a "single source of truth"—all metrics dashboards are reconciled to it and sit under it
- To confirm the viability of planned investments based on reasonable assumptions
- To evaluate the business by employee, by segment, by channel, by product, by marketing program, and by sales type and region

The model is built via inputs:

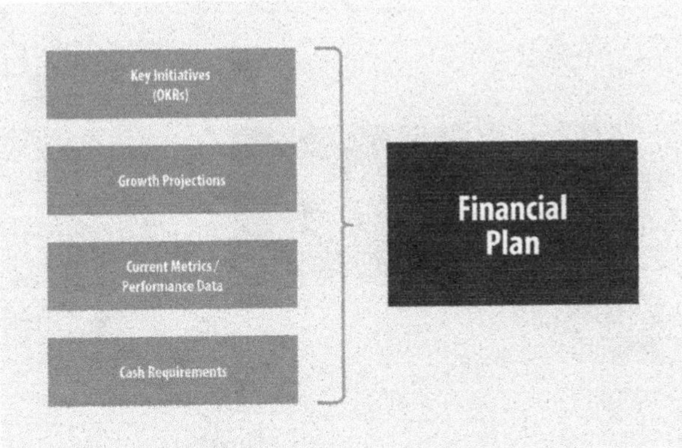

It yields a set of outputs:

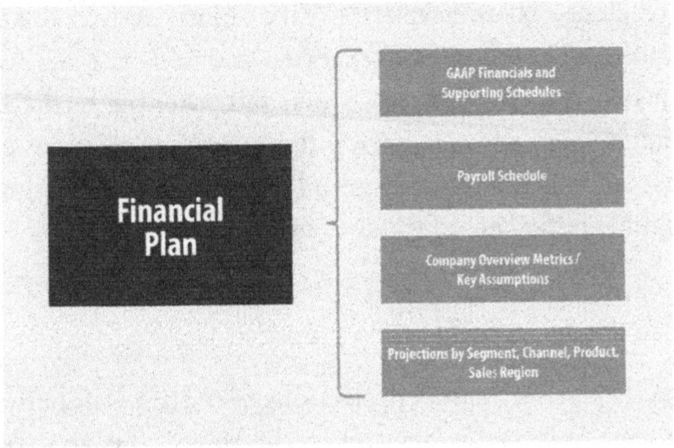

And it links to a set of systems:

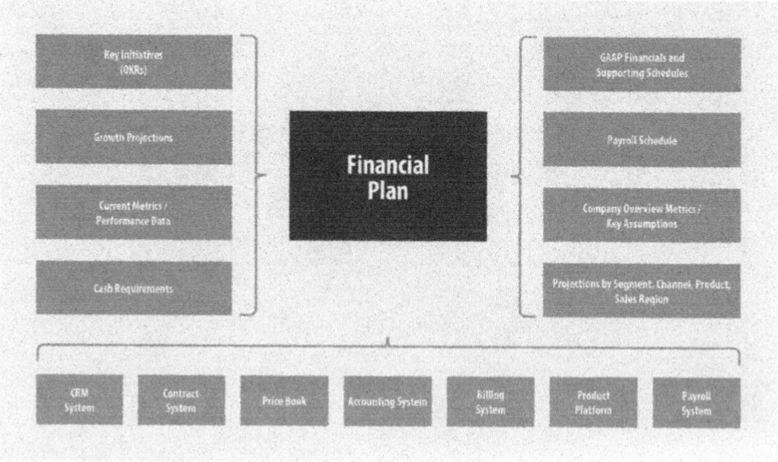

Your challenge is to ensure the data inputs, system linkages, and final outputs are executed to deliver to key stakeholders (your exec team, your board and current investors, and potential future investors) the maximum value while requiring the minimum effort to complete. This takes smart planning and careful implementation if you want to avoid a highly inefficient, continuous mess.

Top-Down vs. Bottom-Up

Your financial plan will model projections over a 2–3 year period. These projections are sure to be "up and to the right." But at what clip? A top-down look will draw comparisons from successful companies with similar business models to yours. For instance, if you are a SaaS business you look at the early performance of public SaaS companies:

Comparable Public Companies

As of 6/16/15

Name	Market Cap	Agg. Value/ Revenue 2015	Revenue 2015	Revenue Growth 2015	Operating Margin % 2015
General SaaS					
salesforce.com	$48,118	7.5x	$6,546	22%	12%
Workday	$15,087	11.9x	$1,145	45%	(2%)
ServiceNow	$12,193	12.0x	$990	45%	5%
NetSuite	$7,449	9.9x	$732	32%	3%
Veeva	$3,516	7.8x	$397	27%	28%
Demandware	$2,621	10.4x	$234	46%	0%
Xero	$1,806	12.4x	$130	55%	(46%)
Zendesk	$2,053	9.0x	$194	53%	(16%)
Hubspot	$1,685	9.3x	$167	44%	(19%)
New Relic	$1,524	8.9x	$148	53%	(32%)
Marketo	$1,238	5.5x	$209	39%	(18%)
Cvent	$1,081	5.0x	$182	28%	(3%)
Jive	$430	1.6x	$197	10%	(8%)
Mean		8.6x		38%	(7%)

Brian Royston, who has served for many years as a temp CFO in Silicon Valley, conducted the following 2015 analysis of public SaaS companies' early year performance. These comparisons can give you a rational "top-down" picture of revenue growth rates, gross margins, and other key financial projections.

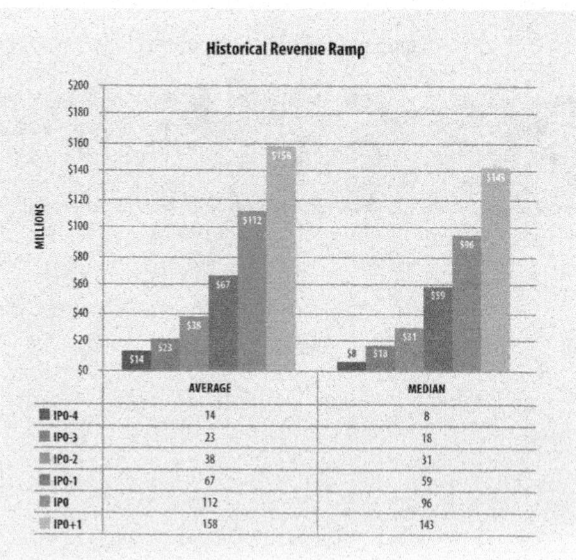

	AVERAGE	MEDIAN
IPO-4	14	8
IPO-3	23	18
IPO-2	38	31
IPO-1	67	59
IPO	112	96
IPO+1	158	143

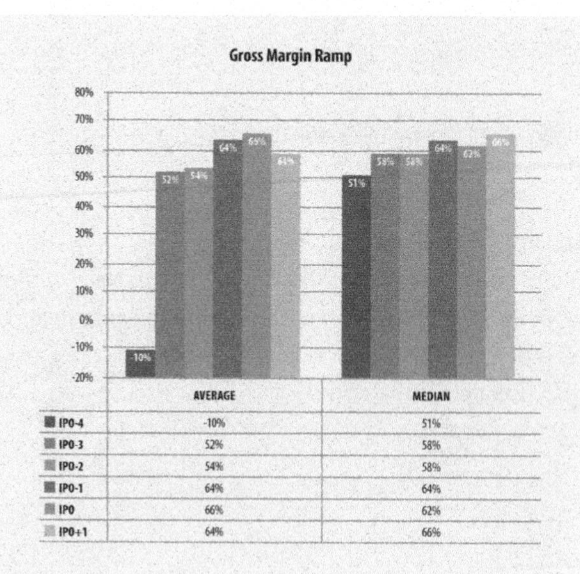

	AVERAGE	MEDIAN
IPO-4	-10%	51%
IPO-3	52%	58%
IPO-2	54%	58%
IPO-1	64%	64%
IPO	66%	62%
IPO+1	64%	66%

But as your financial model builds top-down from these numbers, it's important to work bottom-up as well. This is a key sanity check. How many sales reps are required? Is it reasonable to hire these reps as quickly as the model stipulates? Have you factored in salesperson churn? What assumptions about the average deal size and deals per month are implied? To achieve this, what marketing spend is required, yielding what quantity of MQLs per month? Are the implied conversion rates reasonable? Is the marketing budget sufficient to drive the required number of leads?

A bottom-up model forces you to think through the dependencies between your investments in marketing, sales and customer success, and the outcomes regarding revenue and churn. You must conduct a reasonableness test of projections vs. your current reality. If there is a significant improvement in key metrics implied in your projections, what initiatives have you mobilized to achieve these improvements? Are the projected outcomes reasonable? Have the costs of these initiatives been built into the model?

By working both top-down and bottom-up, projecting into the future while reviewing the past and current performance, you vector towards a reasonable and defensible financial plan.

But a financial plan is not just about projections. A well-designed financial plan presents both plan and actual, after every month's close. The variances between the plan and actuals are alerts that focus exec team attention and drive continuous improvement. There are four building blocks to ensure the efficient comparison of plan and actual:

- Defined customer hierarchy
- Customer unique identifiers
- Customer detailed transaction report
- Pivot tables

Defined Customer Hierarchy

What is the hierarchy of your customer data? Is your customer General Electric? Or is it the Marketing Department of the San Francisco Region of General Electric? You must determine the most atomic level of "customer" you will support, then build the parent / child scaffolding above it. It is vital to structure your data this way, so that reporting is clean and you are able to compare "apples to apples."

Customer Unique Identifiers

With a clear customer hierarchy in place, you are ready to develop a unique identifier protocol to tag customers. It's important that these unique identifiers are maintained as you hand customer data from system to system. By doing so, your CRM, Contract, Accounting, Billing, and Customer Success systems will be in alignment with the Financial Model. This ensures one source of truth.

This is hard, granular work. For each data element in a customer record, you will need to determine which system is the master and which systems are subordinate. But if you think it through carefully and implement it rigorously, you will build a solid foundation for scaling.

Customer Detailed Transaction Report

From the initial contract through every status change along the customer lifecycle, you need to capture the data in the customer record and log the history. This requires a Customer Detailed Transaction Report.

For an SaaS company, the columns of a Customer Detailed Transaction Report include:

- Customer name
- Effective date
- Term start date
- Term end date
- Termination for convenience date
- Cancellation date
- Canceled before recognizing revenue? Y/N
- Booking amount canceled
- Billing amount canceled
- ARR canceled
- Renewal ARR increase / decrease
- Deal type
- Total contract value

- Booking amount
- Term (in months)
- ARR
- Auto renew Y/N
- Billing frequency

Ideally, from the date of company inception all the way through to current day, every single customer's entire history, including all changes in their status at the most atomic detail level, is tracked and reportable. This gives you incredible analytical capability.

Furthermore, when you seek new funding, or you move towards an M&A transaction, the data will streamline due diligence and convey credibility.

Pivot Tables

Since the underlying data sets that make up your financial plan are large, you may wish to use pivot tables so as to summarize data into a few data fields quickly and easily. You can efficiently create multiple reports that draw upon the same data sets.

Summary

The financial plan and underlying metrics dashboards comprise the central nervous system of your business. They reveal the strengths and the failure points, and track progress over time. They give you forewarning of a cash crunch. They force you to think through the implications of your plans regarding expense and revenue, investments and cash, and new headcount and productivity outcome timing. They enable you to articulate your case for funding to investors.

As such, the financial plan is a critical component of the revenue engine. To make your engine a Porsche, a well-conceived and well-maintained financial plan is key.

Plan accordingly.

14

Tools

Key Concepts in Chapter 14:

- In the revenue engine, tools support four key domains: Top of Funnel; Mid and Bottom Funnel; Launch / Stabilize / Expand; and Finance
- Tools are as effective as the leverage they deliver to people and workflows
- Tools exist to efficiently acquire customers (both increasing reach and improving conversion), to serve them effectively, and to measure performance of the business
- Data is at the heart of an effective tools stack; job one is to get the data right
- The federated model of tools adoption must give way to central control so that data standards can be maintained
- Choice of tools is affected by business stage, business model, domain focus and business strategy

This chapter is relevant for the following business models:

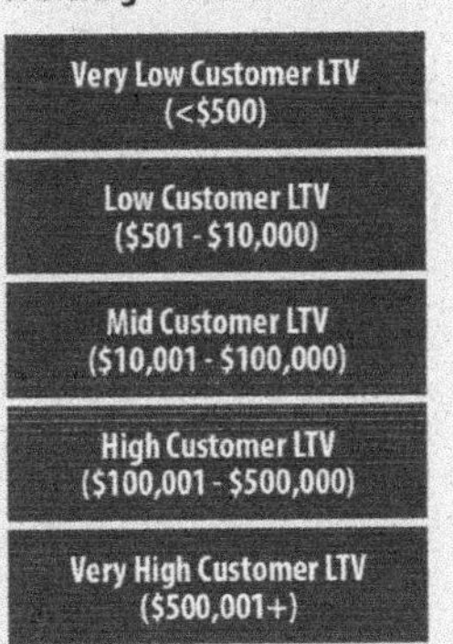

Top teams tailor tools to the task.

Tools are everywhere. In the revenue engine, there are marketing automation tools, sales automation tools, CRMs, customer success tools, and finance and billing tools.

Given the explosion of tools available, it's not surprising that CEOs and their marketing and sales leads find themselves confused about what tools to acquire and what to do with the tools they already have. The factors that drive the choice of tools are so varied it's downright vexing.

Your choice of tools will be influenced by:

- Your stage of company growth
- Your business model (ranging from Very Low LTV—i.e., media, gaming and B2C marketplace companies; to Very High LTV—i.e., B2B enterprise SaaS companies)
- The revenue engine domain you seek to address (Top of Funnel, Mid / Bottom Funnel, Customer Success, or Finance)
- Your business strategy (audience versus leads versus account based)

But when it comes to tools—no matter what your company stage, business model or strategy—some universal principles apply:

- The measure of a tool is the leverage it provides to people and workflows
- If you want to get tools right, first get data right
- Tools don't stand alone—they are linked to workflows and receive, generate, and transmit data throughout a whole system
- The control over data structure, data flows, tools acquisition, and tools configuration must be centralized: it's the only way to keep the whole system integrated
- There is a rational sequence to tools optimization: work outward from the Mid and Bottom Funnels

Very Low LTV Business Models

If you run a media company, consumers enjoy a free product experience. There is, therefore, no separation from Top, to Mid, to Bottom Funnel: a new visitor is an addition to "audience" and immediately monetized. Deeper engagement yields more monetizable page views, but even the first visited page is monetizable.

Tools can support the extension of reach to new visitors and the testing and optimization of site design based on observed visitor behaviors.

For a gaming or marketplace company (i.e., companies with a Very Low LTV business model), your product natively guides a fully automated journey from prospect to customer. Likewise, the free part of a freemium business model—either B2C or B2B. To move prospects along that journey, your most important "tool" is your product. As noted in Chapter 8—Product, for such companies the "first mile" of the prospect's experience is key (the Top of Funnel product utility, the home page, the browsing features, the first required actions, the empty states, etc.). Success depends on the speed with which you can deliver significant customer value.

Once you have achieved a baseline threshold of prospect-to-customer conversion, you can explore marketing automation tools and distribution partnerships to increase Top of Funnel. Tools and vendors can help you increase reach via the following Top of Funnel pathways:

- SEO
- SEM
- Online media (desktop and mobile)
- E-commerce / marketplace
- Email

And there are a wide variety of tools and vendors that help you to take advantage of Top of Funnel amplification levers:

- Advocacy / referrals
- Loyalty
- Public relations
- Community / reviews
- Feedback / chat
- Influencers
- Affiliate marketing

- Interactive content

All Other Business Models

However, if you run a company with a business model that ranges from Low LTV to Very High LTV, human beings are in the mix. People interact with tools to advance prospects and customers along the journey. Here, the revenue engine's horsepower is a function of the people / tools / workflows / metrics flywheel. Tools are essential, but they exist only to support people and workflows as tracked by metrics—all must be in sync.

The rest of this chapter will be dedicated to business models from Low LTV to Very High LTV—i.e., those business models that include people. As the CEO of such a tech company, how do you approach the build-out of your tools stack?

As is often true, it's best to go back to first principles. Revenue engine tools exist for just four reasons:

- To increase reach of prospects most likely to convert
- To convert more new customers more efficiently
- To make the serving of existing customers more effective
- To make the management of the business more metrics driven

The revenue engine is a whole system. Tools apply mainly to the following four broad domains in the system:

- Top of Funnel (marketing automation tools)
- Mid and Bottom Funnel (sales automation tools)
- Launch / Stabilize / Expand (customer success tools)
- Unit Economics / Financial Plan (metrics and business reporting tools, along with the billing and accounting tools that drive financial plan inputs)

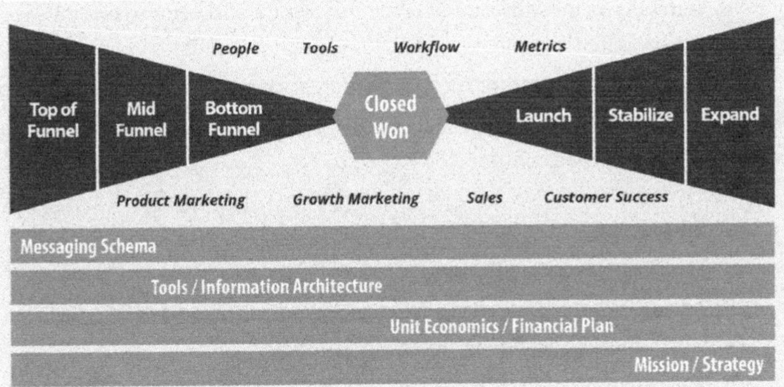

For the tools in these four domains to perform their functions well, the following must be true:

- All steps in the journey of a prospect or customer are clearly defined
- All the data attributes you seek to track at every step of the prospect and customer journey, from top of funnel through transaction-detail accounting records, are clearly defined and universally applied inside tools
- The structure of data (the definition of a lead, definition of an account, the definition of the parent / child hierarchy, the key affiliate relationships, all active account statuses, etc.) is delineated clearly and universally applied inside tools
- In each domain, people, tools, and workflow come together to get work done; this interaction has been mapped out
- Each tool is used in the right way by the right people, making a critical workflow more efficient and effective
- Each tool integrates well with adjacent tools and workflows
- There is centralized control over tools configuration and integration under someone who possesses a comprehensive whole-system design and demonstrable systems integration skills
- Metrics dashboards are in place to make workflow performance visible

- Workflows are rationalized for efficiency and effectiveness

Unfortunately, for many tech companies, the above descriptions do not apply. Too often, a look "under the hood" quickly reveals wiring problems. Problems include:

- Messy data
- Multiple sources of truth
- Thousands of unused or little-used fields in Salesforce
- Ill-defined prospect and customer stages
- Tools that don't speak to each other
- Formal workflows that don't account for all use case permutations
- Poorly trained people working around (not within) formal workflows and existing tools
- Tools configured incorrectly
- Tools used improperly or not at all

Why have so few CEOs successfully solved for these problems?

There are two reasons. First, it's hard to create simple. Few executives have the skill, patience, time, and stubbornness to work methodically from high-level system design down to every atomic-level permutation to get it right. And second, the power to acquire a tool has been delegated to functional teams without visibility of the whole system.

A distributed—as opposed to centralized—decision model results in disconnected systems.

If your company's current state matches the "wiring problem" described above, then you have important work to do: the cost of these inefficiencies is very high. It's akin to a car engine that's missing three spark plugs, has an oil leak and runs with a faulty alternator.

Don't add one more tool until you clean up what you already have. Take control by centralizing tools and information architecture decision making. Go back to basics: assess your data hygiene and data structure, and your prospect / customer journey stage definitions. Starting with Closed Won and working backward, redesign workflows in each domain. Clean up the data. Properly configure the tools. Train the folks. Prove to yourself that each stage is solid before moving to the next.

Once ready, the introduction of tools into workflows has a natural sequence. In building out or fixing your tools stack, the proper sequential order is as follows:

- Mid and Bottom Funnel
- Unit Economics / Financial Plan
- Launch / Stabilize / Expand
- Top of Funnel

Mid and Bottom Funnel

It's important to start here because as you nail down the data elements and data definitions at Mid and Bottom Funnel, you set the data foundation for all other domains. So job one is to align people, tools and workflows towards the task of converting prospect interest into a Closed Won customer.

It starts with data. Your data must be clean. You must define all relevant data attributes, build a clear data structure, tightly delineate the data flows, and establish clear stage by stage performance metrics within each domain. With these data elements nailed down, you then build them into tools such as the contact data repository, CRM system, and sales email system.

If you sweat the details here in the Mid and Bottom Funnel domain, you create a secure foundation for all other domains.

For companies with a Mid LTV business model or higher, in building out your Mid and Bottom Funnel, you might begin with one sales pod—perhaps two SDRs and an account executive (AE). Here's the sequence:

- Ensure all data elements (the first six items on the checklist) are at least at a "level 4" maturity (see assessment tool, below)
- Ensure reporting analytics are at least "level 3" maturity

- Ensure the team's execution of contact prioritization, research, initial outreach, and follow-up disciplines (using LinkedIn and other contact data, the sales email system, and CRM system) have achieved at least a "level 3" maturity
- When conversion rates are financially viable and repeatable, you are ready to expand the team
- As the team grows, you begin to introduce dialing automation, predictive analytics, marketing automation for nurture, and other enhancements—depending in part on your business model

At the outset, you might simply have a sales platform such as Outreach.io or Salesloft, contact data from LinkedIn, and basic email capabilities built into your sales platform or augmented by an email tool such as Campaign Monitor. At scale, you have probably shifted to Salesforce as your CRM tool, a high-end marketing automation tool such as Marketo (with its lead scoring and predictive analytics capabilities), dialing automation tools such as InsideSales, sales intelligence tools such as InsideView, and so forth.

But don't get ahead of yourself: keep the choice of tools aligned with your stage of growth.

Tom Grubb, Chief Strategy Officer for Digital Pi, a company that cleans up the marketing and sales automation tools stack and can directly manage a company's marketing campaigns, asserts that very few companies do the work necessary to take full advantage of powerful tools like Marketo. It takes both knowledge of how to do it, prioritization of the time and resources, and the discipline to get it done. In his experience, too many companies fall short, costing them significant lost revenue opportunity.

For B2B companies, a major problem often exists at the intersection of a lead and an account. Accounts may be linked to multiple contacts. A number of them might have submitted leads. Gaining visibility into the leads associated with accounts is a difficult challenge. These days, vendors such as LeanData and Engagio have taken on this challenge. Both Engagio's CEO, Jon Miller, and LeanData's CEO, Evan Liang, are leading evangelists for account-based marketing (ABM).

Liang built his company on the premise that account-based data (linking leads to accounts) is the key to any account-based strategy.

When contemplating additions to your tools stack, it's helpful to assess your current state. Use the following checklist to determine your Mid and Bottom Funnel maturity from 1 (nascent)—5 (fully mature):

Mid and Bottom Funnel Maturity Assessment	1	2	3	4	5
You have defined all the detail-level stages of a prospect and customer, including all permutations. These definitions are shared across the company.					
You have defined all the data attributes that must be tracked for an individual prospect (a person), from raw lead through Closed Won customer.					
You have defined the parent / child and affiliate relationships of a customer. You have defined an account. You can map multiple individual prospects to an account.					
You have established data hygiene protocols such that you regularly de-dupe your data. Your data accurately defines the actual status of a prospect or customer 98% of the time or more.					
You have incorporated all stages, definitions and data attributes into your CRM system.					
You have defined each step in the workflow of an SDR, Sales Rep and / or Account Exec (consistent with your business model), and the workflow steps align with and are supported by the CRM system and other tools.					
You have a source for contact data that augments and goes beyond LinkedIn data.					
You have the capacity to research a prospect before making contact, gaining an information advantage that increases the likelihood of engagement and ultimate sale.					
You have in place sales email technology that enables you to time and personalize campaigns.					
You have in place dialing automation technology that enables you to eliminate dial time. This technology calls from the local area code ("local presence" feature).					
You have in place the analytics necessary to evaluate reach and conversion at every step of the workflow.					

Unit Economics / Financial Plan

Next up is Unit Economics / Financial Plan (billing, accounting, and business reporting). You must correctly price, contract for, and bill the customer. Sales incentives need to be calculated accurately. The accounting function must execute with precision. The financials must be tracked, and actuals compared to projections in the financial plan. Reporting and analytics must be bolted down end to end.

Tools play a major role here.

Once again, you start with the data—define all data attributes, data structure, and data flow stages. Clean and de-dupe all data. In this domain, the transaction detail record is the litmus test: if you executed the data layer well, this record accurately captures all possible permutations of customer status. Chapter 13 provides more information on the transaction detail report.

Tools such as Docusign (for contracts), Zuora (for billing and payments), Quickbooks or Netsuite (for accounting), Xactly or CallidusCloud (for commission calculations), and a broad range of business intelligence tools are a part of this domain.

Assess the maturity of your finance systems by grading each of the following from 1–5:

Finance Maturity Assessment	1	2	3	4	5
Your transaction detail report captures every detail about the status of a customer necessary to ensure proper billing and reporting. It is 100% accurate across all customers.					
You have transaction detail reporting through history, so that you can track the status changes of a customer through its entire lifecycle. This data is 100% accurate across all customers through history.					
All the data in the transaction detail report is synchronized with other tools and systems, and there is a clear definition of the master source for all data elements. There is only one source of truth for all data.					
The difference between an account and a billing entity is clear. This difference is addressed so that both accounting and billing actions are 100% accurate.					
You have in place a price book that determines the appropriate price for a given transaction, and provides the necessary approvals as appropriate. It is used 100% of the time to determine the price.					
You have in place an online contract system that is linked to the price book, enabling you to execute completion of the contract online.					
You have in place a billing system that addresses all billing activity, determines appropriate state taxes, manages payments and supports proper revenue recognition. Data flows through this system without error.					
You have established a clear workflow to manage renewals-- from Sales through Finance-- and there is a seamless integration of people, tools and workflows to support it.					
You have in place an accounting system that is right-sized for the scale of your business, supporting all necessary accounting functions. Data flows through this system without error.					
You have in place a financial reporting system and a financial plan that ensures actual financial performance can be compared to plan via a mostly automated process. The data is 100% accurate.					
You have clearly defined all critical business metrics. You have in place a company metrics dashboard that tracks the business performance of the whole system. The dashboard has an exec team level view and more detailed functional views. The data is generated via mostly automated means, and is 100% accurate.					

With the data elements clear, you can build out the tools stack, once again working to optimize the intersection of people, tools, and workflows.

Launch / Stabilize / Expand

This is the third domain in the sequence. Now that you can move a prospect to Closed Won with acceptable levels of repeatability; and bill, account for, and report on a customer at an acceptable level of fidelity; it's time to Launch / Stabilize / Expand a customer in a tools-supported, data-driven way. Once again, you start with the data, making sure data hygiene, structures, and flows are solid. Then, you can introduce a tool if it makes people and workflows significantly more efficient and effective. Customer success tools such as Totango and Gainsight are often used by B2B SaaS companies to provide visibility into customer usage rates and to monitor customer health.

Launch / Stabilize / Expand Maturity Assessment	1	2	3	4	5
The definition of a customer (an account?) has been clearly and universally applied, with all parent / child and affiliate relationships clear.					
Every step on every possible path of the customer journey, for every purchasable product, has been defined and universally applied.					
The status of a customer for every product is easily determined and visible.					
The status of every customer in the launch phase, and the overall status of launches, is easily visible via metrics dashboards					
The number of users using the product as compared to the contracted number of users, the frequency of use and the degree of utilization across all important product features can be measured at the individual customer level. Corrective actions are automatically triggered when product use falls below pre-established thresholds. At the overview level, the metrics dashboard tracks usage over time.					
Tools prompt people to intervene if a customer's health is determined to be at risk.					
Tools can track the ROI that a customer experiences by using our product.					
Tools trigger people to engage the customer in advance of contract renewal, and when data points to the potential for expansion or upsells.					

Top of Funnel

In all three of the previous domains, your goal is clear: to optimize people, tools, and workflows so that they perform at high quality, in an efficient, consistent, and repeatable way. The goal, even when undergoing a process redesign, is to arrive at a "standard operating procedure." In these domains, the variables are mostly or completely within your company's control.

This fourth and final domain—Top of Funnel—is different. The mission at Top of Funnel is to create leads by acquiring quality names and initiating early engagement with them. Here, continuous experimentation is the order of the day. Many of the variables that impact performance at Top of Funnel are outside the company's span of control and always shifting—such as customer needs, emerging trends, competitive dynamics, and so forth. So the actions that drive success in one month might prove ineffective the next. Therefore, you must test and iterate campaigns at Top of Funnel constantly. Even tools themselves can and should be the subject of experimentation and iteration.

How do you figure out what's working? If your sales cycle is relatively short, you can apply attribution rules and track the Closed Won performance of each campaign. If your sales cycle is longer—say, four months or more—an attribution approach will be insufficient. There's too big of a time gap for rapid iteration and optimization. In this situation, scoring becomes key. Given the ideal customer profile (ICP), you measure reach and engagement for ICP prospects. You set rules determining how the number and types of engagement (white paper downloads, webinar attendance, email opens, etc.) will impact scoring of the lead. With these rules defined, scoring thresholds can be used to identify readiness to buy and to drive nurture activities and sales interventions.

Top of Funnel Maturity Assessment	1	2	3	4	5
You have a clear definition of the Ideal Customer Profile (ICP), and have determined the data attributes and data values you seek in a qualified lead					
You have de-dupe capability in place, and procedures are in place to ensure all new names are immediately de-duped whenever a new list or set of names is uploaded.					
You have identified the rules for lead scoring, and you are currently scoring all your leads					
You are using lead scoring data to evaluate the status of your funnel.					
You have developed clear attribution rules, and these rules are being used to evaluate all top of funnel campaigns					
You have mapped lead data to accounts.					
You have in place the metrics dashboards necessary to analyze the performance of campaigns and channels					
You are testing and reporting on the performance of every campaign and channel-- via lead score data, attribution data or both					
You have tools in place to augment performance of your website and landing pages, SEO and email					
You have tools in place to augment performance of online media, e-commerce, direct mail, telemarketing, webinars, events, print media, TV and Retail, as appropriate to your model					
You have tools or vendors in place to take advantage of amplification levers such as advocacy, referrals, loyalty, PR, influencers, affiliate marketing, feedback and chat, community and reviews, and interactive content					
A portion of your marketing time and budget is allocated to research and testing of new tools and vendor relationships					
You have testing tools in place, and have a rigorous testing methodology to determine the efficacy of campaigns and tools					

Why is Top of Funnel the final domain to work on? Because to do otherwise is a waste of time and money. If a campaign can't be tracked accurately from Top of Funnel to Closed Won, it's impossible to assess campaign performance.

If your data is unclean (i.e., duplicate data, inaccurate data), if you don't have a consistent data structure, if you haven't defined journey stages, if your Mid and Bottom Funnel tools are misconfigured or don't accurately measure conversion, if prospect conversion is too low, or you can't bill, track, or serve customers well then you are wasting leads, abandoning prospects, and flying blind. So earn your way to Top of Funnel tools by first making the other domains as solid as a rock.

Always remember you are building a whole, integrated system. Here's an entirely built out B2B SaaS tools stack for a Mid-LTV business model. You'll notice everything links together:

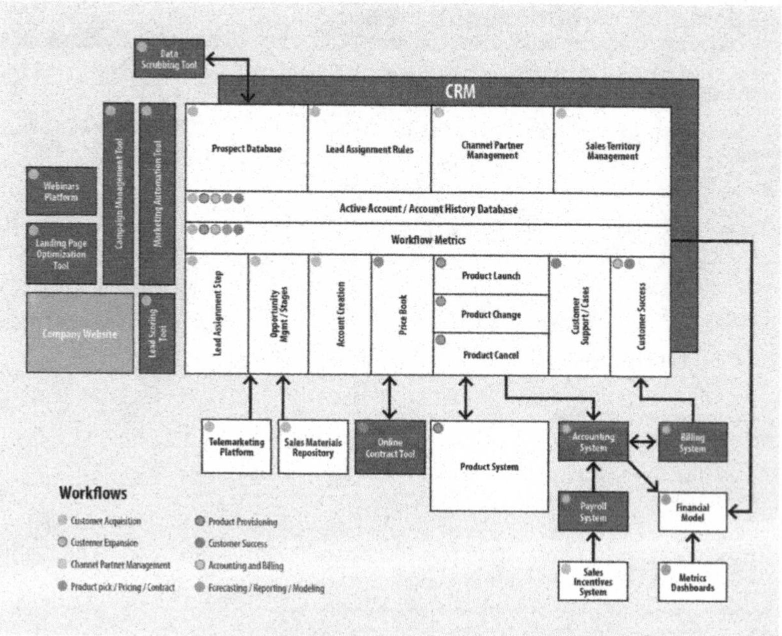

Build vs. Buy

There's a good rule of thumb when you've determined a tool is needed to fix a workflow problem: buy when you can and build when you have to. Building takes time and money and diverts your engineering team from the product road map. While a buy decision forces you to adopt the native workflows within the tool (within configuration parameters) vs. growing your own, that may be a good thing. Be open to the workflow requirements of leading tools. Remember that any market-tested tool has years of development behind it. The vendor has probably thought it through more than you.

Evaluating Competing Tools

When searching for a tool to solve the next workflow bottleneck, it's common to have multiple alternatives. How do you assess them? First list the features you seek then map these features to the features available in the tools you are considering. Phone a friend—seek references. If multiple tools offer all the features you require, have a strong service and support record, and have been confirmed to deliver high reliability and quality, then you're free to choose based on price and "extras."

The Role of Leadership

A high power revenue engine features seamless, efficient workflows. These workflows are powered by tools used correctly by people in service of prospects and customers. Data flows smoothly from step to step and from tool to tool across the whole system.

To make this happen, define workflow stages within each domain. Determine data attributes. Establish the entire data structure with its parent / child and affiliate relationships and the definition of an account. Choose the right tools at the right time, so they are well configured to support the workflow and the people.

How to do this with the rigor necessary?

Expert central control is the distinguishing factor. An executive team member must have the authority to design the whole system, build the data standards, and control tools adoption and configuration. This person must first have a deep understanding of the business and strategy. She must be able to work cross-functionally and be responsive to the needs of various functions. And, she must also possess the rare capability of envisioning the whole system from high level down to the details of data structure and data flows.

It's not an easy hire—the skills to do it well are in short supply. In the beginning, it's probably you—the CEO. As you scale, it might be the VP Finance, or eventually a VP Business Operations. Just make sure that at every stage of growth, someone owns this vital role. It's fundamental to a well-designed tools stack.

Tools yield leverage when smartly selected and implemented with precision.

Lever up.

15

Information Architecture

Key Concepts in Chapter 15:

- Information architecture is comprised of data structure and data flow architecture
- Data elements must be rigorously defined in order for data to flow properly through the whole system
- Specifically, the answers to the questions "what is a prospect?" and "what is a customer?" are critical to the friction-free flow of data
- A customer should be tracked via a unique identifier that is consistently applied across all systems, from the CRM system to contract system to billing and accounting systems to the financial plan

This chapter is relevant for the following business models:

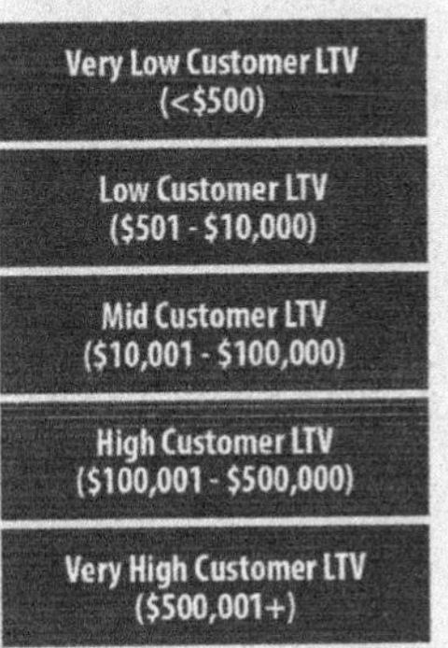

Information informs when architected intelligently.

The revenue engine will cough and sputter, and may even blow a gasket if data does not flow friction-free throughout the system. Yet friction-free is hard won. It requires you to think through your information architecture carefully and to execute flawlessly at every node throughout the entire system. Since it's hard to redo once implemented, you want to get it right the first time. To make that happen, focus on these two things:

- Smart data structure
- Smart data flow architecture

Smart Data Structure

Smart data structure exhibits clear, unambiguous definitions of data elements, and the rules governing the relationships between data elements. The objective of this chapter is not to provide a comprehensive documentation of the factors to consider in your information architecture, but rather to provide a glimpse into the degree of rigor required to get it right.

Let's take the example of a B2B SaaS company. We must start at the very beginning. Here's a simple question: what is a customer?

This issue is not as simple as it seems. Is a customer a person, or a company? Let's assume you determine it's a company (let's use the word "account"). When does an account become a customer? We can't answer that question until we further define an account. Is the account General Electric, or is the account the marketing department in the San Francisco region of General Electric? Let's assume you determine that the parent account is General Electric, and the child account is the San Francisco region, and the grandchild account is the marketing department in the San Francisco region.

We go on. Is an account (whether parent, child or grandchild) a customer the moment you define it as a prospect? Stop right there. What is a prospect? Is a prospect a person, or is a prospect an account? Perhaps you decide the answer is both: a prospect contact is a person, and a prospect account is an account. Prospect accounts are those accounts that fall within the definition of your ideal customer profile (ICP). Prospect accounts include prospect contacts. So is a prospect account a customer?

Let's assume you determine that the status "customer" is only achieved once an account buys at least one product item or package from you. If three grandchild accounts inside General Electric separately purchase a product item from you over a six month period, in three separate transactions, does this constitute three customers or one? And if an account becomes a customer and then later cancels, do they revert to being a non-customer or do they continue to be considered a customer?

Your answers to these questions are imperative. The definitions you establish must be carried throughout your whole system: into your CRM, your product system, your accounting system, your billing system, and your financial plan. Any inconsistency from platform to platform will turn your data into a confusing mess.

There may be no single universal list of "right" answers, but it is critical that your answers are internally consistent throughout your revenue engine.

Here is one example of a set of definitions for a prospect contact and a prospect account:

- A company is a prospect account if it meets the ICP definition
- A prospect account may have a hierarchy: such as parent account, child account, and grandchild account
- A prospect account comprises prospect contacts
- Each prospect contact associates with at least one level in the prospect account hierarchy
- A single prospect contact may be touched by, and may act on, multiple actions or campaigns
- An action by a prospect contact that results in an incoming data packet (lead form, email message, etc.) generates a raw lead
- A raw lead from a prospect contact is designated a marketing qualified lead (MQL) if an automated score (based on contact characteristics, type and amount of data entered and level of activity) achieves a predefined threshold

- Prospect leads (raw leads and MQLs) may or may not be able to be tracked back to a specific marketing or sales action or campaign via an attribution rule
- Since multiple outbound campaigns and connections may yield a single raw lead or MQL, the attribution rule defines the method by which credit attributes to outbound campaigns
- One prospect contact may generate multiple leads
- Multiple prospect contacts may generate multiple leads for a single prospect account
- An MQL becomes a sales qualified lead (SQL) once a sales development rep (SDR) determines that: the account meets the ICP; the prospect contact meets the target persona; the prospect contact meets the thresholds for budget, authority, need, and timing (BANT); and, an appointment is set up between an AE and the prospect contact
- An SQL becomes a sales accepted lead (SAL) once an account executive (AE) has held an initial call with the prospect contact, has reconfirmed the contact meets BANT and is interested in going to the next step
- At the point that the next meeting is held, the appropriate prospect account hierarchy is established, and the lowest appropriate level in the hierarchy becomes a prospect account opportunity (i.e. General Electric—San Francisco region—marketing department)
- All prospect contacts within the prospect account that fit the profiles of decision maker, influencer, user or blocker may be identified and retained in the prospect account record, associated with their appropriate hierarchical level
- A prospect account opportunity goes through four steps: discover, prove, negotiate, and close.

Here's one example of a set of definitions for a customer account:

- An account becomes a customer account with purchase of a

product item or package, at which time an account ID is assigned.

- The account ID is a unique identifier and is used consistently across all systems (CRM, product system, billing system, accounting system, financial plan, etc.).
- An account ceases to be a customer account when no product item or package is live, but it retains the account ID—when this happens, it returns to its status as a prospect account.
- Any level at which the product can be sold and serviced is an account (parent, child, grandchild, etc.).
- Parent / child / grandchild relationships are tracked via a nested set of account IDs
- These account hierarchy relationships are identified in an account tracking system (possibly the CRM).
- The number of customer accounts is measured based on the most atomic level of product purchase capability. For example, the marketing department in the San Francisco region of General Electric might be one customer account, and the marketing department in the Minneapolis region might a second, separate customer account (sitting inside General Electric's nested parent account hierarchy).
- An account (at any level in the account hierarchy) may have one or more external affinities (examples: OEM, ad agency, partner). These affinity relationships are specified in the account record in the CRM system.
- Every account has a unique account ID, which is applied consistently throughout the whole system (the CRM system, the contract system, the product system, the billing system, the accounting system, the financial plan, etc.).
- In an account hierarchy, the parent is a customer account if at least one child / grandchild / great-grandchild account is live with at least one product item or package.
- The system can support reporting of account status for all levels within an account hierarchy under the parent.

- An account is live if there is at least one product item or package that is active, paused, or cancel pending.
- Live vs. not live status is determined at any account hierarchy level (parent, child, grandchild, etc.).

Notice that the definitions are exacting and rigorous. There's no wiggle room. That's the key to a smart data structure.

Smart Data Flow Architecture

Data structures are set up to support workflows. For instance, to manage workflows such as customer acquisition, product selection, pricing, contracting, product provisioning, product launch, and ongoing customer success, four data structure categories are key: prospect account lifecycle stages, customer account lifecycle stages, orders, and billing arrangements.

Prospect Account Lifecycle Stages

The stages of a prospect account can now be defined using the data structure definitions and mapped to the Bow Tie domains as shown below:

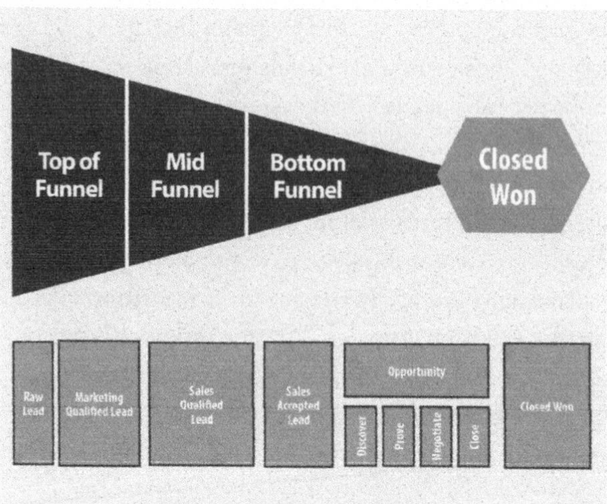

Prospect account lifecycle stages are:

- Prospect contact: raw lead
- Prospect contact: marketing qualified lead (MQL)
- Prospect contact: sales qualified lead (SQL)
- Prospect contact: sales accepted lead (SAL)
- Prospect account: opportunity (discover step)
- Prospect account: opportunity (prove step)
- Prospect account: opportunity (negotiate step)
- Prospect account: opportunity (close step)
- Customer account: closed / won

Customer Account Lifecycle Stages

Similarly, the lifecycle stages of a customer account can now be identified and mapped to the Bow Tie domains as shown below.

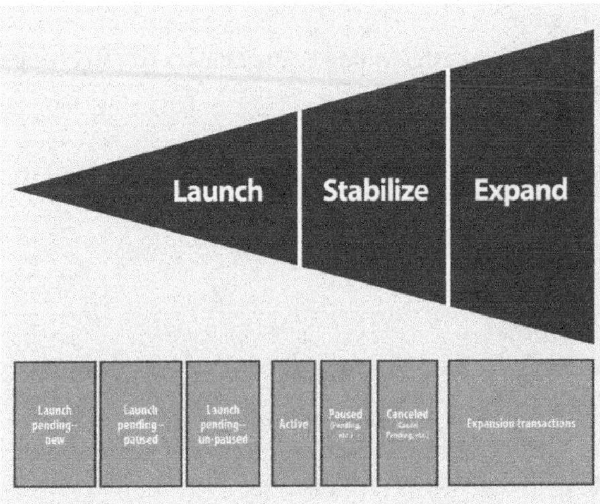

Stages include:

- Contract signed
- Launch pending—new

- Launch pending—paused
- Launch pending—unpaused
- Active
- Pending paused
- Paused
- Cancel pending and pending paused
- Cancel pending and paused
- Cancel pending—no pause
- Canceled
- Expansion transactions

Orders

Orders are the means by which changes are made to the lifecycle stage, term, price, or invoice amount of a product item or package. Order types include:

- New order
- Price / term length / billing arrangements (PTB) change order

Specific PTB change orders may include:

- Pause order
- Unpause order
- Cancel order
- Stop cancel order
- Credit order
- Price change order
- Billing arrangements change order

Billing Arrangements

Billing arrangements touch upon the billing entity or entities, the billing method, the billing type, and the billing cycle.

- Usually, the customer is also the billing entity—but not always. One or more billing entities may exist
- Billing methods include prepay, advance billing, and arrears billing
- Billing types include credit card, check, and automated transfer
- The billing cycle is the agreed start day and end day of service for each period for which the customer is billed

You get the idea. In tightening up your workflows, the same rigor must apply in selecting product items and packages, using the price book, signing contracts, executing product provisioning, managing accounting and billing, managing employee data (titles, hierarchies, departments), etc.

Data elements and their relationships are used daily in the business to manage your workflows.

A critical resource for various teams across the whole system is the customer account record.

The customer account record includes:

- *Customer account ID*. Every customer account has a customer account ID, which is a unique identifier across all systems (the CRM, contract system, accounting system, billing system and the transaction logs that flow into the financial plan). The customer account ID is displayed in the customer account record in the CRM.
- *Contact information*. List all contacts with name, phone, email, mail information. Certain contacts may be designated particular contact roles tied to alerts and other correspondence they are to receive as appropriate.
- *Account hierarchy*. If the customer exists within a customer hierarchy (parent, child, grandchild, etc.), its position in the hierarchy and relationship to other customer account records is recorded via its nested customer account ID structure.

- *Affinity groups*. If the customer is tied to any affinity groups (ad agency, OEM, etc.), these relationships are recorded.
- *Customer configuration*. By product item and package, provisioning configuration detail and current lifecycle stage are identified with orders and billing history. Current and historical invoices and statements are shown. The billing arrangement, billing status, and credit order status are shown.
- *Customer support*. Customer survey data and customer support open cases and history are shown.
- *Communications*. The archive of past communications (email history, etc.) is shown by department (sales, customer success, finance, etc.).
- *Account team*. The assigned account exec, launch rep, customer success manager, and finance contact are identified.

Access to the customer account record is available via a link in:

- The product system
- The contract system
- The accounting system
- The billing system

It's hard to overestimate the power of getting data structure and data flow architecture right. If you step back and think it through then carefully implement it at the most granular level across all workflows, you will build serious horsepower into your engine. Your metrics dashboards will be unfailingly accurate. You won't waste time cleaning up the messes created by bad data, bad handoffs, or uninformed employees. You'll be running a massively more efficient company that is much more prepared to scale.

If your company suffers from ill-conceived information architecture, it's critical to come to terms with the magnitude of the problem. It's a significant drag on your future. To overhaul your engine requires a material investment of time, effort, and money (front-end loaded) to get the payoff (back-end loaded). You may well need to bring in contractors to help you execute the redesign and implementation successfully. It will be worth it. Once overhauled, your engine can begin to perform like a Porsche.

Hit the gas.

16

Messaging Schema

Key Concepts in Chapter 16:

- The Messaging Schema layer is comprised of the orchestration plan and playbooks
- To build the messaging schema you start by creating a message map
- For all business models, playbooks are required for the functions of brand, product marketing, and growth marketing
- For Mid, High and Very High LTV business models, playbooks are also required for sales development, account executives, and customer success
- The orchestration plan and playbooks are the planning tools that enable efficient and effective execution of prospect and customer engagement

This chapter is relevant for the following business models:

- Very Low Customer LTV (<$500)
- Low Customer LTV ($501 - $10,000)
- Mid Customer LTV ($10,001 - $100,000)
- High Customer LTV ($100,001 - $500,000)
- Very High Customer LTV ($500,001+)

Message + method = momentum.

When it comes to chasing revenue, CEOs often spend all their time in execution mode, without dedicating any time to foundation building. This is a mistake. Time wasted delivering poorly considered messages to the wrong people, at the wrong time, in an irrational sequence, leads to disappointing results. If anything is clear by now in reading this book, it's that research, planning, and thoughtful design are essential to effective execution of the revenue engine.

Nowhere is this more true than in the Messaging Schema, the final foundational layer of the revenue engine framework.

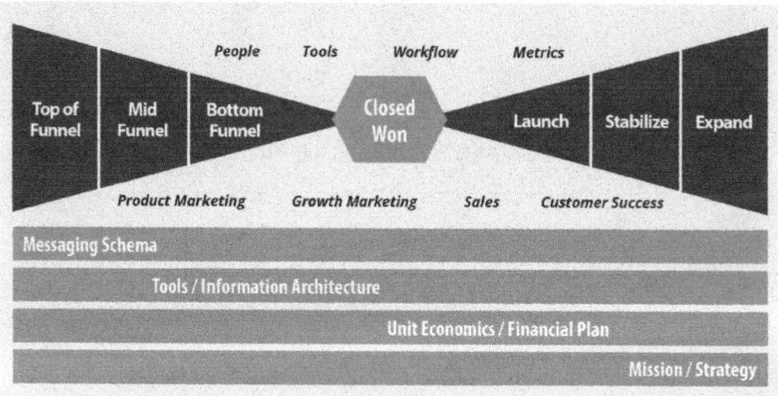

By now you have:

- Defined your mission and vision
- Built a robust segmentation scheme
- Chosen your top priority segments, the ideal customer profile (ICP), and buyer and user personas specific to each segment
- Validated a clear value proposition
- Verified competitive positioning statements
- Developed your brand identity (brand as product / company / person / symbol) and articulated clear "vision lock," "conviction lock," and "advocacy lock" statements (as captured in your brand identity document)
- Mapped the prospect and customer journeys for buyer and user personas
- Determined your channel choices and weightings
- Defined and living within the LTV / CAC constraints of your revenue model

- Built a board-approved financial plan, with specific revenue objectives and a marketing and sales budget (both labor and non-labor)
- Constructed your tools and information architecture

Now you're ready to create your messaging schema—the orchestration plan and playbooks that drive all messaging.

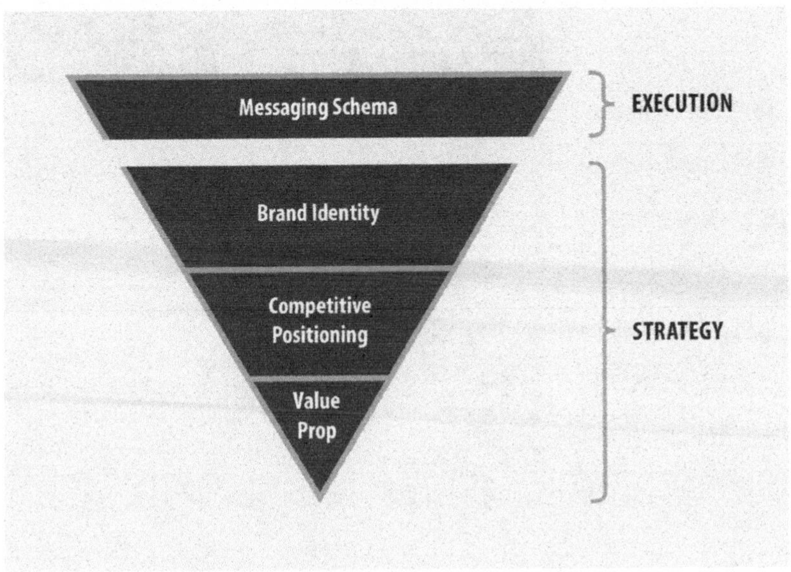

Orchestration Plan

Your orchestration plan is of supreme importance. In this plan, you design the journey you hope to deliver to your target prospect (from Top of Funnel to Mid to Bottom domains in the Bow Tie), and the journey of your customer (from Closed Won domain to Launch / Stabilize / Expand domains in the Bow Tie).

For a Very Low LTV business model, the prospect is a person, and the journey is fully digital. For a Very High LTV business model, the prospect is an account, multiple people are prospect contacts and must be engaged (e.g., buyers, users, gatekeepers, and influencers), and the journey is multidimensional. Regardless of prospect type, the goal is to continuously increase engagement. This begins by defining the key players inside a target account and determining who on your team owns the relationship. In the High or Very High LTV scenario, it's multidimensional, with many-to-many engagement required. Here's an example for a business selling a development platform to enterprise customers:

	Chief Information Officer	VP Engineering	Director, DevOps	DevOps Engineers	Purchasing Department
Marketing: Thought Leadership					
Marketing: Demand Gen					
Marketing: Nurture Campaigns					
SDR: Get Appointments					
Account Exec: Owns Opportunity Stage					
Sales Engineer: Prove Technical Claims					
VP Sales: Owns CIO Relationship					
CEO: Final Deal Support					

With the primary many-to-many relationships determined, your orchestration plan then maps the experience you seek to deliver to each of these key players on the prospect and customer journey, as follows:

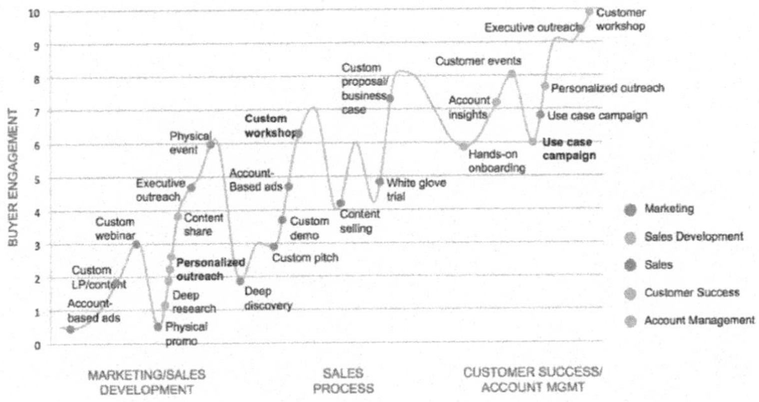

Source: Scott Albro, CEO of TOPO[1]

In this example, a prospect receives a sequence of account-based ads, customized content, a custom webinar, physical promotion, deep research, a personal outreach, an executive outreach, a physical event or trade show, deep discovery, a personalized pitch, a custom demo, more ads, a custom workshop, and content-based selling. After the purchase decision, the customer receives a white glove trial, a custom proposal and business case, hands-on on-boarding, account insights, customer events, use case campaigns, more personalized outreach, and a customer workshop.

Note that along this journey from prospect to customer, contacts occur in a variety of ways with stage-specific messaging.

The various touch points are designed to move the prospect steadily from Top of Funnel domain to Mid to Bottom domains, and then to move the new customer through the domains of Launch, Stabilize, to Expand.

If the orchestration plan is driven by touch points, the touch points themselves are driven by messaging. It's helpful to complete a message map to get the stage-specific messaging right.

A message map is a table with the following columns:

- Prospect / customer step
- Objective
- Barriers
- Messages
- Content formats / vehicles

Prospect / Customer Step	Objective	Barriers	Messages	Content Formats / Vehicles
User problems / pain experienced (Top of Funnel)	Awareness. Relevance. Engagement. An ICP lead.	Ignorance of any viable solution. Ignorance of us.	Value themes:______ Speed to Ah Hah phrase:______ Emotional phrases that convey excitement and novelty:______ Segment and persona-specific problem and positioning statements:______	Thought leadership and product content blogs. Company website content. Landing pages. Public relations. Events. SEO. Paid search. Social search. Display ads / retargeting. Email marketing.
Buyer prioritizes the problem for resolution (Top of Funnel)	Awareness. Relevance. Engagement. An ICP lead	Ignorance of us. Don't understand our value. Negative brand attributes.	Value themes:______ Speed to Ah Hah phrase:______ Emotional phrases that convey excitement and novelty:______ Segment and persona-specific problem and positioning statements:________	Thought leadership and product content blogs. Company website content. Public relations. Events. SEO. Paid search. Social search. Display ads / retargeting. Email marketing.
Buyer researches alternatives (Top of Funnel)	Engagement. Deepen understanding. An ICP lead.	Ignorance of us. Don't understand our value. Negative brand attributes.	Value themes:______ Speed to Ah Hah phrase:______ Emotional phrases that convey excitement and novelty:______ Segment and persona-specific problem and positioning statements:______ Detailed proof statements of product relevance and efficacy:______	Thought leadership and product content blogs. Company website content. Public relations. Events. SEO. Paid search. Social search. Display ads / retargeting. Email marketing.
Buyer discovers Our Product (Top of Funnel)	Engagement. Deepen understanding. An ICP lead. An MQL.	Lack of confidence in our value claims. Lack of confidence our solution maps to customer problem. List of objections.	Value themes:______ Speed to Ah Hah phrase:______ Emotional phrases that convey excitement and novelty:______ Segment and persona-specific problem and positioning statements:______ Detailed proof statements of product relevance and efficacy:______	Company website content. Events. SEO. Paid search. Social search. Display ads / retargeting. Email marketing. Cold call telemarketing. Referral programs. Lead form.
Buyer seeks demo of Our Product (Mid Funnel)	Confirm a target prospect. An ICP lead. An MQL. An Opportunity--Discover	Not a qualified lead.	Automated filter: is customer an MQL? ________	SDR script and plays
Demo of Product held (Bottom Funnel)	Engagement. Deepen understanding. Prove claims. An Opportunity--Discover	Lack of confidence in our value claims. Lack of confidence our solution maps to customer problem. List of objections.	Segment and persona-specific problem and positioning statements:______ Detailed proof statements of product relevance and efficacy:______ Detailed proof statements of product dependability / reliability / SLAs:______ Specification and feature lists:______	Segment and persona-specific sales pitch decks. Persona-specific AE scripts / plays (Discover meeting) Prospect dossier
Buyer talks to influencers / seeks references for Our Product (Bottom Funnel)	Deepen understanding. Prove claims. Overcome objections. An Opportunity.--Prove	Need independent validation.	Segment and persona-specific problem and positioning statements:______ Detailed proof statements of product relevance and efficacy:______ Detailed proof statements of product dependability / reliability / SLAs:______ Specification and feature lists:______ Feature comparisons and benefit statements vs. key competitors:______	Persona-specific AE scripts / plays (evaluation) Prospect dossier

Prospect / Customer Step	Objective	Barriers	Messages	Content Formats / Vehicles
Buyer involves Users in review of Our Product (Bottom Funnel)	Deepen understanding. Prove claims. Overcome objections. An Opportunity-- Prove	Need user validation.	Segment and persona-specific problem and positioning statements:______ Detailed proof statements of product relevance and efficacy:______ Detailed proof statements of product dependability / reliability / SLAs:______ Specification and feature lists:______ Feature comparisons and benefit statements vs. key competitors:______	Persona-specific AE scripts / sales plays (Prove meeting)
Buyer assesses ROI / financial rationale for Our Product (Bottom Funnel)	Deepen understanding. Prove claims. Overcome objections. An Opportunity.-- Negotiate	Need financial validation.	Specification and feature lists:______ Detailed proof statements of product relevance and efficacy:______	AE scripts / plays (Negotiate meeting)
Buyer compares to alternatives Bottom Funnel)	Deepen understanding. Prove claims. Overcome objections. Opportunity-- Close	Need best available alternative validation.	Specification and feature lists:______ Feature comparisons and benefit statements vs. key competitors:______ Detailed proof statements of product relevance and efficacy:______ Detailed proof statements of product dependability / reliability / SLAs:______	AE scripts / sales plays (Negotiate meeting)
Buyer purchases Our Product (Closed Won)	Get to close. Opportunity-- Close. Closed / Won			AE scripts / sales plays (Negotiate meeting)
Product is Launched (Launch)	Prove claims. Best practice adoption. Confirm purchase decision. Customer live.	Launch issues.	Checklists:______ Best practice statements:______	Customer Provisioning Team: Checklists Videos Implementation workflows
Buyer and Users Implement Product (Stabilize)	Prove claims. Deepen understanding. Best practice adoption. Confirm purchase decision.	Implementation challenges.	Checklists:______ Best practice statements:______	Email nurture: best practices and checklists. Webinars: best practices and checklists. Customer success programs. Customer success plays.
Buyer and Users Assess the Product (Stabilize)	Prove claims. Deepen understanding. Best practice adoption. Confirm purchase decision.	Usability issues. Inadequate ROI outcomes.	Best practice statements:______	Email nurture: best practices and checklists. Webinars: best practices and checklists. Customer success programs. Customer success plays.
Buyer and Users either Optimize / Expand or Wind Down / Cancel (Expand)	Deepen understanding. Get to expansion.	Usability issues. Inadequate ROI outcomes. Decision-making process for expansion.	Best practice statements:______ Expansion specification and feature lists:______	Customer success programs. Customer success plays. Sales pitch / scripts / plays.

With your orchestration plan and message map complete, you can now turn to the creation of playbooks.

The Purpose of Playbooks

Playbooks guide day to day actions for your team. If your business has a Very Low or Low LTV business model, there will be three playbooks: brand marketing, product marketing, and growth marketing. If your business model is from Mid LTV to Very High LTV, you will add three more playbooks for sales development, account executive, and customer success. Your playbooks rest on the foundations of segmentation scheme, brand identity, message map, and orchestration plan:

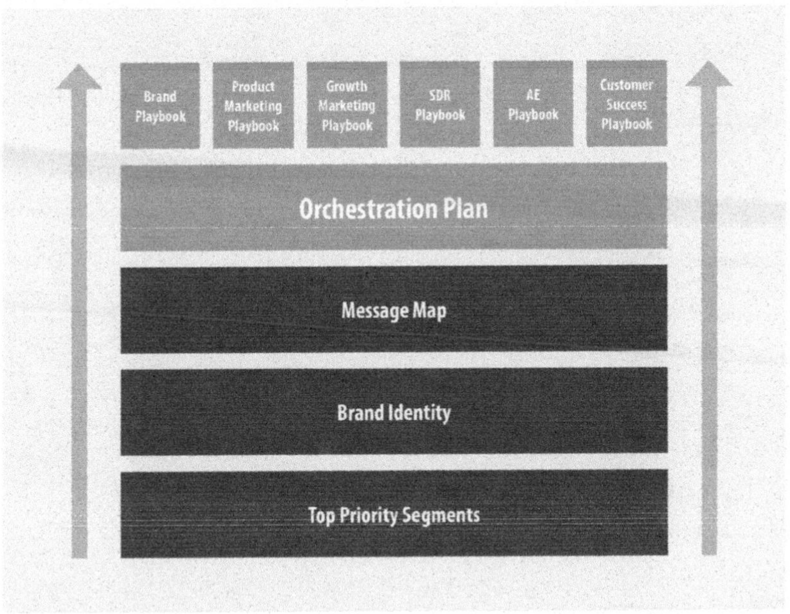

Your brand identity document (see Chapter 7—Brand Identity), with its theme statements and product-specific statements, anchors all messaging. But messages will vary by prospect and customer stage. They will be presented in diverse vehicles and formats. They must be communicated in time and space. And they must be generated and transmitted by different functional team members. So it is the purpose of each playbook to provide each functional team (whether brand, product marketing, growth marketing, sales development, account execs, or customer success) a game plan that coordinates:

Bow Tie domain

- Top of Funnel
- Mid Funnel
- Bottom Funnel
- Launch
- Stabilize
- Expand

Message vehicle

- Media
- Company website
- SEO / landing pages
- SEM
- Email
- Advertising / retargeting
- Trade shows
- Workshops
- SDRs
- AEs

Message format

- Email templates
- Call scripts
- Blog
- Video
- Slideshow
- Articles
- Press releases

- Power points
- Demo platform
- Collateral materials

Time

- Prospect engagement steps and messaging rules
- Editorial calendar

Brand Playbook

The brand playbook includes the style guide. The style guide presents your brand visual expression comprised of your brand architecture, your brand personality, and brand symbols (logo, slogans, iconography, typography, color palette, etc.). It is followed rigorously in all messaging.

The brand playbook also lists the top priority projects that will be completed (this quarter / this year) to improve brand visual expression. The redesign of collateral materials, the website, or other brand assets are good examples.

Finally, in larger companies, the brand playbook includes the plan for any brand campaigns. Brand campaigns are usually big-budget multimedia campaigns with the purpose being to increase brand awareness and brand equity. They live by the motto, "go big or go home." A brand campaign would include the budget, multimedia content creation plan, and the media plan.

Product Marketing Playbook

Product marketing is all about content. The purpose of the product marketing playbook is to provide direction on content creation—the content itself, the format, and the timing. A product marketing playbook might include:

- Value proposition

- Competitive positioning statements
- Theme based and product based value statements for Top, Mid, and Bottom Funnel Domains
- Top of Funnel domain: content production plan by vehicle and format
- Mid and Bottom Funnel domains: the pitch deck; the demo; supporting materials
- Launch / Stabilize / Expand domains: best practice checklists, case studies, and content production plan by vehicle and format
- Company website plan
- Community and partner plan
- Content publication calendar
- PR calendar
- Webinar calendar
- Trade show calendar

Growth Marketing Playbook

Growth marketing exists to execute campaigns and optimize conversion along the domains of the Bow Tie (i.e., from Top of Funnel to Mid Funnel to Bottom Funnel to Launch, Stabilize, and Expand). The growth marketer's work at the Top of the Funnel domain involves using a diversity of messaging vehicles and leveraging a several different message formats in a continuous test / iterate / optimize mode. In contrast, growth marketing work in the Mid and Bottom Funnel domains and in the Launch, Stabilize, and Expand domains is structured more formally. Email nurture campaigns for all prospect and customer use case scenarios are designed, built, and maintained.

The role of the growth marketing playbook is to guide the team in executing this diverse plan. It might include:

- Monthly budget; allocation by product
- Reach and conversion objectives at every step
- Data management plan: data structure in the database and

how data will be tagged, de-duped, and accurately maintained
- Vendors / tools plan (review of existing; new ones to consider; plan to leverage each)
- Value proposition
- Competitive positioning statements
- Key theme based and product based value statements
- Top of Funnel domain campaign plans: SEO, SEM, digital advertising / retargeting, email
- Testing plan: how campaigns will be tested, iterated and optimized
- Prospect email nurture workflow (with templates) supporting the sales development process and the process from Opportunity stage to Closed Won stage for all use case permutations
- Customer email nurture workflow (with templates) supporting the entire post-sale customer experience for all use case permutations

Sales Development Playbook

For those companies with Mid, High or Very High LTV business models, perhaps the most critical—and under-appreciated—function in the revenue engine is sales development. Human engagement with prospects begins here. Therefore, the efficiency and effectiveness of this engagement are vital.

Sales development reps (SDRs) exist to determine whether leads are qualified (regarding budget, authority, need, and timing—BANT) and whether qualified prospects are ready to engage seriously.

In a well-orchestrated plan, there are a wide variety of prospect touch points such as ads, emails, search results, and trade show connects. The first human connection is usually made by a sales development rep (SDR) in the Mid Funnel domain on the Bow Tie schema. Whether SDRs are following up on a marketing qualified lead (MQL) or cold-calling into targeted prospects, the goal is to create a sales qualified lead (SQL). This SQL is turned over to an account exec who reconfirms budget, authority, need and timing (BANT), and it then becomes a sales accepted lead (SAL).

The SDR playbook is used by management and the SDRs themselves to conform to best practice in day-to-day work. This playbook includes:

- Overview of the role
- Overview of the orchestration plan
- Overview of SDR workflow
- ICP description: the key attributes
- Buyer, influencer, and user persona descriptions
- Buyer, influencer and user value propositions and use case stories
- Qualifying questions
- The AE handoff
- SAL criteria
- SDR multi-day, multi-touch campaign specifics, and SDR actions at each step
- Instructions for updating the account and contact status in CRM
- Scripts for voicemails and live calls
- Scripts for emails and guidance on custom content blocks
- Objection-handling plays
- SDR standards and expectations
- The SDR daily calendar

Account Executive Playbook

Given the increased cost of an account executive (AE) as compared to an SDR, AE time is spent in the Bottom Funnel domain. The Bottom Funnel journey is a series of stages from opportunity to closed won—a journey that involves four steps (discover, prove, negotiate, and close). The AE playbook provides the process tools and messaging to help AEs manage their workload and optimize conversion.

The AE playbook includes:

- Description of ICP
- Description of the buyer personas and associated messaging
- Value proposition
- Competitive positioning
- Theme based and product based value statements
- Case study examples
- Competitive feature comparison lists
- Objection handling talking points
- Product feature details
- Product implementation details
- Pitch deck and demo plan (may be variations by segment or product)
- Detailed review of the sales process, including definitions for MQL and SAL
- Discover step: the objective and meeting plan; plays (such as "map the buying process" play)
- Prove step: the objective and meeting plan; plays (such as "proof of value" or "champion enablement" play)
- Propose step: the objective and meeting plan; plays (such as "the ROI" play)
- Close step: the objective and meeting plan; plays (such as "due diligence" or "onboarding" plays)
- Renewal: the objective and meeting plan; plays
- Expansion: the objective and meeting plan; plays

Customer Success Playbook

The customer success function touches three Bow Tie domains: Launch, Stabilize, and Expand. For many products, the successful technical launch of a customer requires completing a series of steps, usually in coordination with the customer. Once technical launch has occurred, user launch comes next—characterized by the achievement of a minimum frequency of use, breadth of feature utilization, and / or number of users. From that point, stabilization occurs when use, utilization, and number of users are consistently at acceptable levels and when the expected benefits of the solution are achieved reliably.

The customer success function, then, is comprised of both programs (consistently repeated work projects that all customers receive) and plays (actions that are taken in response to signals, such as "below minimum use threshold"). These programs and plays are often technical and tactical in nature. Regardless, messaging remains critically important.

With every on-boarding step, FAQ, or intervention "play," your messaging schema must be brand true.

Given these functional requirements, the playbook will include such programs and plays as:

- The customer success launch: handoff meeting from the sales team to the customer success team
- The technical launch program: on-boarding system manual, step-by-step on-boarding guide, integration checklist, testing procedures
- The user launch program: user enablement plan, best practices, FAQ's
- 90/180/360 day program: engagement plan, user webinars, best practice standards, objectives, and outcome metrics
- Feature adoption and usage program: engagement plan
- Play: too few users
- Play: too low rates of utilization
- Play: too low feature adoption
- Play: account suffers from drop in utilization
- Play: users affected by service outage or SLA breach
- Play: customer cancels
- Play: customer inquires about up-sell / cross-sell opportunities
- Play: customer records very high customer satisfaction (NPS) score

Your messaging schema will vary depending on your business model and target customer. How it is applied will vary by channel. Of course, for direct selling, you have full control. If you have resellers or OEMs as partners, then you will need to develop your messaging schema in collaboration with your partners and seek agreement to inspect and continuously improve it.

Messaging Schema is the final foundational layer of the revenue engine. With a fully tested and validated messaging schema, you are now ready to execute the Bow Tie journey.

Unleash your greatness.

17

Organization Design

Key Concepts in Chapter 17:

- Organizations are designed to support company goals
- Organization design builds on the design of data, workflow, and tools
- Keep teams small until product / market fit is proven and workflows are at least moderately efficient
- Different business models have different organization requirements
- The revenue engine leadership team (marketing, sales, and customer success) is responsible for coordinating the whole system

This chapter is relevant for the following business models:

- Very Low Customer LTV (<$500)
- Low Customer LTV ($501 - $10,000)
- Mid Customer LTV ($10,001 - $100,000)
- High Customer LTV ($100,001 - $500,000)
- Very High Customer LTV ($500,001+)

Performance is powered by people.

Your revenue engine is a whole system comprised of all actions that occur across the Bow Tie (see image, below). As CEO, it's your mission to scale and run the revenue engine—and the people within it—so that you achieve optimal performance.

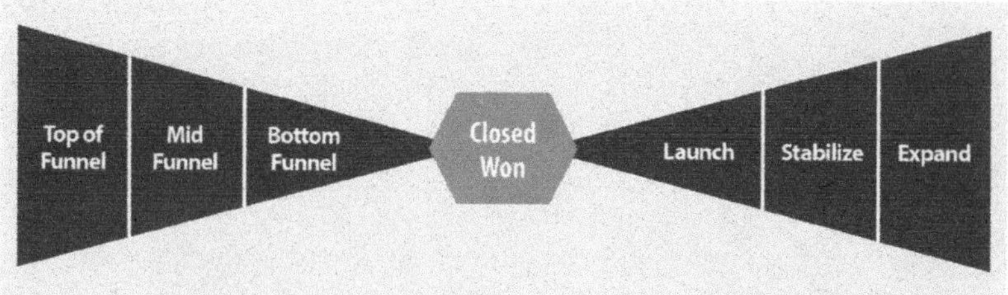

To do this, four aspects must be synchronized: data structure, workflows, tools, and people. To acquire and retain customers, data passes along workflows via tools, augmented by people. Wherever a machine can do the job, it should. Wherever human action is required, your job is to ensure each person's work is executed efficiently and effectively within established workflows.

In previous chapters we have discussed how to develop a tight segmentation scheme. We've reviewed how to achieve smart pricing and packaging, a well-honed channel architecture, intelligent information architecture, an optimized tools stack, and a tightly defined messaging schema.

In this chapter, we will focus on organization design. This draws upon all that's been covered in prior chapters. With data structure, workflows, and tools figured out, you are ready to address organization design.

In your design, the data structure, workflow, and tools come first, and people next—not the other way around.

Organizations are best designed bottom-up, flat, and cross-functional. In support of your workflows, you hire to solve capacity constraints without getting too far ahead of them. Three key factors impact the design and scale of your organization:

- Business model
- Proof of product / market fit
- Workflow maturity

Business Model Variations

Under the Very Low LTV business model (under $500), the entire Bow Tie journey is fully automated. The product drives the journey, so your product and engineering teams are very much a part of your revenue engine organization design. The org chart also includes the growth marketers, product marketers, and possibly brand marketers necessary to achieve broad reach, engagement, and nurture. Given the data volume (millions of prospects), a data scientist may play a prominent role.

If you operate within a Low LTV ($501—$10,000) business model, yours is a high velocity leads based approach. With hundreds of thousands of prospects, data science remains relevant here. You may have a call center in place, populated with reps who provide order fulfillment (this becomes economically viable as your LTV approaches $10,000).

With a Mid LTV ($10,001—$100,000) business model, some account based tactics begin to make sense, but you still must ensure a highly efficient sales development team. Your account exec team is likely inside sales-based. Integrations are highly efficient, with launch teams leveraging tools and automated processes to execute. The customer success team has a high customer-to-CSM ratio (100:1 or greater).

High LTV ($100,001—$500,000) and Very High LTV ($500,001+) business models enable you to adopt a full-fledged account based approach where sales development reps (SDRs) work with inside and field based account executives (AEs) to drive multi-touch engagement throughout a complex, many-to-many, multiple-point sales process. You seek engagement with the right people in the right companies. In this model, content may be highly customized by prospect, which then requires dedicated product marketing support. Sales engineers are deeply engaged in the sales process. Launch teams have the engineering and technical support competencies to execute highly customized integrations. Customer success teams serve customers with a low customer-to-CSM ratio, and provide support to multiple points of contact inside each account. With very high LTV business models, each account may even have a fully dedicated account manager. Sometimes, that account manager is physically located right inside the customer's own office.

Proof of Product / Market Fit

A general principle of organization design is that teams remain small until there is proof of product / market fit. If you can't sell your product or keep customers, it makes no sense to scale. Before you expand, fix the product first and prove it with sales growth and customer retention at steadily improving levels of efficiency. You don't need perfect sales efficiency before you scale; however, you do want validation of product / market fit. Once you have traction (as shown by customer acquisition efficiency and retention), then it is time to build out your teams.

Workflow Maturity

Aggressive scaling of your sales team should not occur until you are approaching an LTV / CAC ratio of 3 or better. As noted above, product / market fit is one reason for falling short of this threshold—but it's not the only possibility. It could also be due to workflow inefficiencies.

Before scaling your team, elevate workflows to an acceptable level of performance. It makes no sense to hire into a broken workflow.

Since workflow optimization is an important precursor to aggressive scaling, let's take a moment and dig deeper. The Carnegie Mellon Capability Maturity Model[1] (see Chapter 2—Revenue Engine Maturity) identifies five levels of workflow maturity:

- Chaotic: workflows unpredictable, poorly controlled and reactive
- Project Centric: broken workflows fixed one at a time; often reactive
- Whole System: workflows linked end to end; proactive approach
- Quantitative: workflows measured and controlled

- Continuous improvement: teams optimize the whole system via ongoing, data driven fine-tuning

To achieve "level 5 maturity," your team must demonstrate that it consistently measures and seeks to improve the capacity, speed, and conversion performance at every bottleneck in every workflow across the whole system. If you are performing at level 5, your team methodically and consistently identifies the most significant bottleneck. It mobilizes an attack on that bottleneck until it is no longer the biggest bottleneck. At that point, the new "biggest bottleneck" is attacked and defeated. In level 5 companies, the workflow improvement cycle operates continuously.

The capacity of the whole system is the capacity of its bottlenecks.[2] An hour lost at one bottleneck is an hour lost throughout the whole system. So the key to workflow optimization is to continuously attack the bottlenecks. The first priority is always the biggest bottleneck.

The High LTV Business Model at Scale

For the purpose of this chapter, let's choose the High LTV business model. Within this business model, the marketing functions bear some resemblance to Low and Very Low LTV business models. Similarly, the sales development, sales, and customer success functions are relevant to the Mid and Very High LTV business models. The information and data noted here is drawn from research into the practices of CEO Quest member companies, and discussions with numerous marketing and sales experts.

Here is an overview of the functions, as they operate at each Bow Tie domain:

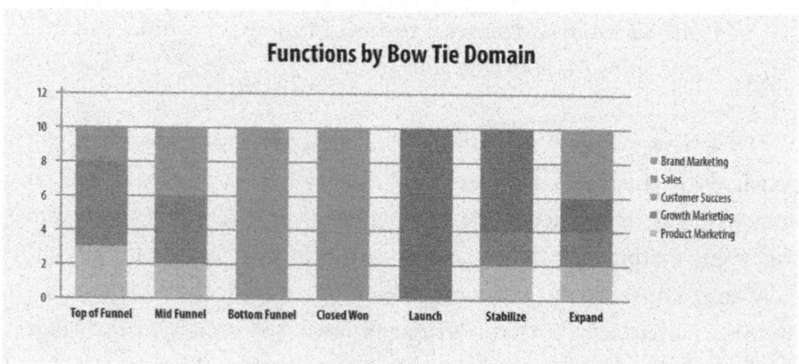

Marketing

At scale, a High LTV business model company is likely to execute a steady stream of product marketing content, a rolling drumbeat of growth marketing campaigns, and, periodically, extensive brand marketing campaigns. At scale, the team that executes this work might contain the following roles:

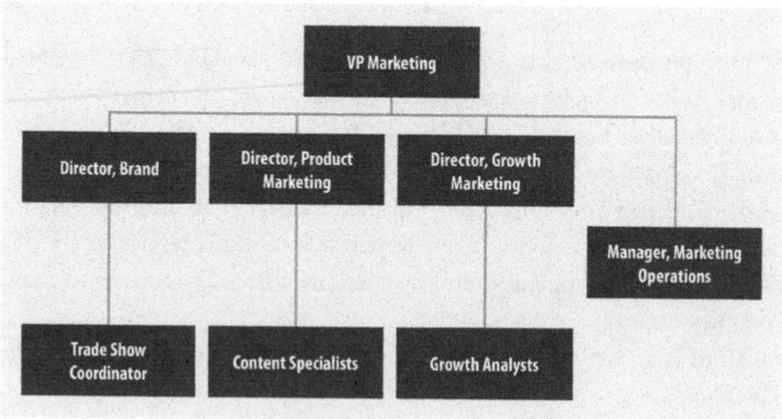

- VP marketing (to define brand identity; marketing strategy and execution; team leadership)
- Director, brand (to build brand equity; fidelity to brand identity; execute brand campaigns)

- Director, product marketing (to lead execution of all content)
- Director, growth marketing (to lead execution of all demand gen and nurture campaigns)
- Marketing operations manager (to manage data / tools)
- Trade show coordinator
- Content specialists (to write, create, and post content)
- Growth analysts (to conduct campaign analysis)
- Growth campaign specialists (to execute campaigns)

The brand, product marketing, and growth marketing playbooks guide the marketing team in their pursuit of reach, engagement, and conversion objectives.

In the base / bonus mix, on-target earnings (OTE) skew heavily towards base. Bonuses often tie to reach and conversion objectives, and occasionally in larger companies to brand awareness and brand equity measures.

Sales

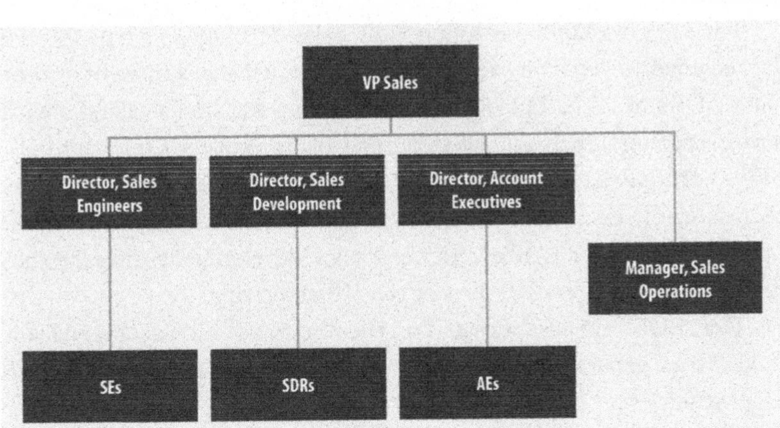

Sales Engineers

Sales engineers provide technical guidance to prospects during the sales process, both for new accounts and for expansion sales. They have the deep technical competencies necessary to clarify all key integration challenges, and how those will be addressed within an account's technical environment.

Sales engineer total compensation can range from $140,000 to $175,000 or more, usually with 15% to 25% of compensation at risk.

The at risk component is usually paid out based on achieving new sales and expansion sales objectives.

Sales Operations

Sales operations maintains workflow and data integrity in the sales process. Data hygiene (lists, de-duping, etc.), tools management (Salesforce, InsideView, Engagio, etc.), territory management, quota management, and commissions calculations are usually the responsibility of a sales operations manager or director. This position usually reports to the VP sales.

Sales Development

The sales development role is vital. Sales development reps (SDRs) are assigned to account executives (AEs), perhaps at a ratio of two or three SDRs to 1 AE. The objective is to fill up each AE's calendar with active accounts that are labeled new or in-process Opportunities. SDRs certainly have accountability to the AE they support. But so as to ensure efficiency and consistency in the execution of the sales development role, there is likely to be a sales development director that reports directly to the VP sales or the VP marketing.

Most SDRs are compensated on the number of sales accepted leads (SALs) they generate and the percent of those that are converted into Opportunities.

SDRs make substantially less than AEs—often half or even one-third the amount. In Silicon Valley, the on-target earning level might be from $60,000 to $100,000 or more.

Elsewhere, it may be closer to $50,000. A 60:40 base-to-bonus split is common for this role.

SDR enablement is of primary importance. The enablement tool of choice is the sales development playbook. The SDR role is especially important in the early part of the orchestration sequence. There are touch points that must be executed in the proper order, with the right content, including calls that follow specific scripts. SDRs are measured on the number of emails sent and the number of calls made per day. SDRs must be held to clear performance requirements. Best practice is to seek steady, positive movements towards minimum requirements over the first three months of employment. If performance stalls below the minimum threshold, quick action should be taken.

In an inside sales model, it's ideal for SDRs to be situated in close proximity to the AEs they support. But for a company based in a high-cost region (such as Silicon Valley or New York City), a key issue will be whether to scale the SDR / AE pods at headquarters or to find a remote location in a lower-cost market (e.g., Omaha, Phoenix, Boise).

Presence at headquarters is a strong positive in ensuring alignment and cultural connectivity, but the economics drive many companies to the remote model.

Without question, the first two to three SDR / AE pods should be at headquarters. Don't scale and don't move remote until you settle into a steady pattern of solid sales performance.

If you do choose the remote office approach, invest time, planning, and money into doing it right. When FiveStars built its Denver office, one of its co-founders, CTO Matt Doka, moved there for six months. He made sure the FiveStars culture was firmly established and that expected performance thresholds were met before he moved back home.

Account Executives

The AE role is vital in the Bottom Funnel domain. AEs must have the skills and experience to move an SAL and its associated account through the four "opportunity" stages: discover, prove, propose and close. For most High LTV business models, AEs also are responsible for renewal and expansion sales. Each stage requires a combination of sales experience, market knowledge, and enablement in the details of the ICP and buyer / user personas. The account executive playbook provides details on the messaging and the plays that AEs must use to execute their roles effectively.

To optimize AE efficiency and impact, territory rules must be established. If it's an inside sales model, how many prospect accounts will you assign? How many customer accounts? If you have a field sales model, how do you define territory boundaries? Are they geographic? If so, how do you deal with accounts that have assets in multiple geographic territories? What are your reassignment rules when an AE exits the company? You must consider all of these factors when you determine AE territory management.

Quota setting is important as well. The following math exercise is one way to determine the AE quota for new customer acquisition:

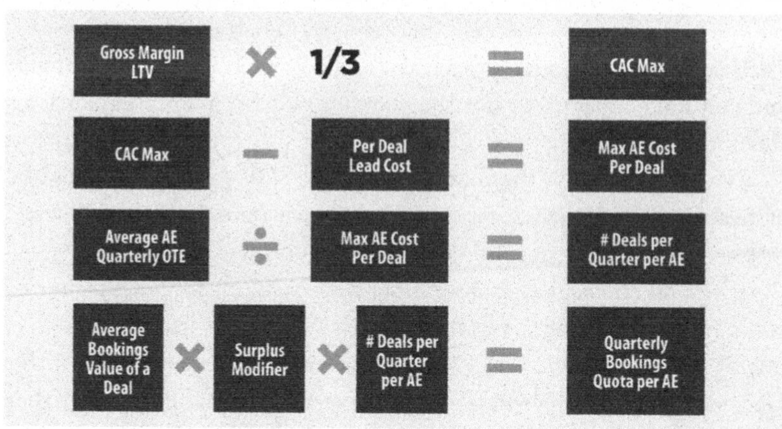

- Determine the gross margin LTV of your average customer
- ⅓ of that number is the maximum you should spend on CAC (CAC Max)
- Calculate Per Deal Lead Cost: the total cost of all lead acquisition and lead qualifying activity (lead gen and sales development labor and nonlabor) in the previous quarter, divided by # of deals in the most recently completed quarter

- Subtract Lead Cost from the CAC Max to get the maximum possible AE Cost per Closed Won Deal per quarter
- Divide the quarterly OTE cost of an AE by the maximum AE Cost per Closed Won Deal to determine how many Closed Won Deals per quarter an AE must sell to achieve minimum positive ROI
- Multiply the minimum number of Closed Won Deals by the average bookings value per closed won deal to determine the minimum bookings quota per quarter
- Decide the "surplus modifier" you will add to the quota to take into account potential AE underperformance, and multiply the modifier by the minimum bookings quota per quarter (i.e. 5% would be 1.05)

AEs are usually compensated at a higher rate for initial customer acquisition bookings, often for the first year ACV. Renewals and expansion commitments are rewarded at a much lower rate, or may even be handled by the customer success team. Performance below quota should yield a rapidly declining rate of payout; it's not uncommon for a 20% quota shortfall to yield a commission payout of $0. Performance above quota should yield accelerating payments.

AE on-target earnings vary widely depending on the complexity and length of sales cycle (OTE can range from $150,000 to $400,000 or more). The base-to-bonus ratio is usually around 50:50.

Customer Success

The customer success team is responsible for the launch and successful stabilization of the customer and either provides support for is fully responsible for expansion. At scale, the team may look something like this:

- VP customer success
- Director, launch team
- Director, customer success team
- Director, professional services team

- Launch managers
- Customer success managers (CSMs)
- Professional services managers (PSMs)

For a software company, a successful launch is both technical and human. "Technical launch" means the system is plugged in and works properly. "User launch" means the intended users are using the system above a defined minimum threshold of use. More specifically, the right number of users are using enough of the key features with high enough rates of utilization to validate that the customer is successfully up and running.

Launch teams must continuously attack bottlenecks and optimize the workflow so as to deliver a high quality new customer experience.

Team members are accountable for both speed of launch and new user health as measured by actual system use. Compensation plans may be designed accordingly. In these positions, a high base-to-bonus mix (80:20 or more) is common.

The customer success playbook is used to support new launch team member enablement.

You will need to decide how to assign accounts to customer success managers (CSMs). At scale, for most B2B SaaS businesses, the number can be high because human engagement is only required when a trigger indicates a problem such as a decline in usage. The customer success playbook includes plays for all the most common trigger events.

In some tech companies, professional services are an important revenue line item. Professional services managers possess strong technical skills and deep product knowledge and are usually compensated with a more significant at-risk component (such as 60:40 base to bonus) tied to revenue generation and customer satisfaction.

Revenue Engine Leadership Team

The VPs of marketing, sales, and customer success possess shared responsibility for performance of all tasks across the Bow Tie—all the way from the Top of Funnel domain to the Closed Won domain, and from the Closed Won domain to the Expand domain. Accountabilities must be clear, but functional dividing lines are less important than cross-functional dependencies. Day to day, the marketing team must generate "right person / right company" MQLs. The sales development team must turn them into SQLs that associate with target accounts. The AE team must convert these accounts into Closed Won stage deals. The launch team must launch the account, the CSMs must stabilize and optimize the account, and the CSMs and AEs must work together to expand the account. These actions require continuous collaboration. Collaboration is also required in the ongoing optimization and redesign of workflows.

If all functional leaders share the same terminology for stages in the prospect and customer journey, if your tools and systems are calibrated accordingly, if everyone uses the same data to assess the performance of the Bow Tie at every step, if bottlenecks are continuously attacked through collaboration at the leadership and frontline levels, and if performance is steadily improving, then leaders are doing their jobs.

In the next six chapters, we will march through the Top of Funnel, Mid Funnel, Bottom Funnel, Launch, Stabilize and finally, Expand domains—the Bow Tie journey itself.

Turn the ignition. It's time for the engine to roar.

18

Top of Funnel

Key Concepts in Chapter 18:

- The goals of Top of Funnel are reach, engagement, conversion, and short sales cycle
- A frictionless product experience, high brand visibility, rapid vision lock, viral effects, channel partnerships, smart introductory pricing, and continuous experimentation are critical success factors at Top of Funnel
- All Top of Funnel actions must be executed consistent with the appropriate CAC boundary given your customer LTV

This chapter is relevant for the following business models:

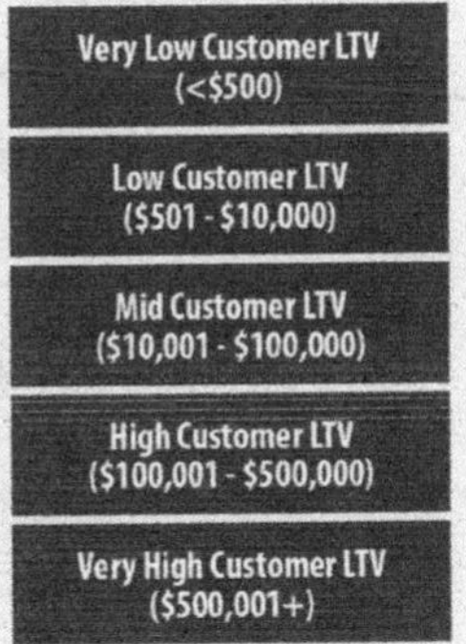

At Top of Funnel, you tackle the total addressable market.

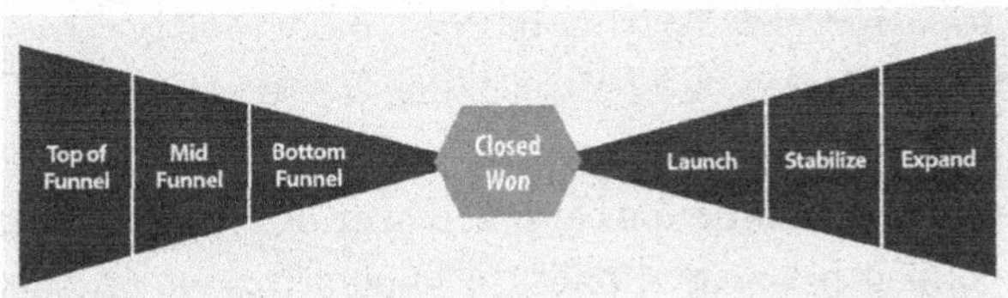

At Top of Funnel, you must quickly gain vision lock with your prospect ("I get what you do and why it's relevant for me"). Four objectives should drive your plan: to maximize reach, to achieve rapid product engagement, to maximize conversion, and to shorten the sales cycle. You must meet all of these objectives within an acceptable cost boundary given customer LTV.

Customer LTV is always the best way to describe a company's business model. The CAC you have available given your LTV determines your choice of customer acquisition tactics.

Even though the money you can spend per customer at Top of Funnel varies dramatically from the Very Low LTV business model to the Very High LTV business model, the primary levers are consistent:

- Frictionless product experience: A lightweight, addictive, easy on-ramp product experience that maximizes engagement as close to Top of Funnel as possible
- Maximize brand and product visibility: Within the constraints of your business model, maximize connections with prospects—optimizing for reach, frequency, and diversity of touch points
- Speed to vision lock: In all messaging, leverage your value proposition and competitive positioning to maximize speed to vision lock—the point at which prospects declare, "I get what you do and why it's relevant for me."
- Viral effects: In the orchestration of Top of Funnel actions, maximize likelihood of social sharing and encourage community building
- High-affinity channel partnerships: The right channel partners bring you established relationships in top priority segments delivering both access and credibility
- Frictionless pricing: Reduce risk and incentivize trial via introductory pricing (your business model will govern whether it's free forever, freemium, free trial, or proof-of-concept)
- Data-driven continuous improvement: At Top of Funnel, ongoing experimentation is the imperative—in product,

pricing, messaging, content formats, and content distribution channels. Instrument metrics into everything, and ensure your teams use metrics to test, iterate, and optimize on a continuous basis

CAC should be no more than ⅓ LTV

For a media company, where the LTV of a unique consumer could be as low as 2 cents, only ⅓ of that LTV (in this example, 6/10ths of a cent) is available to spend per new consumer. Given this extremely low CAC investment threshold, the product experience is king. This "first mile" (to use Scott Belsky's terminology) must immediately capture the user's interest and spark instant engagement. The Very Low LTV business model heavily depends on viral effects. Channel partnerships are one viable option to expand reach. If CAC investments are viable at all, these are fully digital and highly cost efficient.

For a gaming company with a subscription model, there may be more room to invest in CAC. An annual pass for the game World of Warcraft costs about $150; if we assume 90% gross margin and a three year average life, a new customer has an LTV of $405. So using the principle that LTV / CAC should be at least 3, World of Warcraft can spend up to $135 to acquire a new customer.

Take the case of a B2B SaaS business selling to SMB customers with a $21,000 LTV. The CAC boundary (in this case, $7000) might support strong performance marketing at the Top of Funnel, with a high-velocity lead-conversion call center at the bottom. This works only if the product is instantly compelling and the demo draws the prospect into active use.

At the high end of the LTV continuum, a B2B enterprise software company with average customer LTV over $500,000 can spend over $150,000 per acquired customer, enabling a comprehensive, customized, multi-dimensional account-based sales model. At Top of Funnel, highly customized content and thought leadership (sometimes customized down to the individual prospect level), combined with highly personalized 1:1 outreach (to buyers, users, and influencers) makes sense. Multi-touch engagement includes both digital and human forms, with multiple players in your company engaging with multiple players at the target account in a highly orchestrated Top of Funnel plan. Even here, it's best to bring the product as close to the top of the funnel as possible—to give the prospect a tantalizing glimpse into the product experience.

Frictionless Product Experience

It might seem unusual to start a Top of Funnel strategy discussion with product considerations. But indeed it's exactly the right place to start. Regardless of your business model, the closer you can draw your product to the Top of the Funnel, the better. Product is perhaps the most potent Top of Funnel lever of all.

For Very Low LTV business models—media companies, game companies, B2C marketplace companies, B2C e-commerce companies, etc.—the "first mile" of the product experience is everything. It's all about the immediate delivery of recognizable value. Does a first-time user instantly encounter value-creating content? Is early product engagement friction free? When the user is asked to provide data (such as personal information), is it minimal, and is the quid pro quo instantaneous and high-value? Very Low LTV business model companies have no choice but to figure these things out.

Every other business model—from Low to Mid to High to Very High LTV—can learn a lot from Very Low LTV companies. Jim Goetz and other partners at Sequoia Capital contributed to the online book, *The Templeton Compression and the Sales Ready Product*,[1] introducing the idea of the Sales Ready Product (SRP). Goetz et al. argue that minimum viable product (MVP) is not enough. Trying to scale with an MVP yields an excessively long sales cycle with too much human effort required to lead the prospect to proof of value. To shorten sales cycles, increase win rates, and leverage sales investments, companies should invest more time and development cycles to turn the product into an SRP.

Fellow CEO Quest Managing Partner Bill Portelli points out in a compelling paper, "The Sales Ready Product: Compressing B2B Sales Cycles—Part 1"[2] that building the SRP must be a top cross-functional company priority. He references the example of GitHub, which used a public cloud based approach to disrupt the software configuration management market. To start using GitHub, a user only enters their username, email address, and password, followed by the name of a project. Just four clicks and you're up and running.

Contrast that with competitors that require a company to install enterprise grade versioning software on-site. One cloud tool that competes with GitHub requires as many as two dozen clicks to get up and running. In both cases, the competitor is at a huge disadvantage compared to GitHub.

To build the SRP, product and engineering must work in close collaboration with sales and marketing. Deep research into the needs and personas of your top priority segments is required. You need a list of top objections and a list of the most desired features. These are the raw materials that allow you to create a "first mile" experience focused on maximizing immediate conversion. Scott Belsky's work, "Crafting The First Mile of Product,"[3] provides an excellent summation of the critical design considerations to address in the early user experience.

In an SRP, a high-value product utility is presented at Top of Funnel. The utility's purpose is to deliver what Goetz calls a "light switch moment"—when the potential value of the product becomes instantly apparent. The prospect is encouraged to enter real data into the utility and immediately experiences value.

For B2B products, such a utility could embed a self-serve ROI calculator. A Mid LTV product might push out four or five different product utilities addressing different market segments or use case scenarios. Each creates a unique entry point based on segment-specific value drivers, but all are designed to deliver rapid speed to value—to give a tantalizing glimpse into the full product's capabilities. Prospective buyers and users can play with these utilities on their own at the top of the funnel, or experience them during the demo.

For Low LTV business models, the utility might be entirely self-serve. For Mid, High, and Very High LTV business models, customers might enter real data into the product platform during a demo. Regardless of business model, the idea is to push the product as close to Top of Funnel as possible.

Goetz's rule of thumb for Mid to High LTV B2B companies is to continue working on the SRP until you can consistently achieve a 50% close rate within 30 days. The proof is in the pudding: if you haven't hit that level of sales performance, your product is not yet an SRP.

Maximize Brand and Product Visibility

For your company to be successful, it must first be known. Brand awareness is a key objective at Top of Funnel. As buyers and users within your top priority segments wrestle with the problems your product can solve, your brand must come to mind—or you'll never win in the marketplace.

Brand awareness starts with strategy. Are you creating a new market (seeking to change paradigms) or disrupting an existing market (seeking to change buyer behavior)? The levers available to you in building brand awareness include thought leadership, brand campaigns, performance marketing campaigns, events, channel partnerships, and direct account-based marketing and sales. But how you use these levers is based on your strategy, business model, and competitive dynamics which you use to weigh Top of Funnel awareness options:

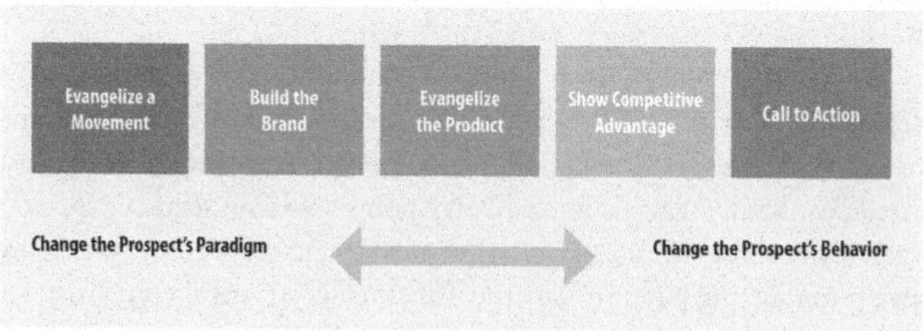

Let's say you're creating a new market. That means you must evangelize a revolutionary, paradigm-changing technology. To do that, you must answer two questions:

- Why do you matter?

- Why now?

When Lightbend built its reactive application development platform, it was working at the edge of innovation. Enterprises were just beginning to confront the problems created by the decentralized, multi-device, spiky-data, cloud-based world we live in today. The whole idea of microservices-based architecture was in its infancy. To break through, Lightbend needed to evangelize a movement. In 2014, Lightbend's CTO, Jonas Boner, co-authored The Reactive Manifesto,[4] laying out the core principles of the Reactive movement. Since its release, the manifesto has garnered over 19,000 signatures. And so a community was born.

Lightbend and key team members continue to be prominent and prolific thought leaders, authoring a steady stream of compelling content to serve this rapidly expanding tech community. Not only does the content feed the movement, but it also catches the attention of the largest players in the ecosystem. Today, Lightbend is widely considered to be at the forefront of this fundamental shift in information technology.

Some companies must change paradigms. But all companies must change buyer behavior if they are to be successful. For this to happen, you must build the brand, evangelize the product, demonstrate competitive advantage, and execute calls to action.

These Top of Funnel imperatives put us into the world of brand marketers, product marketers, and growth marketers. The brand marketer's job is to build brand equity. The product marketer's job is to create product-related content. And the growth marketer's job is to test, iterate, optimize, and scale campaigns.

There are many tools in the toolkit. Variations in content purpose combine with variations in content format, content type, content delivery methods, and delivery platforms to create a wide array of choices:

Content purpose

- Thought leadership

- Public relations
- Brand development
- Demand generation / performance

Content format

- Press releases
- Articles
- Slideshows
- Videos
- E-books
- Photos
- Blog posts
- Printed material

Content type

- Curation
- "How to"
- Reviews
- Interviews
- Quizzes
- Best practices
- Testimonials

Delivery method

- Organic search
- Paid search
- Display / retargeting
- Social advertising

Delivery platform

- Company website

- Facebook / YouTube / Twitter and other social sharing platforms
- Blog sites
- Forums
- Events

Your messaging schema (with its brand, product marketing, and growth marketing playbooks) is your guide for all Top of Funnel content creation. Everything you create must be true to your brand identity. Within those guidelines, your goal is to maximize reach and impact.

Speed to Vision Lock

Speed to vision lock ("I get what you do and why it's relevant for me.") is a function of sharp, lucid competitive positioning. Excellent positioning instantly communicates your value proposition in a way that boxes in your competitors (see Chapter 6—Competitive Positioning). Top of Funnel messaging must deliver instant vision lock. Get to the "aha" moment as quickly as possible. If you don't, prospects simply won't spend time seeking to understand—they'll just move on.

Remember that all roads lead to the company website. So the website itself must present content that quickly moves the visitor towards a frictionless, high-value initial product experience. You want prospects to find instant product value, dig deeper, gain confidence, and move from "interest" to "lead" to "closed won" as efficiently as possible.

Viral Effects

To maximize the impact value of content you must focus not only on initial consumption, but also on total available reach. Online social sharing becomes a force multiplier. But isn't virality, by definition, out of your hands? Not at all. The key is to construct your content with sharing in mind. Known sharing triggers include "funny," "cool," "shocking," "controversial," "illuminating," and "uplifting." In fast-scaling best-practice companies, the content calendar is filled with content plans across multiple content formats, using multiple content types, leveraging all significant content platforms, with liberal use of the sharing triggers to increase engagement. Not everything will go viral—but if you're intentional about it, some of your content will.

Channel Partnerships

Channel is a powerful Top of Funnel tool (see Chapter 11—Channel Architecture).

A channel partnership can transform a company, regardless of its business model.

This is exactly what happened to CareerBuilder when it won the AOL and MSN deals away from Monster.

Channel partnerships can be equally transformational for companies with higher LTV business models. Siebel's Andersen Consulting and IBM partnerships propelled them to global status. In both cases, these partnerships opened doors to thousands of new prospects that otherwise would have been more challenging and expensive to reach.

Frictionless Pricing

Introductory pricing is another key Top of Funnel tool (see Chapter 9—Pricing and Packaging). The objective is to reduce perceived risk so as to accelerate the transition from prospect to customer. There are four variations:

- Free forever
- Freemium
- Free trial
- Proof of concept

Most media models keep the consumer experience free forever, in return for accepting ads on the page. By minimizing visitor friction, media sites hope to maximize visitor growth, then monetize via display advertising on a cost per thousand (CPM) basis.

Freemium models are most common in Low LTV B2C offerings such as gaming and Low to Mid LTV B2B SaaS, where users can use the product for free up to a certain usage threshold. Once usage rises above the defined threshold, users must pay.

A free trial is a widely used pricing method to reduce introductory risk, especially for B2B SaaS offerings. Here, the customer self-provisions and is free to use the product for a short period. When a frictionless initial product experience is paired with a sales ready product (SRP), it can be a powerful Top of Funnel pricing strategy.

For High and Very High LTV products, a free trial is often not feasible. The launch cost is too high. Even so, the objective to minimize risk remains a priority. Here, a proof of concept (POC) approach often makes sense. The customer pays for a single-purpose implementation, contracted to be live for a limited time. Once again, the POC reduces friction, and the offer of a POC, along with an SRP, can be built into Top of Funnel messaging.

Data-Driven Continuous Improvement

What are the three most essential competencies to possess for strong Top of Funnel execution? Analytics, analytics, analytics.

With Very Low LTV business models, acceleration requires (and the volume of data allows) a highly quantified, analytical approach. All fast-growing companies with Very Low LTV business models have developed strong competencies in analytics. These days, many vendors deliver advanced analytical capability. For instance, QuanticMind helps marketers optimize their search and social investments, algorithmically guiding ad buys by manipulating such variables as keywords, time of day, and even geography. The results can be profound in reducing cost per lead at scale.

As you move up the LTV continuum, data must continue to be at the center of Top of Funnel optimization, although as data volume declines statistical reliability does too.

Include on your team at least one data geek with access to the tools and instrumentation necessary to conduct analyses. At Top of Funnel, analytical rigor must be a core competency and a daily discipline.

For Mid, High, and Very High LTV business models, the yield from effective product and growth marketing is steadily growing MQL volume, captured at an efficient acquisition cost. Efficiency is achieved by minimizing cost and maximizing conversion which, of course, requires that you continuously test, iterate, and optimize.

Top of Funnel constitutes the frontline of the battle to survive, scale, and dominate.

Fight intelligently.

19

Mid Funnel

Key Concepts in Chapter 19:

- The focus in this chapter is on business models at the Mid LTV level and higher
- At Mid Funnel, the right people in the right accounts must receive the right messages in the right order to spark conviction
- At Top of Funnel, the goal was vision lock. Now at Mid Funnel the goal is to deliver speed to "aha" moment and speed to trust-- so as to move the prospect towards conviction lock

This chapter is relevant for the following business models:

At Mid Funnel, conversion is king.

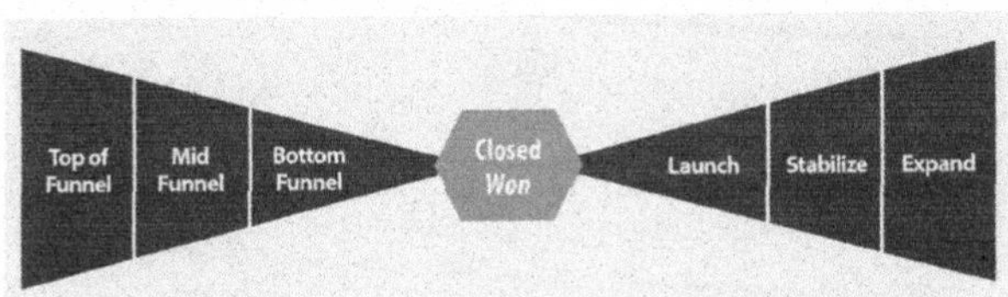

As always, Mid Funnel design varies by business model:

- Very Low LTV: Millions of consumer prospects; fully automated Mid and Bottom Funnel ("first mile" of the product experience)
- Low LTV: Hundreds of thousands of consumer or business prospects; lead-based demand generation, possibly with a call center for Bottom Funnel conversion
- Mid LTV: Thousands of prospects; high velocity, mass-customized, account-based marketing
- High LTV: Hundreds to thousands of prospects; moderately customized account-based marketing (ABM)
- Very High LTV: Hundreds of prospects; highly customized ABM

Business model variations can be seen in the research data. Note how the percent of CAC dedicated to marketing vs. sales varies based on the type of sale—from field sales to inside sales to internet sales:

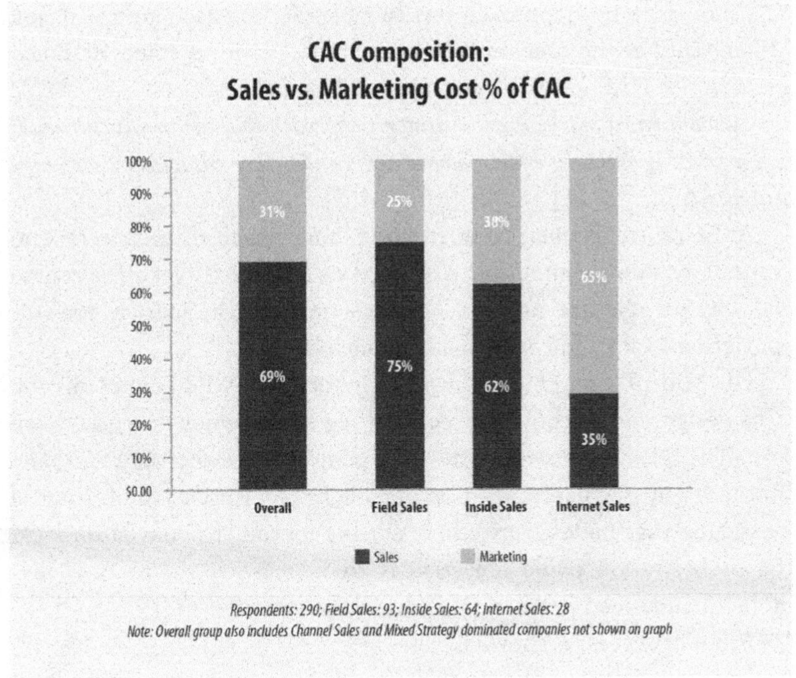

Source: David Skok, "2016 Pacific Crest SaaS Survey"[1]

Here, we focus on businesses with Mid LTV business models and higher.

Prospect engagement strategy has evolved. Just a few years ago, the role of marketing in a tech company was to drive leads. Marketing generated the leads and sales sold them. No thought was given to business model variations.

For Very Low and Low LTV business models, this lead generation approach makes sense. Leads come from individuals. Since at the low end of the LTV spectrum decisions tend to be made by one individual (either a consumer or an SMB owner), leads are what's needed.

But for higher LTV business models, a leads-based marketing approach that's not closely connected to the prospect account is ineffective. In the enterprise, multiple individuals make buying decisions. There's the decision maker, the influencers, the users, and (sometimes) the blockers. Leads don't buy products—accounts do. For these business models, a new approach has gained traction: account-based. Jon Miller, CEO of the account-based marketing platform company Engagio, describes the account-based approach as follows:

"Account-based marketing is a strategic approach that coordinates personalized marketing and sales efforts to open doors and deepen engagement at specific accounts."[2]

At Top of Funnel, you reached and engaged prospects and customers. Your mission was to achieve vision lock ("I get what you do and why it's relevant to me"). Now it's time for the journey towards conviction lock ("I'm convinced. Sign me up").

For Mid LTV and higher business models, the Mid Funnel mission is to design and effectively execute a high-engagement orchestration plan. This plan must swarm the right people inside the right accounts in the right segments with multi-touch connections and spot-on messaging that builds conviction. On the journey to conviction lock, the orchestration plan's objective is to increase speed to the "aha" moment and speed to trust.

Proof of success is shown by:

- High conversion
- Increased bookings
- Sales cycle compression
- Cost efficiency

The Fundamentals

Step One: Build a Sales Ready Product

To deliver speed to "aha," get the product in front of the prospect as quickly as possible. The light bulb moment only happens once a prospect has seen the product and started using it. To achieve this, you need to build a product utility that provides a glimpse into the full product experience, is available via an online link, and can be sent to prospects. A prospect that has already experienced part of the product experience is significantly more likely to advance along the funnel. This idea was explored more fully in Chapter 18—Top of Funnel.

Step Two: Build the Tools and Workflow

A core principle of cost-efficient Mid Funnel execution is this: everything that can be automated should be automated. The ratio of automated to human activity shifts steadily to favor human intervention as LTV increases. However, even for Very High LTV businesses, automation is important. For instance, your orchestration plan is sure to include a catalog of nurture campaigns—created by product marketers and growth marketers—that executes automatically based on various contact or account states. In the Mid Funnel workflow, the sales development rep (SDR) role comprises the human activity which is sparked by automated triggers from sales automation tools. Product marketers, growth marketers, and SDRs need the right tools and platforms to power the workflow.

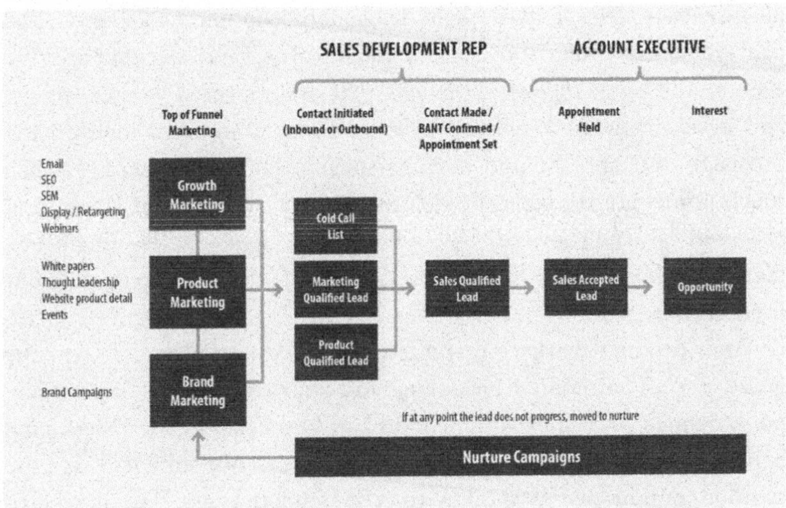

The SDR function is vital. Under the canopy of digital—and sometimes analog—campaigns, SDRs execute both cold and warm MQL follow-up calls and custom emails to contacts that fit the ideal customer profile (ICP) target personas. These live connections are central to building prospect engagement. SDRs are on the frontline ascertaining whether prospects exhibit the right budget, authority, need, and timing (BANT) to qualify as a sales qualified lead (SQL) so that the account executive (AE) demo call can be scheduled.

Leads come from people, but accounts buy. So leads must be associated with accounts, following the principle of "right person, right company." You seek to touch multiple people within a target account. Of course, the result is multiple leads from multiple people from a single account.

Sales engineers play an important role in providing technical validation throughout Mid Funnel the sales process.

Step Three: Build out your Orchestration Plan and Messaging

Your orchestration plan defines how you will engage your ICP personas and in what sequence.

This includes all Mid Funnel digital marketing such as email nurture campaigns and thought leadership content campaigns. The plan includes trade shows, lunch-and-learns, and account-specific events. You build digital campaigns that are triggered when contacts and accounts achieve certain states. These campaigns deliver the prospect state-specific and persona-specific nurture content. Human touch points are triggered by defined contact and account states, and executed as appropriate by SDRs, AEs, Field Sales Engineers, managers, VPs, and even the CEO. All of these are part of your orchestration plan.

Your product marketing and growth marketing playbooks are the guides for all automated messaging and your sales development playbook defines your SDR scripts and plays (see Chapter 16—Messaging Schema). Automated messaging is necessary, but not sufficient. It's the custom content that is the key to ABM effectiveness. The degree of effort put into content customization rises steadily from Mid LTV to High LTV to Very High LTV business models.

For Mid LTV, where lifetime value is between $10,000 and $100,000, CAC can range from $3,000—$30,000. Here, short blocks of custom content sit inside email templates or white paper templates comprised primarily of standardized content. Custom content is gathered from public data in a highly efficient (probably off-shore) workflow, quickly converted by high-speed writers into prose, and uploaded to the platform for auto-merge.

For High and Very High LTV business models, there is a greater degree of content customization. For instance, in the Very High LTV business model, business analysts might execute a comprehensive ROI analysis or competitive alternatives analysis for a single prospect. Or develop a completely customized market trends or maturity assessment white paper. Or all four. If the LTV is greater than $500,000, more than $150,000 is available to spend to reel in a single customer. As you can see, the customization effort needed in these higher LTV business models is significant.

Step Four: Find your Prospects

Everything hinges on finding the right people. Your ideal customer profile (ICP) emerges from top priority segments in your segmentation scheme (see Chapter 4—Customer Segmentation). You define your ICP attributes with specificity in order to pinpoint the prospect accounts you seek to target. You build your prospect database with both account and contact details. You align messaging to your buyer, influencer, and user personas.

For the Mid LTV business model, you generically define the roles and titles of your buyers, influencers, and users. Here, data gathering focuses on account discovery and contact data capture. Lists may be purchased to expand your prospect database. Predictive scoring tools may be used to support optimization of the ICP definition and to find "accounts like this." You may deploy a team (for cost purposes, often located offshore) that augments your account data in preparation for active engagement.

In Very High LTV business models, however, the universe of accounts is, at most, in the hundreds. So, data gathering is highly customized. You need to know the exact names, titles, and contact details of the buyers, influencers, users, and blockers inside each company. For each prospect account, a "mole" is required to provide insight into purchase decision steps, decision participants, key company priorities, and other decision-influencing factors.

Step Five: Train your People

SDR enablement is fundamental if you are to achieve your key objectives of high conversion, a compressed sales cycle, maximization of customer spend, and cost efficiency. It's not uncommon for an SDR to be expected to execute 40 or more phone calls and 40 or more emails per day. Doing it well requires training.

Since most phone calls go to voicemail or result in an immediate hang-up, live connections must be executed effectively. Once the prospect says "hello," an SDR has five seconds to win 30 seconds, 30 seconds to win 2 minutes, and 2 minutes to win a demo. Therefore, train SDRs effectively to deliver carefully developed scripts. Ensure that SDRs can execute these phone-based "moments of truth" to positive effect.

Measure your SDRs on number of calls made, number of emails sent, conversion of calls to scheduled demos, conversion of scheduled demos to demos held, and conversion of demos held to sales accepted lead (SAL). It is critical to establish performance thresholds for the second week and the first month with consistent above-threshold performance expected by the third month.

The SDR's primary enablement tool is the sales development playbook (see Chapter 16—Messaging Schema).

Managing Channel Partnerships at the Mid Funnel Stage

If your business depends on the effective execution of channel partnerships, then you will face a different challenge. Success depends, of course, on best-practice Mid Funnel prospect engagement via a well orchestrated ABM strategy. But the strategy and its execution are beyond your control. What can you do?

Start with a vision of best practice. If you don't understand ABM best practice, you can't influence your channel partner to adopt it.

Once you have vision clarity, you need to accurately pinpoint the current state of your partner's Mid Funnel engagement effort. Visibility is vital. To achieve visibility, best practice is for you to place a partner manager inside your partner's offices. Co-location is by far the best way to ensure you know what's really going on.

Transparency and trust are the foundational requirements for collaboration.

Once you know "the good, the bad, and the ugly" in your partner's Mid Funnel engagement execution, your job becomes one of communication and influence.

It's possible that some of the levers of Mid Funnel prospect engagement are controlled by you. You might manage the thought leadership and product marketing content that provides the canopy under which your partner engages. If so, then orchestration, communication, and coordination all become even more critical and challenging to a successful partnership.

In the end, it comes down to your partner's competency and willingness to collaborate. If you have a strong partnership, both companies will be highly motivated to continuously improve.

Summary

At the Mid Funnel stage, executional discipline is the order of the day. Multiple people in your company must execute multiple touch points with multiple people in your target accounts. Everything needs to follow the orchestration plan in volume and at scale. To get there takes time and difficult, granular optimization work.

Keep at it. Rigor wins.

20

Bottom Funnel

Key Concepts in Chapter 20:

- At Bottom Funnel an Opportunity progresses from discover, to prove, to negotiate, to close-- the final stages on the road to conviction lock
- With Very High LTV business models, top prospect accounts have been prioritized based on a rigorous "rifle" approach
- The AE playbook guides the approach to prospect engagement, and prospect account dossiers identify account-specific plans
- AEs are "top guns" who sell using the "challenger" approach

This chapter is relevant for the following business models:

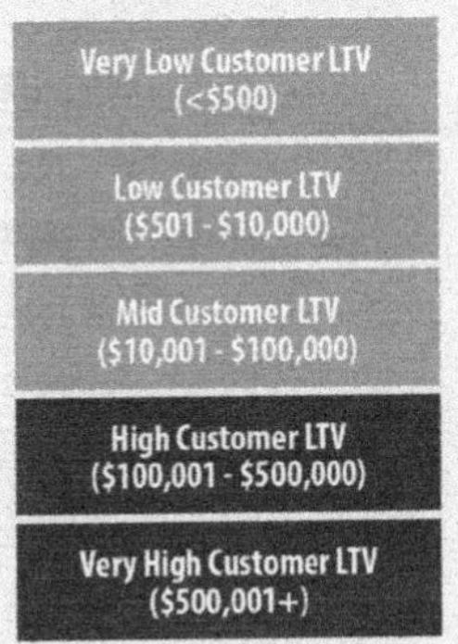

The bottom line is the bottom line. Deal or no deal?

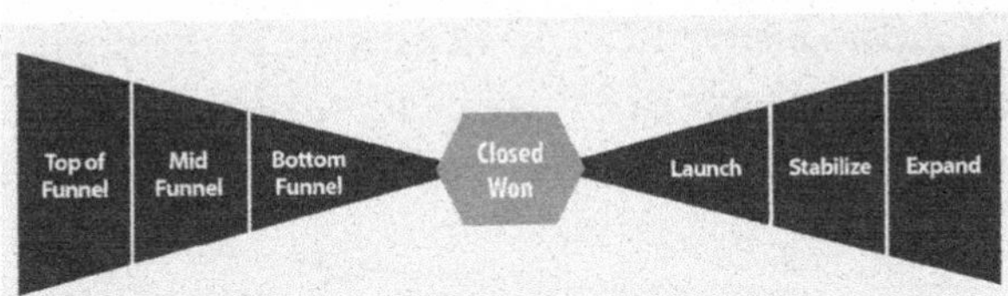

It took a lot to get to the "opportunity" stage. Now it's time to finish strong. Great sales teams execute the journey from "opportunity to closed won" with a runner's kick. The key, of course, is to complete the journey to conviction lock ("I'm convinced. Sign me up."). Painstaking preparation results in strong execution, which results in the deal. Time and time again.

The sequence of steps from "opportunity" to "closed won" varies based on business model. For the Very Low LTV business model, it's all automated—from the login page to inventory pages to shopping cart to "confirm purchase" page. For a Low LTV business—for instance, a B2B SMB SaaS business—a single demo leads to a trial close, with a follow-up call to finalize only if necessary. For a Mid LTV business, 2–3 meetings may be required to move from "opportunity" to "closed won."

In this chapter, I'll focus on the High and Very High LTV business models. These are the realms of the complex enterprise sale.

There are five building blocks to a successful enterprise sales strategy:

- Rifle prioritization
- Playbooks
- Prospect dossier
- Challenger sales approach
- People

Rifle Prioritization Model

Vinod Khosla of Khosla Ventures developed what he refers to as the "rifle" prioritization model.[1] This model provides an analytically rigorous method for determining where to focus enterprise sales investment and effort. Ideally, all the data points necessary to conduct this analysis are accessible from previous work in the development of your segmentation scheme (see Chapter 4—Customer Segmentation).

Khosla summarizes the rifle prioritization model in four slides:

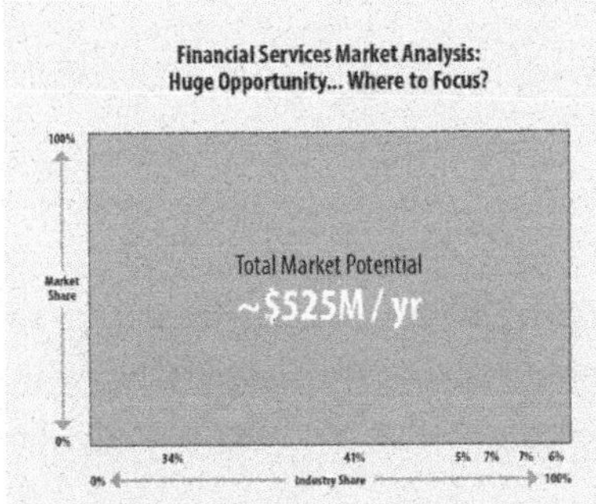

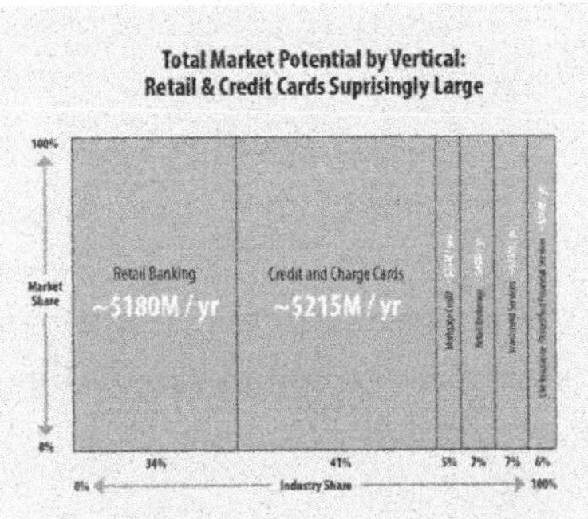

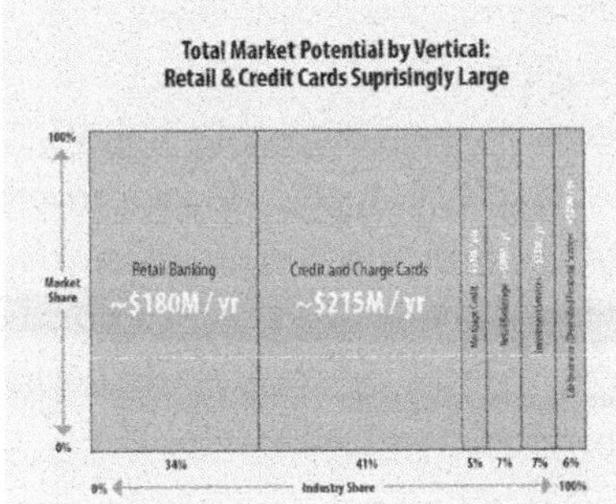

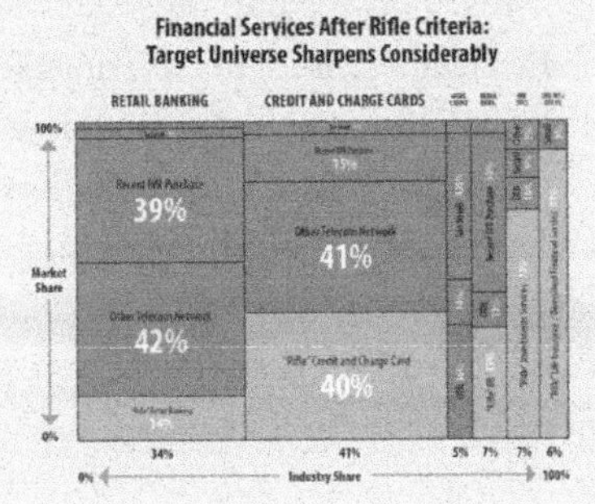

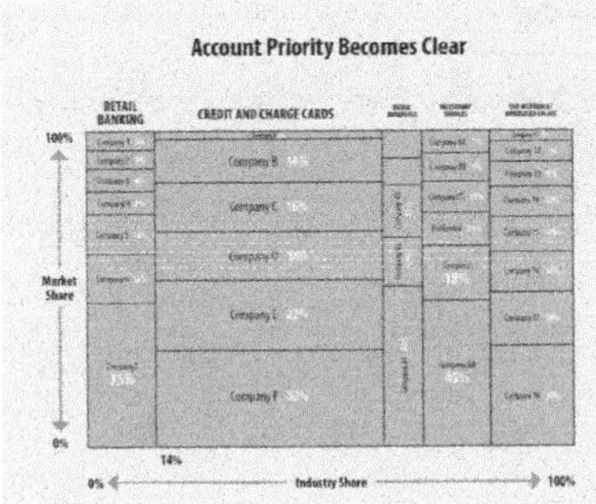

Notably, segments are first prioritized by market potential. Then within these segments, sub-segments are assessed via a weighted numerical assessment of attractiveness, considering six criteria:

- Sales model required
- Marketing model required

- Decision-maker attributes
- Competition level
- Product requirements
- Market size

The resulting top-priority sub-segments are further analyzed to determine the companies within the sub-segments that offer the most significant opportunity. The same rifle criteria are applied at the company level.

This analysis results in a small number of high priority companies (20–30). These companies demand a sharp focus and an intense, multi-dimensional, multi-person engagement approach.

The rifle approach fits well with account-based marketing (ABM).

Account-based marketing has evolved to a company-wide approach called account-based everything (ABE) as coined by leading research and advisory firm TOPO.[2] In account-based frameworks, with a prioritized and limited set of prospect accounts, you can engage the right people in the right companies with a focused attack plan.

AE Playbook

The AE's Playbook (see Chapter 16—Messaging Schema) contains all an AE must know to be prepared to engage an enterprise customer.

Here's how meeting plans and sales plays chart the journey from "opportunity" to "closed won" through the discover / prove / propose / negotiate steps:

	Discover	Prove	Propose	Negotiate
Meeting Objective	· Decision Maker meeting · Discover pain points · Confirm BANT · Determine readiness to progress	· DM and Decision Influencer (DI) meeting · Prove we can address pain points	· DM meeting · Present details of product / service offering · Present price and terms	· DM / DI / legal meeting · Get to Closed Won
Meeting Plan	· Intros · Purpose, Agenda, Outcome · Discovery questions · Relevant value statement · Use case stories · Validate level of commitment to address pain · Next step summary · Email recap	· Intros · Purpose, Agenda, Outcome · Summary of key claims to validate · Demonstrations of proof · Check in: does the prospect agree? · Next step summary · Email recap	· Intros · Purpose, Agenda, Outcome · Restate pain and proof of our ability to fix · Review of specific product / service / price / terms · Q&A · Restate value · Agreement in principle · Next step summary · Email recap	· May be multiple meetings · AE brings legal docs, knows negotiating authority, knows negotiating position & strategy · Purpose, Agenda, Outcome · Terms review / negotiation · Always have data advantage
Sales Plays	· Decision process complicated: Map Process Play · Need further validation: Demo Play	· More stakeholders: Prove it Again Play · Question Value: Prove Value Play · Competitive: Head to Head Play	· Question value: Prove ROI Play · Need other approvals: Propose Again Play	· Stuck on legal points: DM Break Logjam Play · Stuck on price: Review of Value / Alternatives Play
When Can Exit	· BANT confirmed · "Prove" meeting scheduled	· DM: you fix our pain · "Propose" meeting scheduled	· DM: Intent to buy · Budget and timeframe · Vendor authorization · First "negotiate" meeting scheduled	· Signed contract · First launch meeting scheduled

At Bottom Funnel, the sales engineer is often the AE's best friend—in attendance at all opportunity stage meetings, ready to answer any technical concerns raised by the prospect.

Prospect Dossier

With 30–40 strategic prospects, you can now turn to the development of your prospect dossier for each.

The dossier includes a pain point thesis, the history of interactions, decision requirements, the organization chart, the key player profiles and an engagement plan.

Pain point thesis

- What are the specific points of pain within this company

- What is the impact of the pain, both short-term (tactical) and long-term (strategic) on the company
- What are the tactical and strategic impacts if the company buys our product / service

History of interactions

- Indicators of interest (leads data: number of leads; number of contacts engaging; recency and frequency)
- Past correspondence
- Past product usage

Decision requirements

- Contract signer
- Decision maker(s)
- Decision influencers
- Product users
- Blockers
- Company decision process (detailed map of the steps)

Organization chart

- Entire hierarchy down to the decision influencer level
- Location on org chart of the users of our product / service
- Key players highlighted and color coded by role

Key player profiles

- Name
- Title
- Role in decision
- Relevant responsibilities
- Motivations
- Persona

Engagement plan

- Who / what / when steps, with outcome objectives
- Your plan to move the account through the discover, prove, propose, and negotiate steps towards the "closed won" stage

The completion of a dossier requires data and significant research. If you see a pattern of increased lead activity from multiple people at your target prospect company (such as white paper downloads), that may signal active interest. Trade show booth visits, correspondence, and SDR notes are also important parts of the data set.

But raw intelligence gathering is necessary too. In the enterprise sale, it's highly valuable to identify and cultivate a "mole." A mole is someone who is "on your side" but sits inside the prospect company, with enough visibility to give you insight. A mole can help you firm up your pain point thesis, decision requirements, organization chart and key player profiles.

Challenger Sales Approach

The sales and marketing consultancy firm CEB researched the sales performance of thousands of sales executives across hundreds of companies. The company found that salespeople fall into one of five profiles, captured in the book *The Challenger Sale* by Brent Adamson and Matthew Dixon:[3]

- The hard worker
- The lone wolf
- The relationship builder
- The problem solver
- The challenger

The research found that particularly in complex enterprise sales, the challenger profile performed substantially better than all other profiles.

Forty percent of high sales performers used the challenger approach and more than 50% of all-star performers fit this profile.

So what exactly is the challenger profile?

Challengers are intelligent and confident—bordering on arrogant. They know so much about their customers, companies and markets—and the product they sell—that they can and do engage their customers in contentious debate. A challenger sales exec seeks to provoke a paradigm change in the prospect such that the prospect gains a new insight leading to a reframing of the current state and desired future.

So how does this challenger approach align with the "opportunity" to "closed won" journey (the discover / prove / propose / negotiate steps)?

In the *discover* meeting, the challenger starts by first confirming BANT, the prospect's pain points, issues, and opportunities. Next, the challenger frames these in a new light. Reframing paints a picture of an alternative future for the prospect, where pain points are relieved and new ideas emerge. This teaching phase seeks to move the prospect rapidly to the "aha" moment, where the prospect begins to see a potential future free of pain and filled with opportunity. The first goal is simple: the "aha" moment. This step is significantly advanced if the company has built a sales ready product (SRP).

This teaching phase leads into a tailoring phase. Using the discover / prove / propose / negotiate steps, this may occur in the second meeting—the *prove*step. Here, the challenger asks "leading the witness" questions, encouraging the prospect to acknowledge how difficult life is with these pain points, and how risky the future looks if they continue unresolved. The challenger's goal here is to listen, learn, and build constructive tension.

In the *prove* step, the challenger takes control. All decision stakeholders move through the proof points that justify the claims made about the pain relief capabilities of the proposed product / service. Depending on the complexity of the sale, there may be multiple such meetings. With proof points confirmed and accepted, the challenger moves on to the *propose* step, laying out terms and persistently moving the conversation away from price and back to value.

Finally, the challenger works through the negotiations in the *negotiate* step. Here, the challenger moves the prospect to conviction lock ("I'm convinced! Sign me up!"), ending in a "closed won" deal.

In an enterprise sale, the four steps (discover / prove / propose / negotiate) often must be revisited multiple times at several levels to help decision-makers and decision-influencers achieve internal consensus and create momentum towards a deal. The engagement plan anticipates this iterative, multi-stakeholder sales motion by laying out a path for effective execution.

People

Like fighter pilots, it all comes down to the people. Are your enterprise sales executives top guns?

- A top gun is wicked smart. You can't engage in a productive debate with a smart, confident senior executive prospect if you don't possess high intelligence.
- A top gun is confident, bordering on arrogant. She fully believes she understands the customer's problem better than the customer.
- A top gun is emotionally intelligent. He can read reactions and sense power relationships. Using these insights, he can adjust his approach to optimize his position.
- A top gun is thoroughly trained. She deeply understands the product and has committed to memory the key components in the messaging toolbox.
- A top gun is genuinely prepared. He has studied the prospect dossier. He helps to architect the engagement plan and knows how to execute it. Before each meeting, he has assembled all necessary data and support tools and has researched the profiles of every attendee. He is exacting in his knowledge about how to manage the agenda for each meeting and how to lead towards a defined outcome objective.
- A top gun is competitive. She wants to win. She wants to

post bigger results than every other enterprise sales executive, every time.
- A top gun yearns for recognition. When excellence is achieved, he expects public accolades from top leaders.
- A top gun is well-paid. Depending on deal size, complexity and domain knowledge requirements, a top gun may earn from $300K OTE to $500K OTE or more, with upside.

To build a team of top guns requires the following:

- A highly promising, competitively advantaged product / service offering
- A VP sales to whom top guns will look up to and learn from
- Rigorous recruitment practices
- Market-based compensation programs

Role of the CEO:

The CEO is the hub of the enterprise sales wheel. She must ensure the rifle analysis is precisely accurate, resulting in the prioritization of the right prospect accounts. In best practice High LTV and Very High LTV companies, the CEO is directly engaged in the development and execution of prospect engagement plans. For example, early on in his company, Geoff Nudd, CEO of ClearCare, held a weekly meeting with his VP sales to review the status of each of the company's top 10 industry prospects. Within an 18-month period, 9 of 10 had purchased his product.

Role of the VP sales:

Who's your Viper? In the movie Top Gun, Viper was the commander and chief instructor of the US Navy Fighter Weapons School (aka the "Top Gun School"). He oversaw the classroom training and led the training sorties, taking the pilots through engagement after engagement to hone their skills and prepare them for the real thing.

If enterprise selling is key to your company's success, then your VP sales is your "Viper." Your "Viper" should be the ace of aces. And must be a "best in class" developer of top gun talent.

The VP sales and CEO partner together to oversee sharp enterprise sales execution. The VP sales drives weekly oversight, always ready to jump right in if the situation requires it.

Summary

Effective enterprise selling is a game-changing competency. If one new deal is worth $500,000 or more, 200 could make you a public company. As CEO, it's on you to build the team capable of making that happen.

Design for excellence, and execute accordingly.

21

Launch

Key Concepts in Chapter 21:

- The customer launch is the first opportunity post sale to prove your value
- A customer launch is really two launches: the technology and the people
- Launches must be tightly orchestrated and efficiently executed: track customer status at every step and act fast if issues arise
- A launch occurs when the technology works and the product is being properly used (by the right users at the right frequency using the right features with the right outcomes)

This chapter is relevant for the following business models:

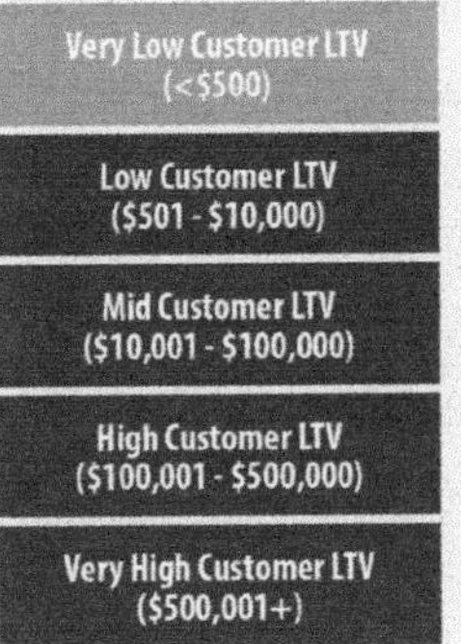

Customer love lessens when a launch lingers.

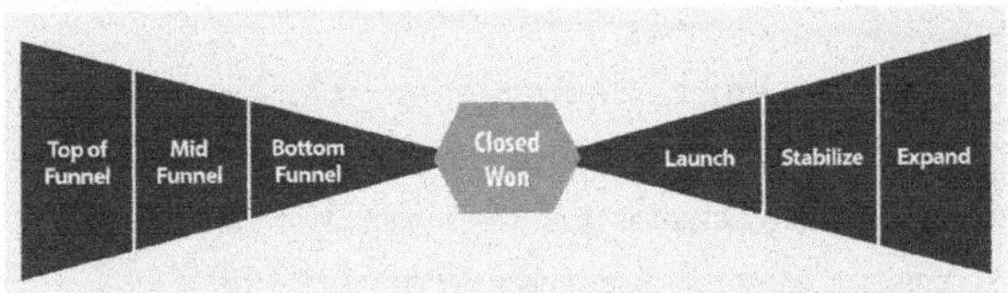

You just closed another deal. Awesome! Now what? With receipt of a signed agreement, the stopwatch begins on a customer's satisfaction half-life. Your next steps are vital. To keep satisfaction high, you now must initiate an efficient, successful launch.

"Launched" does not mean "flipped the on switch." "Launched" means "customer happy."

Launch requirements vary, depending on your company's business model. For a B2C e-commerce site, launch happens with the click of a mouse. For a complex enterprise B2B SaaS or licensing sale, a six-month project to ensure integration, training, and user adoption may be required. In general, companies operating B2B business models from Mid to Very High LTV tend to sell products that require a launch. When a launch is required, your new customer expects brisk execution.

What does that execution look like? First, your product must technically plug into the customer's legacy environment. Then your customer's employees must begin to use the tool inside their native workflows. This combination of technical and human launch factors underscores that there are, in fact, two launches:

- The technology launch
- The people launch

To deliver both successfully requires that you:

- Define the launch workflow—Tightly define your launch workflow with a precise sequence of customer engagement steps (managed in the CRM system or some other tool)
- Minimize human steps—Automate as many steps as possible
- Track customer launch status—Track launch status and act on delays
- Document technical requirements—Document in detail all technical integration requirements for all supported permutations of customers' legacy technical environments
- Instrument usage indicators and define launch—

Instrument usage indicators and define what "launched" means regarding user adoption (number of users, level and frequency of usage, etc.)

- Train the launch team—Train your launch team to handle all use case permutations with confidence

Define the Launch Workflow

The on-boarding of a new customer touches multiple company systems, such as contracting, pricing, sales incentives, the product system, billing, accounting. So it's crucial that the technical steps and data handoffs are clear.

Launch workflow definitions must be rigorous to support effective execution.

Here's an example:

- Launch stages exist at the product item or package level
- These stages identify the service status (not the billing status) of the product item or package
- The first launch stage is "opportunity / negotiate"
- The "opportunity / negotiate" stage begins with the choice of a product item or package from the price book and an online contract generated and presented to the customer for signing
- The "opportunity / negotiate" stage ends when the required order entry data fields are complete and the contract is approved, indicating that the product item or package is ready to move to the "closed won / launch pending" stage (the system defines all order entry data requirements and specifies who approves contracts)
- When multiple product items and packages are listed in one contract, each of these exits the "opportunity / negotiate" stage at the same time, since contract approval marks the end of this stage
- The "closed won / launch pending" stage begins when a contract is approved for a product item or package

- The approval triggers all appropriate product provisioning tasks in the CRM system and the billing system
- The technical launch processes commence and are complete when the product item or package is active for a customer
- At this point, the technical launch step turns to system active; this is the end of the "closed won / launch pending" stage
- The "system active" stage begins when a product item or package turns active
- The product item or package remains active independent of billing status
- The training of executive, administrative, and functional users is initiated and completed
- The "system active" stage ends when the product item or package moves to "users trained / system live," "pending paused," "paused," or "cancel pending"
- The "users trained / system live" stage begins when product usage has hit the required threshold for user adoption and usage frequency

Notice the level of rigor in this documentation. This rigor is at the heart of an effective configuration of systems and execution of the onboarding process for new customers. Along the way, workflow bottlenecks inevitably emerge, but they can be minimized. Best practices to compress the launch timeline include:

- When customer data and system access approvals are required for successful technical integration, capture these data elements as early as possible in the launch workflow—ideally in the first post-sale meeting
- In the first post-sale meeting, ask your customer to appoint a technical lead to be your primary point of contact (has necessary skill / authority / responsibility / time). If relevant, invite your pre-sales field team into the first post-sale meeting to ensure a seamless handoff to the Customer Support team for your customer.

- Have a clear roadmap and checklist defining every sequential step—ideally supported by an online tool that tracks step-by-step completion. Assign owners and responsibilities for all members of the launch team—both your team and your customers
- If a step is not complete or if too much time passes between one step and the next, make sure the system triggers action alerts to the launch rep and management

No matter how tightly defined the launch process, customer launches will sometimes go "off the rails." For those situations you need plays:

- What is the success play for "customer unable to use the product after launch"?
- What is the success play for "customer unhappy with launch process"?
- What is the success play for "too low percentage of users trained"?

If you establish plays for the most common "off the rails" scenarios, then you are prepared to get the customer back on track quickly.

Minimize Human Steps

Automate everything possible. Remember that each human step is a potential failure point. Where human steps are required, measure activity and results at each step and drive continuous improvement. The fewer actions required by a human, the faster you'll launch. A rapid, error-free launch assures high customer satisfaction.

Track Customer Launch Status

The customer is considered launched once the customer is happy—and properly using the product. All too often, especially at scale when tens or hundreds of customers are simultaneously in the launch process each month, some customers can get stuck. In the chaos, you lose track of them, and they stay stuck for too long—creating customer frustration. If you wish to avoid that disaster, it's critical that your dashboards signal the status of every customer's launch stage and set off alarms when a customer slips past the normal time window for a given stage.

If you catch launch slippage quickly and take immediate action, you're more likely to get the customer back on track. Otherwise, your customer will be on the way towards cancellation.

Here's an example of a launch team dashboard:

	Stage 1	Stage 2	Stage 3	Stage 4	Stage 5	Stage 6	Stage 7
Customer A							
Customer B							
Customer C							
Customer D							
Customer E							
Customer F							
CustomerG							
Customer H							
Customer I							
Customer J							
Customer K							
Customer L							
Customer M							
Customer N							

In the above example, the data shows four blocked customers (customers B, C, H, and J). Another two—G and M—were temporarily blocked, but then were brought back on track. We can also see that stages 2, 4, and 5 (especially stage 5) seem to be places of recurring issues (stage 4 exhibits regular slowdowns, and 2 and 5 seem to be major bottlenecks). If this pattern is observed over a sustained period, it indicates the need for redesign work.

By carefully tracking the status of each launch at a customer by customer level, you can quickly catch and recover the "black hole" customers, while discovering stages in the process that might benefit from a redesign.

Document Technical Requirements

For many companies, especially B2B SaaS companies, your software must fit into the customer's legacy environment. Integration with other software systems is required. To execute a successful integration, you must have:

- Total clarity as to every technical integration requirement for every supported use case permutation
- Identified the necessary sequence of steps to meet these integration requirements
- Built these steps into a checklist sequence that your launch system follows
- Required testing at multiple stages in the integration process to confirm successful completion of each stage
- Defined test failure protocols, including technical escalation procedures

Instrument Usage Indicators and Define Launch

The proof of your product's value is usage. If you offer a B2B SaaS product used by executives, administrators, and functional users, then you need to compare each customer to a "healthy customer" standard on dimensions such as:

- The % of users trained by user type
- Frequency of use by user type
- The % of purchased seats utilized at all
- % of features used at all

A launch is successful once your data tells you the right users are using the product at a predefined level of success.

Train the Launch Team

The launch team usually sits inside the Customer Success function. Its mission is to deliver a successful integration of the product into the customer's technical environment, and to successfully onboard all users (executive, administrative, and functional) such that these users show a pattern of use that at least meets minimum thresholds.

The required skills of the launch team depend on the requirements of a launch. Based on your business model and your product, it may be a simple plug-and-play process. Or it may require complicated steps demanding advanced technical skill to execute. Tools are useful in supporting this process. Depending on your business, tools such as Gainsight, Totango, Pendo, Aptrinsic or others may be relevant in providing insight into customer launch and usage adoption. Your staff design and recruiting efforts must match the skills to the problem. The customer's first post-purchase impression of your company and its products will depend on the people you choose for this team—so choose well.

Assuming you have a talented team in place, it is best practice to train and certify them regularly. Create competency levels: "assistant," "regular," "senior." Ensure that people earn their progression. Above all else, make sure each one of them is fully ready to interact with the customer.

Top talent is most important at the top. Your director of customer operations (head of the launch team) must be a process champion, a data hog, a fitness trainer, and an execution fanatic. Anything short of "excellent" is not good enough.

Precision yields perfection.

22

Stabilize

Key Concepts in Chapter 22:

- Within the constraints your business model imposes on customer success investments, your objective is to quickly move your customer to increasing dependency on your product, where ongoing value is derived by all intended users
- Customer success teams respond to "health risk" alerts by executing predefined "plays" that address problems and bring customers back to health
- Product and growth marketing staff create the content and execute the campaigns to support customer success -- from best practice sharing to feature adoption and usage reporting

This chapter is relevant for the following business models:

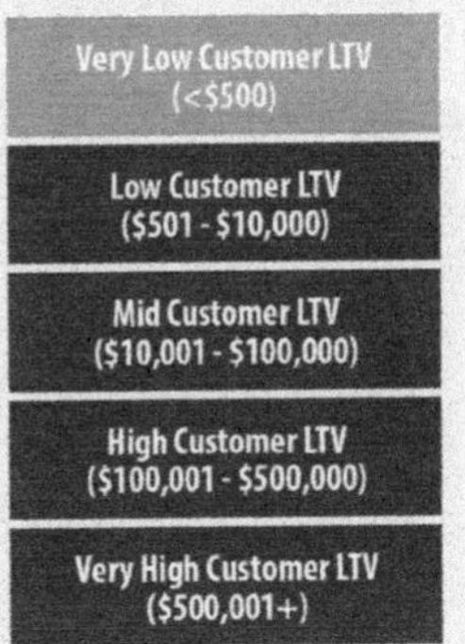

"They set me up, settled me in, and showed me success."

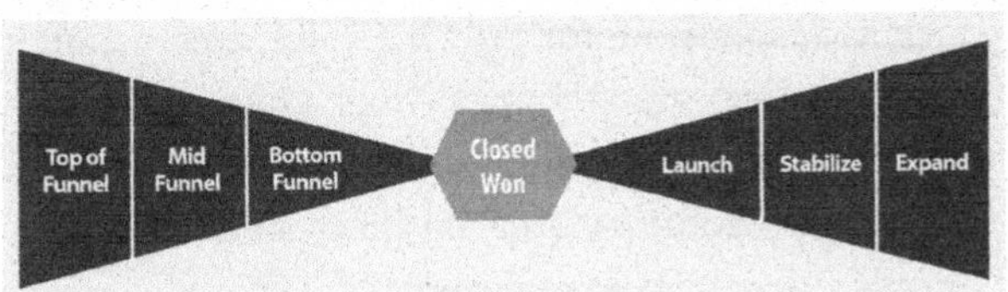

Let's assume you have sold a B2B SaaS product to a customer. You've just completed the launch in which you successfully activated your product inside your customer's technical environment. You trained the users (executive, administrative, and functional), and confirmed that they are regularly using the product in a way that at least meets minimum thresholds.

Good job. You have passed your first test. Now you need to move your new customer deliberately from "fingers crossed" to advocacy lock ("I'm a raving fan"). You have just eight weeks or so to do it before your customer's first impressions—good or bad—harden into cement.

These eight weeks comprise the Stabilize domain in the Bow Tie framework. Here, you rapidly grow your value to your customer, as manifested in rapid adoption of users, usage rate, and functionality. Guy Nirpaz, CEO of the customer success platform Totango, maps it like this:[1]

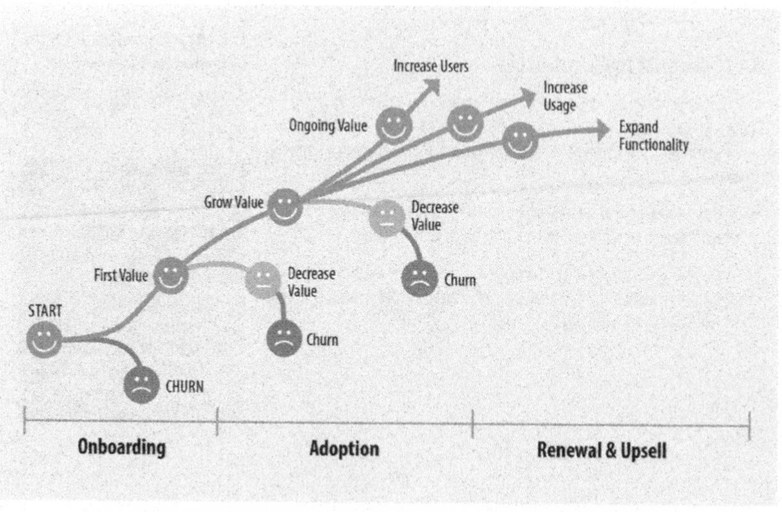

The functions responsible for growing value are customer success, product marketing, and growth marketing. Once you prove success and create a happy customer, sales may be presented with up-selling and cross-selling opportunities. Your business model will gate the level of investment placed into these functions.

Driven by your business model, the stabilize strategy begins with some fundamental questions:

- Given LTV and the financial impact of reduced churn and increased up-sell and renewal revenue, what monthly investments in customer success are possible?
- Within these financial constraints, what high-level actions for nurturing, harvesting (renewal / up-sell / cross-sell), and saving activities deliver optimal customer success outcomes?
- How do these actions impact organization design, including customer-to-staff ratios?

The answers to these questions will help you determine the mix of customer success, product marketing, and growth marketing initiatives required to optimize customer satisfaction and the sales resources necessary to exploit expansion potential.

In the Stabilize domain of the Bow Tie, the playbooks for customer success, product marketing, and growth marketing include the following programs and plays:

		Customer Success	Product Marketing	Growth Marketing	Sales
PROGRAMS	Feature Adoption Program	■	■		
	Usage Reporting Program	■		■	
	Periodic Business Review Program	■			
	Customer Feedback Program	■		■	
	Best Practice Sharing Program	■	■		
	Renewals Program		■	■	■
	Upsells / Cross Sells Program		■	■	■
PLAYS	Too Few Users	■		■	
	Too Low Rates of Utilization	■		■	
	Too Low Feature Adoption	■		■	
	Drop in Utilization	■		■	
	Service Outage or SLA Breach	■		■	
	Key User Leaves Company	■			
	Support Storm: Multiple Similar Cases Filed	■		■	
	Slow Ramp Up in Use After Launch	■		■	
	Customer Not Seeing Business Results	■			
	Too Many Escalations	■			
	Customer Cancels	■		■	■
	Customer Approaching Contract Capacity	■		■	■
	Customer Inquires about Upsell / Cross Sell Opportunities			■	■
	Customer Records High Customer Satisfaction (NPS Score)	■		■	■

Customer Success

The old model for customer care was the "account manager" model. The idea was to maintain a consistent human connection with the customer via scheduled monthly calls. These calls were part "check-in," part "on-the-spot training," part "up-sell opportunity detection"—sort of like an annual doctor checkup. To staff adequately for the regular calls to all customers, ratios above 60 customers per account manager were not possible.

The problems with this model are that it's rigid, inefficient, and poorly timed. Not all customers are alike. Some are already happy, productive users and don't need to waste time talking with you. On the other hand, for the customer who has fallen into a low-use pattern, quick intervention is critical: you can't wait until the next monthly call pops up.

The new customer success model is proactive and data-driven.

It requires that you can report, by customer, the percentage of intended users that are using the system at all, utilization rate by user and overall, feature adoption by user and overall, and, if possible, measured business outcomes resulting from your product's use.

At the department level, the metrics dashboard tracks both activity and outcome metrics.

Activity metrics:

- Utilization (# / % customers at 25% / 50% / 75% of purchased seats used)
- Frequency of use (daily or monthly average use: # of customers at 0 / 1 / 5 / 10 uses per day)
- The percent of features used (# / % of customers with 25% / 50% / 75% of features used)
- Types of features used
- Escalations (by revenue / by % of base / by first-time escalation vs. multiple escalations / by length of open escalation)
- Launch took too long (over 30 days / over 60 days)

Outcome metrics:

- Customer satisfaction data such as Net Promoter Score (NPS) (right after launch, at three months and ten months)
- Customer business outcome metrics (proof of value)
- Retention rate
- Up-sell / cross-sell rate
- Churn rate

- Revenue

Turn these metrics into your customer success dashboard and manage the business accordingly. Continuous improvement should show up in the metrics (higher rates of utilization, use, and adoption; higher customer satisfaction, retention, expansion, and LTV scores).

The activity data enables you to act. If your business model supports it, you can send customer success managers (CSMs) alerts when a threshold is crossed. The CSM can then reach out to the customer right away, with a precise understanding of the problem. The fix happens quickly. It is confirmed by data. And it's super efficient.

With High and Very High LTV business models, even though the planned meetings may be less frequent than under the old account manager model, CSMs still do hold them. In these meetings, you can execute the following programs:

- Feature adoption program (to review customer data on feature use, discuss value of underutilized features and, if necessary, train)
- Usage reporting program (to communicate value provided during a period of time)
- Periodic business review program (to discuss / review business outcomes)
- Customer feedback program (to discuss customer feedback / NPS score results)
- Best practice sharing program (to discuss best practices, especially in areas of underutilization)

It is also possible to send "health risk" alerts to CSMs. Here it's important to execute the right play. Document and train CSMs on your success plays for:

- Too few users
- Too low rates of utilization
- Too low feature adoption
- Account suffers from drop in utilization

- Users affected by service outage or SLA breach
- A key user leaves the company
- A support storm—multiple similar cases from multiple customers
- Slow ramp up in use after launch
- Customer not seeing business results
- Too many escalations
- Customer cancels
- Customer approaching utilization capacity
- Customer inquires about up-sell / cross-sell opportunities
- Customer records very high customer satisfaction (NPS) score

Product and Growth Marketing

Product marketing generates the content, and growth marketing executes the distribution for a series of programs and plays.

Programs

- Usage reporting program (send usage reports to customer)
- Feature adoption program (nurture email campaign)
- Best practice sharing program (nurture email campaign)
- Customer feedback program (send surveys to customer)
- Renewals program (nurture campaign underscoring customer value, timed ahead of renewal date)
- Up-sells / cross-sells program (nurture campaign to communicate value of up-sells / cross-sells)

Plays

- Too few users
- Too low rates of utilization
- Too low feature adoption
- Drop in utilization
- Slow ramp up in use after launch

- Customer cancels
- Customer approaching contract capacity
- Customer inquiries about up-sell / cross-sell opportunities
- Customer records high customer satisfaction

The growth marketing team will also be enlisted to support communications to customers regarding unexpected events:

- Service outage or SLA breach
- Support storm: multiple similar cases filed

Summary

At the end of the day, the mission of the Stabilize domain is to create customer success, through smart, customer-centric programs and plays, informed by data.

If you can reach the "third month live" with a happy, highly product-engaged customer, you've conquered the toughest, most critical leg of the journey.

From then on it's about staying ahead of the customer—continuously adding incremental value until the opportunity arises to expand use.

If you can execute this mission day in day out, with every customer, you open the door to a rapidly scaling growth path.

Scale on!

23

Expand

Key Concepts in Chapter 23:

- A happy customer is the starting point for customer expansion
- A strong product plus a smart expansion strategy yields negative churn
- Negative dollar churn yields hypergrowth
- Expansion strategy is anchored by pricing for expansion, product line expansion, smart execution of expansion programs and plays, and expansion incentives
- Creating strong expansion outcomes doesn't just happen: it must be a top leadership priority

This chapter is relevant for the following business models:

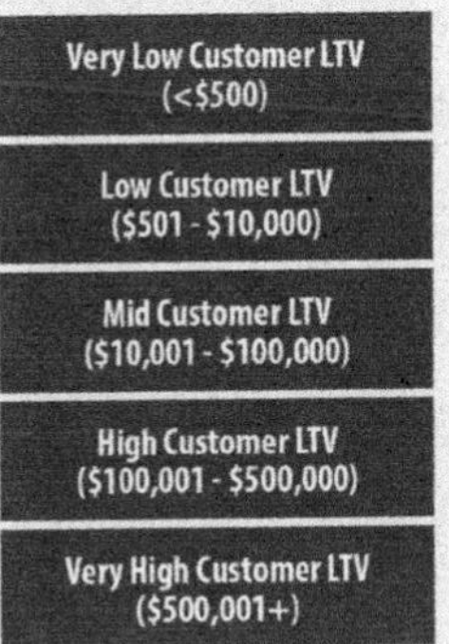

Expansion is explosive.

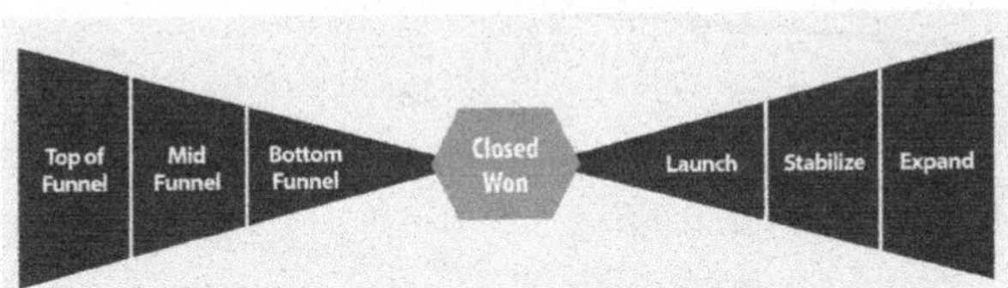

Consider the happy customer. Once upon a time, this prospect knew nothing about your company or product. First, you had to create awareness. Second, you had to create relevancy—we called that vision lock ("I get what you do, and why it's relevant for me."). Third, you started leading your prospect on the journey towards conviction lock ("I'm convinced, sign me up."). Time was your enemy, so you focused on speed to "aha." Finally, you focused on speed to trust until the eureka moment when you held in your hand (or saw on your platform) a Closed Won deal.

Soon enough, your customer is launched, stabilized, and beginning to derive sustaining value from your product. She has reached the advocacy lock stage ("I'm a raving fan."). Great work!

Now, your customer is poised for expansion.

Companies of every business model, from Very Low to Very High LTV, can design for the Expansion domain of the Bow Tie. For a media company, expansion involves increasing page views per visit and visits per month per visitor. For a marketplace company, it's about increasing the number and size of transactions per month per customer. B2B SaaS companies seek to increase users and usage levels and expand products. Most businesses can leverage expansion to drive growth.

Expansion is your secret scaling weapon. The math of your business explodes if your expansion efforts yield the outcome of negative dollar churn.

SaaS expert David Skok, General Partner at Matrix Partners and author of the popular blog *forentrepreneurs.com,* modeled MRR (Monthly Recurring Revenue) at zero, and bookings from new customers at $10k in the first month, increasing by $2k every month after that. In the graph, net bookings grow with negative churn.

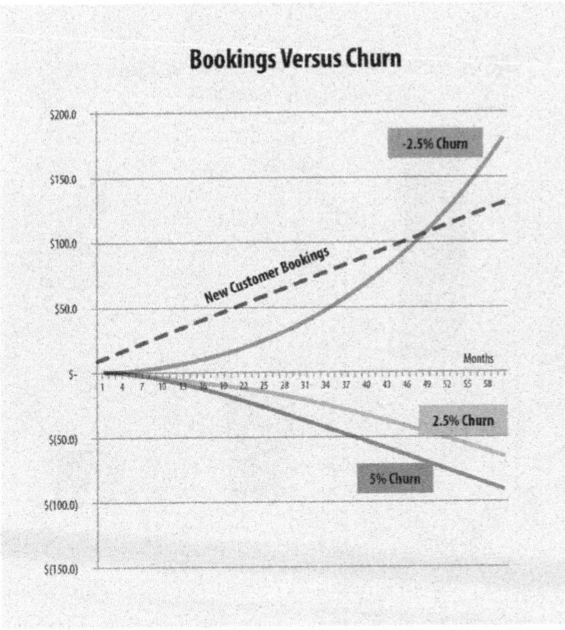

Based on data from the "2016 Pacific Crest Saas Survey,"[2] Skok reported that to acquire an incremental $1 in ACV from a new customer, it costs $1.13. However, an upsell dollar from an existing customer costs just $0.27. Moreover, an expansion dollar costs $0.20, and a renewal dollar costs even less—$0.13.

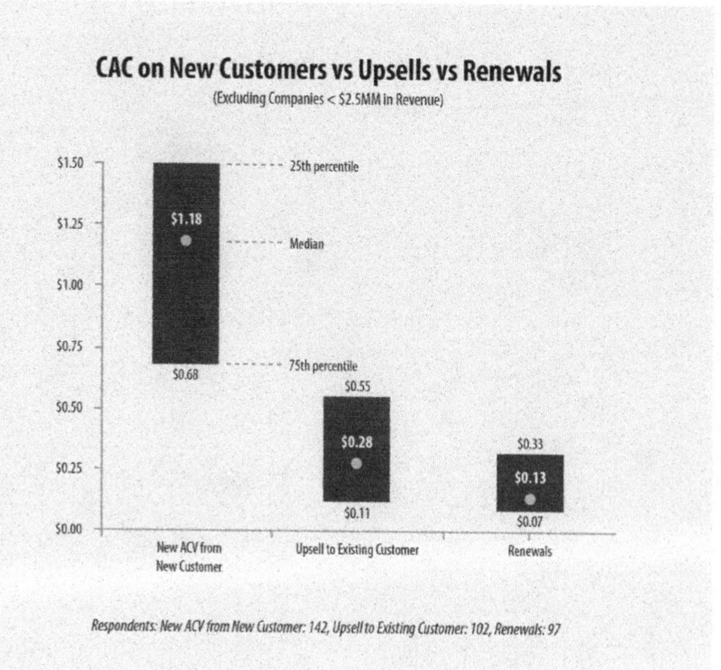

Given the substantially lower CAC associated with renewals and upsells, negative churn transforms your LTV / CAC ratio. So how do you get there?

A successful expansion strategy requires that you:

- Deliver a product with superior sustaining value
- Price for expansion
- Expand the product line
- Execute smart expansion programs and plays
- Incentivize for expansion

Superior Product

No expansion strategy can succeed unless the product delivers superior value. As discussed in Chapter 8—Product, your product needs to genuinely connect to the needs of the customer in order to win in the marketplace. This is true for a media website, a marketplace company, a B2C e-commerce site, a B2B SMB SaaS company, or an enterprise software company. Expansion starts with the value your product delivers to your customers.

Price for Expansion

You expansion strategy informs pricing and packaging decisions. At its essence, pricing is the quantification of your leverage in your relationship with your customer. You have created value, and through pricing, you capture back some of that value. The more value you create, the more leverage you have.

Cash up front

If you are a SaaS business, the best practice is to offer annual or multi-year contracts and receive cash up front (see Chapter 9—Pricing and Packaging).

Cash up front significantly reduces the amount of funding required to scale. Cash up front also locks the customer in for the 12 months.

Of course, the cash up front approach results in the customer receiving another big bill at renewal time. Depending on your leverage, you may be able to capture an increase, or you'll renew at the same price, or you may require a discount. If your leverage is low, you may be forced to go to month-to-month billing as well.

So a smart pricing plan builds on a realistic understanding of your leverage and structures the renewal offer (cash up front or not; price up, same, or down) accordingly.

Automatic Surcharges

For expansion optimization, the automatic surcharge is a powerful pricing lever. Mobile companies employ this strategy to great effect. In a SaaS offer, pricing is usually based on a use threshold: either # of users or # or quantity used. If the customer buys "up to" a monthly threshold level, then you can bill for surcharges.

For example, you sell an annual contract for $200K, receiving the cash up front. The contract enables the company to use up to 10,000 "widgets" (processing power, queries, leads, etc.) a month for 12 months. In any month where the widget use exceeds 10,000, there is a $5 per widget charge. In February, if the company uses 14,000 widgets, the customer is sent a surcharge bill for $20,000.

Multi-Year Deal

The multi-year deal locks in the expansion, especially if the cash is up front. To calculate the percent discount you might be willing to offer the customer for a multi-year deal, consider the logo (accounts) churn rate you might otherwise experience and the time value of money. Discounts of 5% to 10% may be fully justified by the math of your business in return for a cash-up-front, multi-year deal.

Expand the Product Line

Of course, product line expansion opens the door to cross sells. If you can create products that expand upon your core product to create new tiers of value for customers, then you can diversify your package bundles, and you'll create cross-sell potential.

The secret to successful product line expansion starts with value and relevancy. Because your customer has already bought your core product, you know a lot about her or his needs. You understand not just the pain points you already solve, but also the nearby pain points you do not yet solve. If your product extensions tackle these next pain points, and if those pain points are significant enough, you have a viable cross-sell product.

Execute Smart Expansion Programs and Plays

Product marketing, growth marketing, sales, and customer success functions all have a role in expansion programs. Product marketers produce the compelling content:

- Thought leadership content, reminding customers of the strategic rationale for your products and services
- Core product best practice videos
- Core product Q&A
- Cross-sell product feature / benefit videos for website and email campaigns
- Renewal, upsell, and cross-sell pitch presentations and collateral

Growth marketers execute the nurture campaigns and webinars to current customers. The nurture campaigns are versioned for different use cases (e.g., low levels of use, some users not using the system, under-utilization of certain features, to name a few). For instance, if it's an under-utilization case, an email campaign might include a link to a video showing how to use a key feature currently not utilized by the customer.

Customer success managers (CSMs) maintain the health of the customer, using data to engage intelligently and efficiently.

Moreover, sales (AEs) will act on tips from the CSM, alerts, and thoughtfully defined workflows to initiate sales engagement and move the customer towards a renewal, upsell, or cross-sell.

Renewal

A smart renewal program starts with data. Is the customer healthy, as measured by the activity and outcome numbers? Is the customer happy, as shown by NPS score and CSM feedback? The faster you act on data to care for and nurture the customer, the better positioned you are for renewal.

Regardless of customer health, if your business model supports a dedicated CSM, your customer should receive a full business review meeting six months ahead of the renewal date. This meeting should include the CSM and the AE responsible for renewal and up-sell / cross-sell. The following preparation is required:

- Review activity and outcome metrics trends / data

- Review customer notes / cases
- Review customer satisfaction measures
- CSM and sales exec discuss the buyer and user personas
- A documented meeting plan (introduction, data review, key value points, questions, next steps / commitments)

After the meeting, the CSM should execute on any commitments made and closely track ongoing health indicators. A second business review meeting should then be held three months before renewal, again with both the CSM and the AE. In this second meeting, the AE reminds the customer of the upcoming renewal date and probes as to the level of satisfaction and readiness to renew on existing terms.

Then a month before renewal the AE holds the renewal meeting, with the objective to gain an online signature by the end of the meeting if possible (or a clear finalization / signature path defined with dates, if necessary).

Up-sell and Cross-Sell

As is true with all expansion activity, accurate data is required to execute up-sells and cross-sells successfully. By knowing the health of a customer on the core product, you can infer the customer's openness to expansion through up-sell, cross-sell, or both.

The data will surely lead you to up-sell opportunities. However, depending on the nature of your add-on product, there may be core product utilization data that will also directly point to the relevancy of the add-on for a given customer.

With the data in hand, it's all about workflows. These "propensity to buy" indicators must be built into alerts, and the alerts built into workflows. The role of the CSM as a trusted advisor means that it is usually best practice to separate this role from direct selling. However, the CSM should certainly alert the AE to initiate a sales action when the opportunity emerges.

Ultimately, CSMs and AEs need to act quickly and decisively on "buy signal" alerts, coordinating the customer interventions that yield an up-sell or cross-sell agreement.

Incentivize for Expansion

Two actors must execute their roles successfully to ensure optimized selling in pursuit of expansion: the CSM and the AE.

CSMs are incentivized significantly for retention. Consider additional kickers for average customer satisfaction scores above a certain threshold. It's also important to have a kicker for successful up-sells and cross-sells. This will encourage CSMs to probe for the opportunity and to alert AEs of buy signals.

For the AE, the "2015 Pacific Crest SaaS Survey" indicates that median commission rates on renewals were 2% of ACV. For up-sells, it's 8%, and for multi-year deals, 32% of companies included an additional percent-of-ACV commission past the first year. Meanwhile, for 26% of the others, the multi-year deal was rewarded with a nominal kicker.

The point is that incentives motivate. Point your dollars where you want action.

Summary

In summary, expansion is the most cost-efficient way to grow revenue. Customer spending has the potential to increase by 400% or more in one year if the product delivers sufficient value and the expansion strategy is conceived and executed well.

A surprising number of companies under-invest in expansion. Don't do that. Be the CEO that gives expansion the focus it so rightly deserves.

Expand like fireworks.

24

Building the Revenue Engine While Running It

Key Concepts in Chapter 24:

- You scale the revenue engine while you run it
- To prioritize where to focus, you assess the current state of your market position, your business economics, your infrastructure, and your Bow Tie execution
- The work to scale the revenue engine involves day to day management, Bow Tie optimization projects and foundation layer projects
- Project teams are built based on the competencies and knowledge required--from strategic to tactical

This chapter is relevant for the following business models:

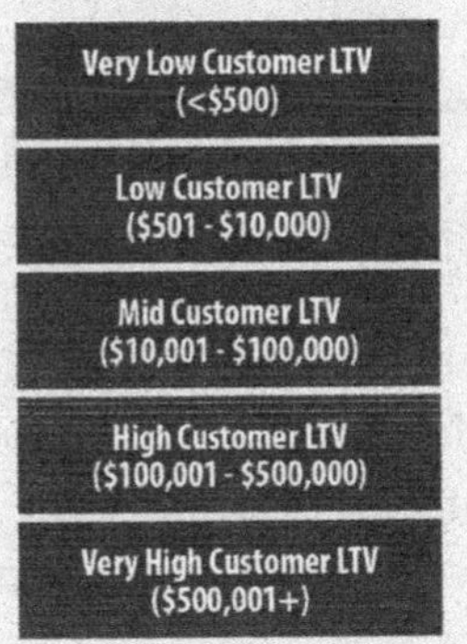

As you redesign the revenue engine, you must run it.

Over the past 23 chapters, we've painted a picture of revenue engine best practice. Now it's time to answer the question, "how do you get there?" The answer is simple. You scale the revenue engine while you run it.

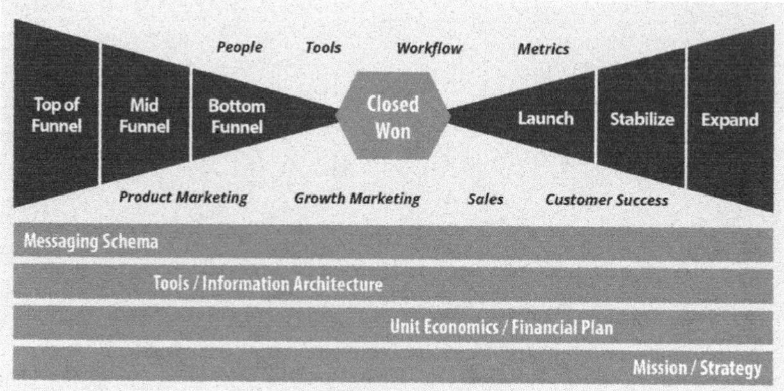

Your revenue engine is a whole system, bounded by unit economics. Workflows, tools, data, and people must work together to orchestrate effective prospect and customer engagement. Functional managers and frontline employees must manage the handoffs from workflow to workflow. When executed well, you maximize reach at Top of Funnel and relevant messaging leads to vision lock. You drive conversion and sales cycle compression at Mid and Bottom Funnel, which leads to conviction lock. With proactive interventions as you Launch, Stabilize, and Expand, you guide the customer to advocacy lock.

But it's never that easy. The engine coughs and sputters. Components are missing, or they break. Frontline employees encounter workflow bottlenecks. Prospects slip off the hook. Customers get frustrated and cancel. Marketing campaigns fail. Salespeople fall short of sales goals. Week by week, you find yourself playing a never-ending game of "whack-a-mole."

It's so very easy to be consumed by these day to day fires.

As CEO, you can find yourself barely keeping pace with the crisis du jour. But firefighting doesn't provoke fundamental change. To create fundamental change, you must stand back from the chaos.

Take stock. Determine what change is required. Then get down to it.

Taking Stock

It starts with your market position. Are you so far in front of the wave you haven't been able to catch it? Are you languishing in its wake? Or are you surfing at its crest? It's important to know. Take an outside-in view:

- Seek the insights of your board of directors—what are their perspectives?
- Regularly engage a customer advisory board—what do customers see on the horizon?
- What do key industry analysts say about you?
- Listen carefully to your marketing and sales teams—what do they hear, and what friction are they discovering?
- Review conversion and churn metrics—what are the trends?
- Listen in on customer calls—what are the objections and complaints?
- Visit customers in their setting—is your product aligned with the customer's reality?
- Go to trade shows—is yours the hottest booth at the show?
- Engage in thought leadership, and read the thought leadership of others in your field—are you ahead of the innovation wave or trying to catch up?

This outside-in data will inform your mission and strategy (customer segmentation, value proposition, competitive positioning, brand identity, product, pricing and packaging, prospect and customer journey, and channel architecture).

Then consider the economics of your business and the status of its infrastructure (unit economics, financial plan, tools, information architecture, and messaging schema).

Finally, take a look at each domain of the Bow Tie journey, from Top of Funnel to Expand.

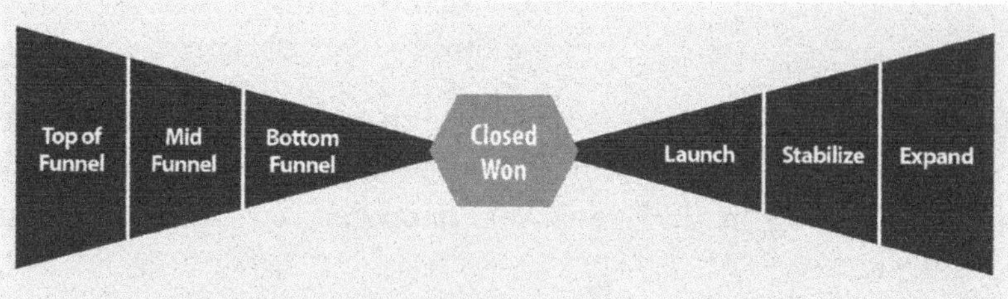

What's the status?

To make these assessments, it's helpful to conduct a revenue engine assessment (see Chapter 2—Revenue Engine Maturity Model). You can assess each component of the revenue engine, using the Carnegie Mellon Capability Maturity Model 1–5 rating system:[1]

1. Chaotic: workflows unpredictable and poorly controlled
2. Project Centric Fixes: broken workflows fixed one at a time
3. Whole System: workflows linked end to end; design considers dependencies
4. Quantitative: workflows measured to improve control
5. Continuous improvement: ongoing, data-driven fine-tuning

Once you have identified the strengths and weaknesses of your engine down to the component level, you can force-rank the weak points.

Scaling the Revenue Engine

Revenue engine scaling falls into three categories of work:

- Day-to-day management—all activities in your company
- Bow Tie optimization projects—Top of Funnel, Mid

Funnel, Bottom Funnel, Launch, Stabilize, and Expand domains
- Foundation layer optimization projects—Mission/Strategy, Unit Economics/Financial Plan, Tools/Information Architecture, and Messaging Schema

Day-to-day management is where the rubber hits the road. This is the world of average MQL follow-up response times or the time it takes from the opening of a customer support case to its resolution. It's the number of cold calls per day, the launch of the next email campaign, and the completion of the day's scheduled demo presentations.

Execute management of day-to-day work as close to the real workflow as possible. In the best run companies, frontline employees take a primary role in managing daily execution. At handoff points in the workflow, frontline employees work across functional boundaries to identify bottlenecks. Self-managed teams review metrics for continuous improvement.

Bow Tie optimization projects tend to be more tactical than strategic. At Top of Funnel, a project might be an A/B test on an email campaign, or a ramp-up of spending for a promising marketing channel, or the launch of a new ad campaign. At Mid Funnel, it might be the rollout of new SDR training or a hiring project. At Bottom Funnel, it might be an update to an email nurture campaign. At Launch, a project may be initiated to document new technical integration protocols. At Stabilize, a new customer best practice email campaign may be initiated to address a new use case scenario. At Expand, a new incentive program for CSMs or AEs might need to be rolled out. These projects are the stuff of routine marketing and sales management and, when executed well, they have meaningful short-term impacts on results. Mid managers are usually well positioned to lead Bow Tie optimization projects.

Foundation layer projects are more strategic than Bow Tie projects. You might need to revisit your segmentation scheme and ideal customer profile (ICP). Or you might need to redesign pricing and packaging. Or your channel strategy. Or your messaging schema. Or rebuild your information architecture. These are heavy lifting projects that take executive vision, coordinated planning, and multi-level, cross-functional implementation.

Because the results of foundation layer projects are usually back-end loaded, it's easy to de-prioritize them. Resist that temptation. The leverage that these projects can yield is orders of magnitude greater than Bow Tie optimization projects, even though their impact may take more time to realize. Foundation layer projects involve a sequential series of steps:

- Envision the end state
- Architect plans to achieve the end state
- Build to the plan
- Implement
- Stabilize
- Optimize
- Scale

These steps require coordinated handoffs of leadership throughout a project, as follows:

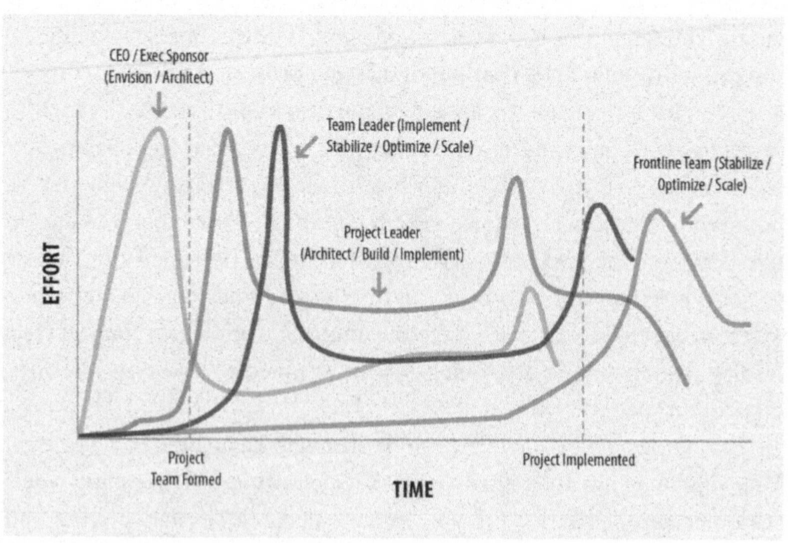

As CEO, you are the "chief envisioner." Most of the time you'll engage the executive team, seeking consensus on the vision. Once you have clarity as to the change you want to create, you can assign an executive sponsor and a project leader to drive it forward from "architect" to "build" to "implement." Others may become involved once the project moves through "implement," "stabilize," "optimize," and "scale."

Once you've prioritized your foundation layer projects, stick with them. Press forward until you've achieved your key project milestones, then move on to the next one. By doing so, you slowly but steadily strengthen your revenue engine. In time, your engine will become highly efficient and robust.

Summary

No matter the state of your revenue engine, it can always be improved. Whether you are an early stage startup, a mid-stage growth startup or a public tech company, your work to scale the revenue engine is ongoing.

Regardless of business model, the core principles of scaling remain the same.

Conceive of your revenue engine as a whole system. Think through how your marketing, sales, finance and product teams will work together. Orchestrate the prospect and customer experience. Understand your unit economics boundaries, and the levers available to you given your business model. Make sure you have in place the data and infrastructure to scale. Do the work to create and execute a winning strategy.

As a tech company CEO, you are the captain of your destiny. Will you build a great company? One that has a profound impact in your chosen field? Will you heartily reward your investors, your employees, and yourself with the fruit of your hard labor?

Your revenue engine is the means by which all of these things are achieved. Make yours a Porsche.

Zoom towards the sunrise on the road to freedom.

Notes

Chapter 1

1. Aileen Lee."Welcome to the Unicorn Club, 2015: Learning from Billion Dollar Companies." *TechCrunch* Web. 18 July 2015.
2. Carmen Nobel. "Why Companies Fail—and How Their Founders Bounce Back." *Working Knowledge* Web. Harvard Business School, 7 March 2011.
3. Diane Mulcahy. "Six Myths about Venture Capitalists." *Harvard Business Review*. May 2013.

Chapter 2

1. Steve Blank. *The Four Steps to the Epiphany: Successful Strategies for Products that Win*. K&S Ranch, July 2013. Print.
2. Tien Tzuo. "Climbing the Mountain." Blog post. *indexventures.com*. n.d.

3. Wildcat Ventures. “The Traction Gap Framework.” White paper. *wildcat.vc*. June 2016.
4. Carnegie Mellon Univ. Software Engineering Inst. The Capability Maturity Model: Guidelines for Improving the Software Process (SEI). Addison-Wesley Professional, 1994. Print.

Chapter 4

1. Vinod Khosla. “Project Rifle: A Quantified Decision Making Framework.” Slide deck. *khoslaventures.com*. March 1, 2010.

Chapter 5

1. Geoffrey Moore. *Crossing the Chasm, 3rd Edition: Marketing and Selling Disruptive Products to Mainstream Customers*. HarperBusiness, January 2014.

Chapter 6

1. Steve Blank. *The Four Steps to the Epiphany: Successful Strategies for Products that Win*. K&S Ranch, July 2013. Print.
2. Gartner Group. “Gartner Magic Quadrant.” Post on website. *gartner.com*. 2017.
3. Jonas Boner. “The Reactive Manifesto.” Post on website. *reactivemanifesto.org*. September 2014.

Chapter 7

1. David Aaker. *Building Strong Brands*. Free Press, December 1995. Print.

Chapter 8

1. Scott Belsky. "Crafting the First Mile of Product." Blog post. *Positive Slope*.Medium.com, June 2016.
2. Geoffrey Moore. *Crossing the Chasm, 3rd Edition: Marketing and Selling Disruptive Products to Mainstream Customers.* New York: HarperBusiness, January 2014.

Chapter 9

1. Steve Blank. *The Four Steps to the Epiphany: Successful Strategies for Products that Win*. K&S Ranch, July 2013. Print.
2. Bill Gurley. "A Rake Too Far: Optimal Platform Pricing Strategy." Blog post. *abovethecrowd.com.* 18 April 2013.
3. David Skok. "2016 Pacific Crest SaaS Survey." Blog post. *forEntrepreneurs.com*. 2016.
4. David Skok. "2013 Pacific Crest Saas Survey." Blog post. *forEntrepreneurs.com*. 2013.
5. Nino Marakovic. "Getting More Cash out of SaaS: Timing is Everything." Web article. *techcrunch.com.* 12 January 2015.

Chapter 12

1. David Skok. "Sales Metrics 2.0—A Guide to Measuring and Improving What Matters." Blog post. *forEntrepreneurs.com*. n.d.
2. Provided by Paul Albright, CEO of Captora.

Chapter 16

1. Scott Albro, CEO of TOPO. "Account-Based Everything."

San Francisco, CA. September 2016. Private presentation to CEO Quest members.

Chapter 17

1. Carnegie Mellon Univ. Software Engineering Inst. The Capability Maturity Model: Guidelines for Improving the Software Process (SEI). Addison-Wesley Professional, 1994. Print.
2. Eli Goldratt & Jeff Cox. *The Goal: A Process of Ongoing Improvement*. North Rivers Press, January 1992. Print.

Chapter 18

1. Sequoia Capital, Jim Goetz & others. *The Templeton Compression and Sales Ready Product*. Online book. Inkling.com, 2015.
2. Bill Portelli. "The Sales Ready Product: Compressing B2B Sales Cycles—Part 1." Special Report. *CEO Quest*. Medium.com, November 2017.
3. Scott Belsky. "Crafting the First Mile of Product." Blog post. *Positive Slope*. Medium.com, June 2016.
4. Jonas Boner. "The Reactive Manifesto." Post on website. *reactivemanifesto.org*. September 2014.

Chapter 19

1. David Skok. "2016 Pacific Crest SaaS Survey—Part 1." Blog post. *forEntrepreneurs.com*. 2016.
2. Jon Miller, CEO of Engagio. *The Clear and Complete Guide to Account Based Marketing*. Booklet on website. *engagio.com*. 2017.
3. Scott Albro, CEO of TOPO. "Account-Based Everything."

San Francisco, CA. September 2016. Private presentation to CEO Quest members.

Chapter 20

1. Vinod Khosla. "Project Rifle: A Quantified Decision Making Approach." Slide deck. *khoslaventures.com*. March 1, 2010.
2. Tom Scearce. "The Account-Based Everything Framework." Blog post. *blog.topohq.com*. n.d.
3. Matthew Dixon & Brent Adamson. *The Challenger Sale: Taking Control of the Customer Conversation*. New York: Penguin Group, 2013. Print.

Chapter 22

1. Guy Nirpaz and Fernando Pizzaro. *Farm, Don't Hunt: The Definitive Guide to Customer Success*. Self-published, 2016.

Chapter 23

1. David Skok. "Unlocking the Path to Negative Churn." Blog post. *forEntrepreneurs.com*. n.d.
2. David Skok. "2016 Pacific Crest SaaS Survey—Part 1." Blog post. *forEntrepreneurs.com*. 2016.

Chapter 24

1. Carnegie Mellon Univ. Software Engineering Inst. The Capability Maturity Model: Guidelines for Improving the Software Process (SEI). Addison-Wesley Professional. 1994. Print.

Acknowledgments

In my preparation for writing this book, I conducted deep research into the revenue generation practices of high-performing CEO Quest member companies — FiveStars, ClearCare, Healthline, Qubole, Lightbend, DispatchTrack, AcademixDirect and more.

Additionally, I completed in-depth research with non-members such as EventBrite (whose revenue engine is finely tuned and highly impressive). My thanks go out to these companies for giving me the access and visibility I needed into their structures, tools, workflows, and daily practices.

Practitioners such as Matt Curl, VP Sales and Chris Luo, VP Marketing at FiveStars; Chris Aker, VP Sales at EventBrite; Bruce Cleveland, founding partner at Wildcat Ventures and executive director of the Traction Gap Institute; Tom Grubb, Chief Strategy Officer at Digital Pi; Scott Albro, CEO of the sales and marketing consultancy Topo; Andrea Tucker, a leading messaging expert and CEO of StrategyApplied; David Puglia, CMO of Jive Software; Jon Miller, CEO of Engagio; Evan Liang, CEO of LeanData; Paul Albright, CEO of Captora; Mark Brewer, CEO of Lightbend; and many others critically evaluated the framework and provided further insights. Bill Portelli, my work partner at CEO Quest and the former founding

CEO of CollabNet, has read every word and has made major contributions. Thanks to my trusted editor, Trish Heald. She was a ceaseless advocate for fit and trim writing. And finally, I thank Jacob Sandler for his tireless work to actually get this book published.

These are just a few of the folks who've significantly contributed to this book. I am deeply indebted to them.

About Tom Mohr

Tom Mohr has a diverse background as a CEO coach, serial entrepreneur and Fortune 500 executive.

In his role as founder and CEO of CEO Quest, he leads a team of tech CEO coaches in Silicon Valley, New York and Los Angeles. CEO Quest coaches provide expert advisory support to CEOs on their journeys of company building.

Prior to CEO Quest, Mohr co-founded Digital Air Strike. Over six years, he raised a lot of VC money and scaled the company from whiteboard concept to profitability, with 2000 auto dealer customers. Previously, he was president of Knight Ridder Digital, a Fortune 500 subsidiary, and sat on the boards of CareerBuilder, Cars.com, Apartments.com and ShopLocal. He has been at the helm of companies and divisions at every stage of company building, from zero revenue to $300M.

Mohr is author of two other books-- *People Design* and *Funding & Exits.* He is currently at work on his fourth book.

Mohr lives in San Jose, CA with his wife Pageen (CEO Quest's controller). They have two adult children, Jack (married to his beautiful wide Ellie), and Mary Catherine.

About CEO Quest

CEO Quest provides elite advisory support to tech company CEOs. The mission is to help CEOs accelerate company growth by leveraging the applied science of company building.

CEO Quest Managing Directors bring to their work with member CEOs extensive experience in tech company leadership, venture fundraising, and participation on boards. In their work with tech CEOs, they leverage their own experiences and CEO Quest's extensive research into the applied science of company building.

As a result, CEOs make sharper decisions, sparking accelerated growth.

To learn more, go to http://ceoquest.com/

The CEO Quest icon describes the five domains of company building:

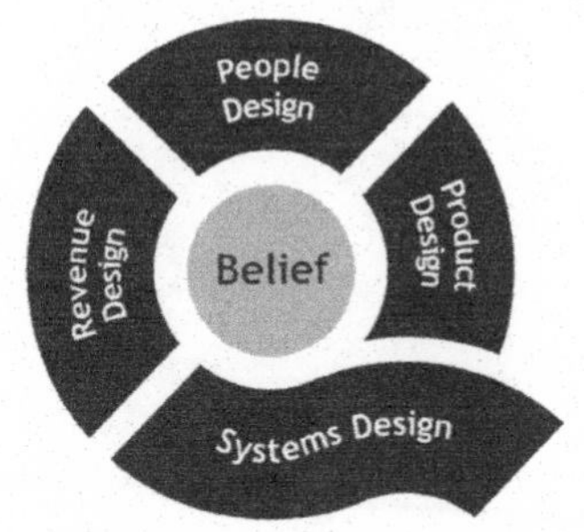